Group Tutoring
Concepts and Case Studies
Wyn Bramley

This book applies insights from American
and British experience in relation to the
theory and practice of small group teaching in
higher education. For the purpose of this
book, personal tutoring is defined as 'all
those professional activities, attitudes and
personalised relationships which characterise
all the teacher's dealings with all students'.
Attention is focused upon the personality
and skills of the tutor himself, in relation to
his group work — with students, colleagues,
and in his institutional training/development
programmes. The book enables tutors to
define in depth one aspect of their role, that
of conducting tutorials, seminars and other
groups. There is also a discussion relating to
the staff groupings to which tutors belong,
institutional dynamics, and the need for in-
service training. Six of the chapters illustrate
the theory by means of case study.

About the Author

Wyn Bramley has been counsellor to
students at University College London since
1976. Prior to this she established the
students' counselling service at the
Polytechnic of Central London and in
addition helped set up a multidisciplinary
team of student services there from 1969-76.
She is currently involved in the training of
student counsellors, and often acts as
consultant to other educational
establishments. She has written *Personal
Tutoring in Higher Education* and many
articles for professional journals.

ISBN-0-89397-059-X

GROUP TUTORING

CONCEPTS AND CASE STUDIES

Wyn Bramley

Kogan Page, London/Nichols Publishing
Company, New York

First published in Great Britain 1979
by Kogan Page Limited, 120 Pentonville Road, London N1

Copyright © by Wyn Bramley 1979
All Rights Reserved

ISBN 0 85038 203 3 (*hardback*)
ISBN 0 85038 238 6 (*paperback*)

First published in the United States of America in 1979
by Nichols Publishing Company, Post Office Box 96, New York,
NY 10024

Library of Congress Cataloging in Publication Data
    Bramley, Wyn.
    Group Tutoring: Concepts and Case Studies.
    Bibliography: p
    1. Tutors and tutoring. 2. Group work in education.
    3. Forums (Discussion and debate). I. Title
    LC41.B69   371.39'4   79-2140
    ISBN 0-89397-059-X

Printed by McCorquodale (Newton) Limited

Dedication

This book is for all those teachers who participated in the case studies, and who appear (in disguise) in the second section. I am deeply grateful for their allowing me to share their work experiences, ideas, and feelings. Mine is the hand that wrote the words, but in effect this work represents a group enterprise.

Acknowledgments

I wish to acknowledge my debt to my secretary José Dunn for the typing of the manuscript. Her patience and care are much appreciated.

I am also grateful to my colleagues and ex-teachers at the Institute of Group Analysis, who have for several years greatly facilitated the development of my conceptual framework, with regard to groups.

The evolution of educational aspects is due to all those staff and students, at University College and elsewhere, who have permitted me to watch them at work, or lead them in training discussions.

Contents

'He saw that the individual can only be understood when he is taken in his social context. He stressed rightly that democracy is not so much the triumph of the free individual, as the triumph of the free group through which the individual gets his freedom.'

Professor R Battegay of S R Slavson

In deference to publishing convention I have been asked to use the male pronoun throughout. I wish to make it clear that this pronoun always refers to both sexes, and in no way indicates gender bias on my part.

Concepts

Chapter 1
Introduction:
the meaning of group tutoring,
and its ethical foundations

Personal tutoring

For the purposes of this book, personal tutoring is defined as all those professional activities, attitudes and personal relationships which characterize all the teacher's dealings with all students. This panoply of functions includes formal teaching. Academically oriented group work is extracted here from this vast range of tutoring responsibilities and studied in some depth. In my previous book, *Personal Tutoring in Higher Education*, those tutoring transactions with individual students which are not principally academic were examined and group work was touched upon only briefly. The two volumes therefore complement one another and together comprise a fairly comprehensive discussion of all tutoring work. Each can be read independently of the other but a balanced view of tutoring is gained by reading both.

The first book introduces thoughts about the tutoring system itself: its design, purpose and procedures. It considers the role of the personal tutor and investigates his predominantly individual and pastoral relationships with students, as well as with specialist agencies. The scope of this second book is much narrower and, I hope, more detailed. Attention is focused upon the personality and skills of the tutor in exclusive relation to *group* work — with students, colleagues, and in institutional training/development programmes.

Some elaborations of the definition: (A) Professionalism
The above definition of personal tutoring demands some qualification. Let us take the idea of professionalism for instance. Teachers engage in many interchanges with students which are not professional but which may have developed out of the professional relationship. A teacher may become a personal or family friend, helpful beyond the call of duty; he may volunteer for quasi-parental responsibilities far beyond those expected of him by his employers; or he may find himself involved in a romantic or sexual liaison. Such relationships are not to be confused with the tutoring job, which, however intimate or intense it grows, remains in essence professional. Many tutors believe 'personal' and

13

'professional' to be antagonistic, as if these qualities could never co-exist for fear of one impairing the other. I hope the ensuing chapters will correct this fallacy, and show how each is a facet of the other *so long as both remain encircled by the boundary of tutoring*.

The teacher is asked to promote education. This occupation cannot be managed without emotional involvement with the learners, regular scrutiny of the teacher's own feelings, and a repeated assessment of his relations with colleagues. All these activities are intensely personal. However, when a personal relationship no longer connects with the educational goals espoused by the tutor, and the relationship is able to exist independently of its educational background, it can no longer be regarded as professional. I hasten to add that a non-professional involvement is not to be automatically regarded as undesirable. However, it often causes confusion and divided loyalties on the part of the tutor if he is not clear about the status of the relationship. It may become difficult and embarrassing to retain the necessary professional control in a situation where the source of ferment is a mutual attachment (or impending loss of attachment) which has long ago lost its contractual nature and abandoned any links with educational objectives. This relationship may be played out in the institutional arena where it originated, but it could just as easily be carried on elsewhere. Tutors with a clear concept of professionalism do not fear the personal commitment required by the work as they can draw their own limits beyond which their conduct becomes estranged from their occupational aims and standards.

Sadly, many teachers have interpreted the increasing interest in personal tutoring as a movement which threatens to violate their privacy and expose their personalities to the critical glare of students. However, I see this renascent movement as indicating a growing awareness that teaching and learning can greatly benefit from a new educational approach. This new approach is no longer based upon the paternalistic hierarchical 'moral tutor' model, nor the allegedly democratic model of 'counselling', but draws upon the growing body of knowledge about how people and institutions organize themselves, both deliberately and unconsciously, to carry out, or fail to carry out, their several jobs and sub-tasks within those jobs. As culture-carriers of the institution, tutors might begin to provide the minimum sufficient conditions in which fulfilling learning-and-living (which are inseparable) can flourish of their own accord. The new approach encourages tutors to become social engineers, rather than moral instructors or amateur counsellors.

(B) Teaching and tutoring: a comparison

The second elaboration of this definition refers to the term 'teaching', which many who practise humanistic education take to be synonymous with personal tutoring. This is true in many respects, but it leaves out the important fact that teaching is often antecedent to personal tutoring which takes place outside the classroom, within the confiding and trusting atmosphere of the tutor's office or home perhaps, or in a bar. The title 'teaching' does not subsume such interactions.

Again, the term 'personal tutoring' specifies a particular type of education. It is a model of education which fosters and authorizes personal as well as academic development in the interests of the society it serves, and in which many of its graduates will play an influential role. 'Teaching' is a word easily misconstrued as meaning only the process by which academic information is transferred from the academician to the student. Thus teaching is safely reified and becomes an object of scientific evaluation; it can be measured in various ways, certain criteria can be laid down for success and failure, and certain techniques and practical aids developed to assist the teacher in carrying out his duties. Turning teachers into mechanics like this encourages practitioners to avoid sensitive issues such as the teacher's own human relations potential: his feelings about himself, his students and the course, as well as the institutional mores within which he must function. It can be painful and distressing to have to examine one's motives and one's behaviour in teaching. Much more reassuring is the ability to convert teaching into a technology which can then be mastered without loss of face or uncomfortable truths one may have to countenance if one begins to explore oneself as a teacher in more subjective ways. If teachers cope with fear of self-knowledge by abusing technology like this, they will teach students to do the same.

A cursory glance at contemporary social and industrial relations reveals an alarming amount of alienation. Much of the cause is traceable to well-meaning attempts to provide technological solutions to non-technological (ie, human) problems. If we are to propel students into industry and the professions, taking human solutions to human problems with them, they must first be exposed to educators who themselves have been liberated from empty teaching techniques, procedures and prescriptions. Max Frisch once wrote, 'Technology is the art of so arranging the world you do not have to experience it'! If teaching technology prevents tutor and student from 'experiencing' the world of higher education, that is experiencing *each other*, what hope is there for our society's future? The tutor's own personality is his most sensitive instrument; he must find the courage to use it. The term 'personal tutoring', then, is an ideological statement and a declaration of bias, whereas 'teaching' can be interpreted in many ways and its meaning is often obscured.

(C) Structure and process

In my definition I have said that personal tutoring is extended to all students, so that readers whose jobs involve accepting responsibility for a student 'caseload' may feel confused by it. Let me make it clear, therefore, that in making statements about personal tutoring I am referring to a network of interpersonal *processes*, not a series of institutionalized structures, procedures, and roles. All staff and students are enmeshed in this social network, irrespective of the overall design superimposed upon it, the nature of which will vary from college to college. Organizational details of tutoring systems such as allocation of students to tutors demonstrate an attempt to convert the personal tutoring philosophy into method and practice. It is these fundamental tutoring *values* with which we should be chiefly concerned; for the instituting of roles and procedures is comparatively easy once the *raison d'être* of the tutoring system is understood by its personnel. This is not to say that roles and structure are irrelevant. Titles such as 'personal tutor' can be viewed as messages and slogans, conveying far more than just factual data to the members of the community. These labels and the duties suggested by them advertise the staff's desire for personal interaction thus promulgating ethical stances which will hopefully be absorbed into the college culture, eventually rendering these crude labels and roles obsolete. A very important administrative function is also served, in that the mass of staff-student information in circulation is ordered, and its exchange regulated, in what would otherwise seem an alienating and amorphous environment. The fact remains that the tutor acting as an essential channel for communication, and the formal tutoring system to which he subscribes, are in themselves merely structural devices for information gathering and dissemination. They are also in receipt of student experiences not catered for by other structures (such as the class, union, or specialist helping services). This artificial social system is a crucial device, manufacturing kinship networks so that everyone belongs somewhere. This tutoring *structure*, no matter how sophisticated, interacts with rather than supplants the tutoring *process*. The various sub-*structures* contain and channel the exchange of feelings, ideas and learning at many levels, which constitute the interpersonal *process*. Where structure operates without attention to process, we find tutoring systems which exempt those teachers with no students officially consigned to their care from personal interactions with students and colleagues. This distinction between structure and process is highly pertinent for group work, as a common error in group teaching springs from excessive reliance on increasingly refined structures at the expense of process. This occurs because an emphasis on process is more emotionally taxing for the teacher and may even be frightening. Large bureaucratic organizations demonstrate how easily surplus structures choke and clog any real communication. Almost always the extra structures are brought about by a genuine wish to improve the organization's output, yet the amount of energy expended in conceiving new, complicated structures seems to be in inverse proportion to the results!

(D) The tutoring continuum

I have been asked 'why not simply say "tutoring", instead of "personal tutoring"?' For the sake of brevity 'tutoring' alone often appears in the text but 'personal' is added periodically to remind the reader that tutoring, no matter how academically slanted, always transpires in a personal context and is coloured by the personalities and feelings of all parties involved. In the following chapters great emphasis is placed on academic learning, but these introductory pages are meant to remind the reader of the necessity for a wider tutoring perspective. 'Personal tutoring' also makes the distinction between the wide range of student/ staff relations discussed in these pages, and the 'tutoring' which many suppose occurs only in the tutorial, and which therefore has a much narrower meaning. My definition of personal tutoring makes room for a tutoring continuum, along which this specific but narrow tutorial activity can be placed. At one end of the continuum lies 'academic' tutoring, which is contained by the lecture structure. This 'academic' process blends gradually into the tutoring process which happens in the seminar. Though still subject related, this structure offers more opportunity for informal contact with the teacher. 'Borderline' tutoring permeates the tutorial, and here the process is midway between 'academic' tutoring at one end of the spectrum, and the 'counselling' style of tutoring at the other. (Usually, the tutorial is a less organized and formal affair than is the seminar, lab, or lecture. In helping students look at *how* they learn, write, read, or study, rather than *what* they learn, more chances are created for closer, emotional contact between the students themselves and between teacher and taught.) Further along the continuum still is 'social tutoring' which comprises all those interchanges and relations occurring in non academic situations between staff and students. The effects of social tutoring are often felt, both positively and negatively, in subsequent academic settings! At the opposite end of the spectrum there is the 'counselling' category. Many tutors run 'adjustment groups' of one sort or another; possibly for induction purposes, career planning, social skills training, or preparation for examinations. Others set aside 'counselling hours' to discuss in private any personal problems students may be suffering. Those relationships with students which result in referral to specialist agencies could also come under this heading. Thus the personal tutoring continuum reads 'academic-borderline-social-counselling.'

Summary of the book's contents and exclusions

This book is addressed primarily to two groups of people: tutors and their trainers, whether counsellors, visiting consultants, or staff development committees who influence the design of any in-service programme. The trainer will find no outline of courses or summary of my training methodology here. Instead, he will come upon reports of staff training groups in which the understanding of group functioning is facilitated for the members by their subjective experience of being in a group. The trainer's task is to assist the participants to identify and use the manifest and latent processes which they themselves spontaneously generate by meeting as a training group. The training 'method' then, is demonstrated by the manner in which I conduct these in-service sessions. Also in the section of the book on case studies, routine tutorials and seminars in the academic department are analyzed from my vantage point as observer. After each teaching group session was completed, discussion took place between myself and the group tutor, and major issues emanating from these important conversations appear in the text. Readers are advised to resist the temptation to peruse the case studies first, for without the previous chapters on concepts as a frame of reference, they are nothing more than anecdotes about other tutors' practices, and as such claim only curiosity value.

Neither in the concepts nor the case studies section, do I look at T-groups, gestalt, encounter, behaviorally oriented, or social or study-skills training groups. The reason for this is that whilst these disciplines are all relevant to learning in the widest sense, my intention in these pages is to assist tutors to study familiar groups. Thus I concentrate almost exclusively upon the large institutional group, the seminar, the tutorial and staff groups. The special approaches to group work listed above tend to be used in social science departments, (with the exception of social or study skills training which has a very wide application). The effectiveness of teaching in these modes depends upon the proficiency of the tutor and the willingness of students to engage in a degree of intimacy not usually associated with straightforward undergraduate work. The climate in a social science department may well be conducive to such group work where the study of group processes is often part of the curriculum itself. However, this does not mean that duplication of such approaches is essential or desirable in other college settings where the atmosphere between staff and students is very different. Many other teachers, however, wish for insight into and advice on the management of routine small teaching groups, and this is what I endeavour to provide. The book is for *all* teachers in tertiary education, without preference being given to any one academic discipline. I should like to offer conceptual assistance to all specialisms by enabling group tutors to understand common aspects of group life. I hope that the conceptual material set out will point towards more effective practice when readers are themselves leading groups as part of their professional work. The case studies will, I hope, enlighten those who have as yet little experience of working with groups and will encourage them to persist with their attempts. Case studies of verbal groups only are offered; as drama, role-play, simulation, games and other techniques are used in special circumstances and in particular disciplines. The success of these specialist groups in any case depends on the sensitive manipulation of those group forces explained in the 'concept' chapters. To discuss a group employing specialist techniques could easily obscure the basic principles of group functioning shared by all groups, and it is these I have tried to clarify by presenting case studies.

This is not a scholastic treatise, surveying the enormous field of group literature. I have read many voluminous works and have tried to distil from them that which pertains to tutoring. I must confess to having added my own thoughts and experiences, and to having made many modifications and revisions of other people's work. Much of the literature on groups was produced in medical environments very different to those of higher education. I have extracted from what I know as a group therapist only those ideas and observations which, once translated and refined, I have found to be particularly relevant to the tutoring process as well as to in-service training of tutors.

Although leadership is vital (and one chapter is devoted entirely to leadership), I should like to stress that training for constructive membership is of equal significance to the success of the group and that this is one of the chief duties of the group tutor. Membership is not the same as 'followership' and the *quality and amount of group production is as much the responsibility of the students as the tutor, unless he removes that obligation from them.* This tendency to assume responsibility for tasks which are not theirs is by far the most common mistake made by new tutors. This central question of who bears the responsibility for learning and quality of group discussion should be borne in mind throughout. The tutor must be skilled at providing and maintaining suitable learning conditions. He is a marshaller of resources, and a teacher, but he cannot be a student too and carry out functions the students must perform for themselves. He must help them find their own way of using the group in order to learn and grow, and train them in membership roles, as surely as he must search toward a subjective understanding of his own leadership style. This leadership-membership motif is developed in the early chapters on the small group.

The reading list at the end is arranged in sequence parallel to the chapters, so that readers can select material of personal interest which will amplify points made in a particular portion of the book. The list includes seminal papers and books, which I believe will not date and which explain enduring group concepts.

Unfortunately, very little is written about group work in higher education — hence my desire to produce this book. Therefore, much of what appears in the reading list, though selected for its resemblance to group work in tertiary education, was in fact written for or by group therapists, or therapy trainers. The central group theories were established some years ago and some of these original texts are included in the reading list. Refinements and embellishments of the basic theories are mainly found in the medical literature and are of limited value to teachers. I have therefore left them out.

The names of all tutors in the case studies, and a few other minor details, have been altered to preserve anonymity, but otherwise the narratives are authentic and all took place between 1976 and 1978. The opinions expressed are entirely my own and do not reflect any official college policy in my own institution.

I have coined a few new expressions and these are elucidated as they appear. Other terms which once had an exact clinical meaning are used, but they here express the lay usage. ('Unconscious' for example is the equivalent of 'unaware of'.) A good deal of the technical language is clumsy. This is unavoidable, as the personal tutoring field is still in the early stages of being developed, and all emergent disciplines must struggle with this language problem.

Chapter 2

Systems theory:
an aid to understanding the institution
as a large group

The success of any formal tutoring provision will largely be determined by the amount of convergence between individual tutors' aspirations and the values and traditions permeating the culture in which these tutoring arrangements are set. This chapter will investigate briefly this large group in which tutoring is rooted, along with its subsidiary contexts. Designing complicated tutoring procedures, without even a cursory look at the large-group culture in which they are planted, is as fruitless as trying to understand students' needs and problems without inspecting the dispositions and qualifications of the staff or the nature of the curriculum. Painstaking observation and understanding of how certain teaching methods, the course content, the committee/consultative structure, the assessment procedures, the staff's own morale, constantly influence the way students think, feel and behave, in relation to one another, to teaching staff and to their work, is far more valuable to tutors than a hasty adoption of do-it-yourself 'counselling' whenever a student is in trouble. If tutoring encompasses personal teaching and the creative deployment of course content, and if advantage is taken of potentially supportive teaching situations, tutors will not need first aid counselling kits nearly so often. Nor will students find themselves sent to 'experts' so often as psychological cases. Emergency tactics only help the student put up with an untenable position for longer, rather than affecting the environment which produced or exacerbated the difficulty in the first place.

Tutors are a sub group of a larger departmental group which in turn relates to other groups of groups ('faculty' for example, or 'administration'). It is the responsibility of the tutors to design the local (departmental) culture, both in terms of its actual visible structures (such as teaching groups, personal tutor allocation, committees and so forth), as well as in the more intangible but equally vital terms of shaping attitudes and values concerning the work and staff-student relations. If the staff collectively strive for informal and supportive contact with students, and if they regard academic work as important, but not the only criteria by which people ought to be judged, then students will absorb and perpetuate these attitudes, and will pass them on to freshers.

They will then automatically expect such responses from their tutors and the culture will gradually evolve into one of positive mutual reinforcement. A productive culture cannot be forced into existence by committee decree; it is a matter of tutoring attitudes and consequent behaviour over time.

What is a large group?

Let me go back to basics and ask, 'why call the institution a large group? Why coin a different term when "institution" seems perfectly comprehensible?' The answer is that an institution brings to mind bricks and mortar, rules and regulations, and a fixed set of mechanized unchanging activities going on within it. When we say something, or some person or some idea has been institutionalized we recognize that we are suggesting the impossibility of change. 'The large group' though, reminds us of the small significance of the campus *per se*, compared with the vast organization of bustling persons who populate it for study or job purposes, and whose personalities are affected by the norms and traditions which imbue all their dealings with each other. The *institution* is merely a physical boundary, an inanimate 'thing', comprising physical sub boundaries. Within it though, many *groups* of people, (such as teachers, students, administrators, caterers, and porters) interrelate, altering, developing, modifying or maintaining the other groups' functions and functioning. When we speak of a large group then, we are referring to a *field of interpersonal forces* which change, grow and/or decay. This is opposed to the idea of a timeless lifeless mass called 'the institution', which merely houses the force field (the large group). Another very basic but apposite question, if we are to use 'large group' as a descriptive phrase, might be 'what *is* a group anyway?' There are several ways of describing a group. Perhaps the simplest is by using a map (see diagram 1 page 23). A group (whatever size) is *any social aggregation that has an external boundary and at least one internal boundary*. Seven people sitting in a doctor's waiting room, lost in their own private thoughts do not constitute a group, because there is no social factor; the people in it do not interact. However, they may become a group if they get together to exchange symptoms or to complain about how long they have been waiting. A group has to have some purpose however ill-defined. Some kind of leadership will emerge in relation to this purpose, so that in our waiting room Mrs Smith may find herself 'elected' to go and complain to the receptionist about the long wait, when, sitting alone before the inception of the group she may well have lacked the courage to challenge the receptionist's authority.

Boundaries and boundary maintenance

The external boundary is simply a line dividing members from non-members. The boundary can be time, a place, a shared precept; it is a set of material conditions, and/or of notions within which the group must carry out its business. Boundary distinguishes 'inside' from 'outside', and it can be rigid or flexible in varying degrees at different times. For example, the upper echelons of a university will undoubtedly have fairly rigid boundaries around its long standing committees, and very little immigration or emigration of members occurs. They may be seen by those outside the boundary to be sealed off groups, tightly guarding their secrets and policy decisions. A more flexible boundary might enclose a staff/student consultative committee where members are elected and stand down regularly. Here, it is fairly easy to get in or out providing one is prepared to abide by all those rules, expressed and implied, which have grown up over time as boundary stabilizers. A very loose boundary encompasses the large lecture — almost anyone can attend, and membership may become quite casual; it is hard to identify who is inside and who outside the group.

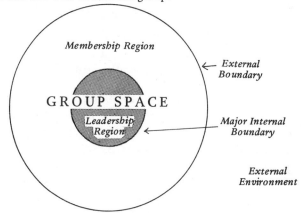

Figure 1: A Simple Group System

Boundaries can shrink or expand, and become stretched or pulled by rebels within and invaders without. A staff meeting for instance, may expand its boundaries to include free discussions about teaching effectiveness, in addition to going through the usual business agenda. Towards examination time a tutor may shrink the boundaries of a seminar so that only subject related work may be studied within its perimeters, where formerly a casual social-cum-work culture prevailed. The students, anxious about assessment, may welcome this contraction and cooperate with the tutor to strengthen this new tighter boundary in order to get through the syllabus.

I visited one college as an external consultant where feelings were running high among the staff of one particular department. Within the staff meeting, which met for a whole afternoon once a term, two factions waged war on one another. Members of faction A wanted more training in identification and referral of students' problems, and felt they could not cope with all those students who, though they were assigned to tutors in faction B, kept approaching them whenever they had personal problems. There were teachers 'in the middle', members of neither faction, the 'silent majority,' who could not understand what all the fuss was about, and were neither inundated with, nor studiously avoided by, problem students.

Instead of a comfortable boundary:

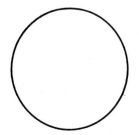

around the staff group, what had happened was that faction A had stretched the boundary in the direction they felt it should go, and faction B (who seemed to support the view that academics should teach and not counsel, and that students should learn to face their own problems without running for help all the time) had pulled it the opposite way, leaving the silent majority in the centre. The boundary was thus:

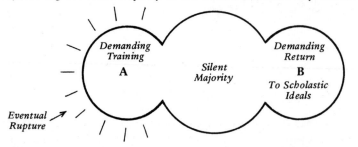

Faction A became so indignant that they ruptured the boundary and formed a côterie of like-minded tutors who held their own meetings. This left the rest of the original staff group with the problem of healing the torn boundary. A particularly dogmatic woman emerged as leader and persuaded most of the silent majority that they had been spared a dreadful fate by the retreat of faction A, though one or two of these middle-of-the-road people were looking longingly at the rupture in the boundary and wondering whether to slip through before it was repaired to join faction A. However, the group pressure which resulted from the new leader making the boundary more rigid prevented them from leaving or daring to air dissident views. The department ended up with two separate groups, A and B, both operating within impenetrable boundaries, and with no group ambassador allowed to emerge from either to negotiate. Very rigid boundaries, or loss of them altogether, is always symptomatic of an ailing group. Faction A thought it had given birth to a new healthy group, but its defensive rigidity excluded co-operation with other members of the department, and the staff group could no longer function as a unit. Student unrest soared during this time, as one sub group fought against another. As matters improved, following external intervention, it became clear that the members of faction A were genuinely afraid of being forced into the role of amateur counsellors and beneath their angry demand for more training was a wish to be protected from these psychological pressures and a request for support from senior colleagues. Faction B mainly consisted of powerful senior staff members. They had not seen or appreciated the fearfulness or the insecurity of the junior staff, and found them to be rebellious and subversive. As a result, they felt so threatened that rather than assisting the junior staff, they retreated to a familiar entrenched position, that of advocating a return to scholasticism and discipline. Faction A failed to understand how damaging was the hostility masking their fear to the older staff members; they saw in their colleagues only reactionary attitudes and a refusal to move with the times. It took a long time for boundaries to loosen, for ambassadors to cross borders and negotiate and finally for the two groups to reconvene as one, with a larger, more flexible boundary around it and the silent majority beginning to use their voice at last. Whenever the former polarized situation threatened to recur it was usually someone from this middle population who would look after the boundaries and prevent rupture by getting the two factions to talk to one another more honestly and directly rather than using abstract political and educational debate as weapons with which to beat the opposition.

It is the duty of all tutors, whether they are teaching students, taking part in a departmental meeting, or representing the department at some other gathering, to maintain, repair, rebuild or renegotiate group boundaries, so that the purpose for which the group has come together may be more easily achieved. People who fall through boundaries, or who feel boundaries around their most important groups are unsafe (and this applies to everyone, staff and students) can become quite alienated, lost and depressed. Other people, despite really serious personal, professional, financial, academic or other problems can function extremely well if they inhabit a series of stable groups — family, friends, colleagues, teacher/student groups, to mention but four of the most common. A student's mental health and his academic motivation are not innate and static. Neither are the tutor's! Motivation and health will improve or regress depending upon many factors, not the least of which is the person's feelings about membership of the various sub groups of the large group that makes up his college life. A student may hate Professor X's seminar, but makes up for it by going to Dr Y's thrilling lectures, attending dramsoc, drinking in the bar with close friends and sitting on Union committees in the evening. He revises with friends from his tutorial group in the library and then goes home to what for many would be an appalling family situation of deprivation and brutality. That he can live there and study for a degree is possible because of his group membership, and the recognition of safe reassuring boundaries all about him in his college life. Another student, after losing a new girlfriend, may cave in altogether and require psychiatric treatment. A brief glance at his group life often reveals an existence so arid that one begins to understand why his brief affair with this girl had meant so much and why her loss triggered off his total despair. He misses tutorials because he is self-conscious; he cannot concentrate on lectures, as he is too preoccupied with his social isolation in the lecture theatre; he belongs to no social or political groups; he studies in solitude and spends his evenings alone in a bedsit miles from the campus. He does not know how to negotiate boundaries.

Tutors are boundary builders, looseners, reinforcers and repairers and may help students more than they know by performing this duty well, continually preventing casualties without realizing it. The majority of students will somehow survive an ailing group without boundaries, or a group where the boundaries are much too rigid, but even so, they will have to adjust to countless new group contexts in the future and a bad experience in one year or section of the course, be it in a small or large group, may predispose them to desperate survival behaviour in new contexts where it would be quite unnecessary, and in which it would only serve to make them unpopular or even rejected. This would confirm these students' suspicions about groups being hostile places and henceforth they would be on the slippery slope to isolation. The tutor needs to take more care in looking after the whole group, its culture and its boundaries than in selecting individuals for his special attention. When students do come to him privately as a personal tutor and confide personal problems, of loneliness or unpopularity perhaps, the wise tutor will help the student look at his group life inside and outside academic structures, across all his experiences within this huge university group of which he is now a member. He will ask the student to pause and think about how he might gain entry across new borders and how he might learn to deserve his membership within these precincts, at last belonging somewhere through his own efforts rather than by the patronizing intervention of the tutor. Encouraging exclusive dependency on the kind, sympathetic personal tutor will not of itself help students to manage group living.

The leadership zone

All groups, whether simple, or large and complex comprising dozens of other interlinking sub groups, are structured enclaves which distinguish between membership and non-membership, and contain at least two classes of people, leaders and members, who may be officially or unofficially labelled as such. Those in the membership region may attack or be invited into the leadership region. On a large group scale we are familiar with student sit-ins, which nearly always seem to represent an occupation of the leadership zone. The choice of territory to be occupied is almost always that of some august personage or committee. Occupying the lavatories would cause far more disruption but does not have the necessary leadership status attached to it! Students who graduate, however, and become teachers in their old university are invitees into rather than invaders of the leadership region The leadership zone itself has a boundary which is pliable (see diagram 1 page 23) unless the leadership area is undergoing great stress owing perhaps to conflict between the leaders which may result in greater rigidity of the boundary or its destruction. If changes within or without menace this major internal boundary the total group is in real jeopardy. It is therefore essential that the boundary round the leadership zone is kept flexible enough to accommodate strife within, between leaders, and attack or appeals for help from the membership region, as well as stress from the community outside the group boundary. Tutors are placed in the leadership region by virtue of their profession. They are therefore obliged to ensure some degree of harmony between themselves and other colleagues and to guarantee the student members enough space and opportunity to trade across the leadership boundary and also to renegotiate it when it becomes inflexible. Otherwise apathy or rebellion sets in and the leadership zone is no longer able to function adequately.

Tutors should also be aware of the world outside the external boundary which brought the students to the campus and which soon will receive them once more. Students ought to be enabled by their staff leaders to help themselves and fellow students manage the entry into and exit from the external boundary and the transitional upheavals, both practical and psychological, which beset them as they cross this boundary at the beginning and end of their university membership. In some institutions, special groups for those arriving and those preparing to leave are organized by tutors to help the students share feelings and thoughts about their situation. These groups are designed to help the students overcome anxieties, and foster confidence in their emergent strengths. The students also discover the value of peer support and learning.

The interdependence of individual and group

Individualistic minded readers may feel irritated with my predilection for groups and fear that I am denying the existence of individuals who

27

have a right to differentiate themselves from the various group masses to which they are forced to belong. My belief is that we do not have a dichotomy here at all. A great many of us assume that 'individual' and 'group' are separate concepts, but in fact the two are so inextricably linked that one requires the other for itself to exist. Without groups (the family, tribe, culture) no individual can survive, and without separate identity, aloneness, there can be no sense of belonging, no attraction toward the formation of a group. To ignore or minimize the relevance of group teaching and staff-group functioning in a university is foolish and anti-educational.

The very notion of 'self' is social. We tend to evaluate our 'selves' according to how we were treated by our primary groups. We learn to be human within the family, the playground, the school, with our brothers and sisters, our teachers and our friends. If we have been loved and respected, our self concept is that we are lovable and worthy and we feel we are able to love and respect other people. It is in groups that we learn to fight, share, communicate, love, lose and win; we learn to to support others, reduce their pain, join in their exultation; to lean and be leant on, to give and to take.

In the myriad groups to which a child belongs he learns not from one parental source but from many; he can compare, contrast and assess others' ways of managing feelings and experience, not just his mother's. He has a wide choice about whom he will imitate and learn from, endlessly modifying his conclusions to fit in with his changing perceptions of himself, until eventually he develops personality traits which make him feel equally at home with himself or with others in a group situation. Given that we learn so many vital things about ourselves in groups it seems a natural step to educate our students in manageable comfortable groups, with which they can easily identify, and in which they can acquire new and exciting insights about themselves and the world they live in. This is not to say that small group teaching is the only worthwhile method of teaching, but that without it a central educational experience is lost, to both teachers and taught. A variety of learning groups, differing in size, function and teaching techniques used, creates opportunities for individual needs to be met. Some students love small cosy tutorials while others prefer a formally structured seminar. The same goes for the tutors. The greater the range of groups offered and the more fluid the teaching policy, the more chance there will be for students and staff to learn, unlearn, relearn and experiment with all manner of relationships with each other.

Such fluidity alarms many tutors who cannot bear to make errors, and who feel they must keep up academic appearances at all costs. They clamour for more course structure and rely heavily on desks, notes, blackboards and other teaching accessories to bolster their authority image, because they are really afraid of not coming up to some standard of perfection which they, or their own parents or teachers, have instilled into them. The students taught by such a tutor copy his style because they assume they must enact the stereotype of the perfect student, a role which they cannot fulfil either. Desks, notes and blackboards can be used to better ends by a tutor who can consent to the group being in actuality a group, rather than rows of silent receptacles waiting passively for information. Even in huge lecture auditoriums, skilled tutors versed in a group approach can secure participation by such methods as forming working sub groups (often sending ambassadors to one another across the lecture hall), encouraging joint note-taking, shared blackboard scribbling and other personal learning transactions. Thus it may be seen that the group ethic is just as useful in large situations as small ones, and that the lecture has an important place in the teaching repetoire.

Groups as natural phenomena

An awful lot of nonsense is talked about groups and group jargon can sometimes give the impression to a neophyte that a group is a profoundly mysterious organism understood only by a highly trained specialist. In fact we have all lived our lives in groups, but have been conditioned to think in individualistic terms. We all possess a huge store of data relating to groups in our memory banks; if only we could gain access to it, we could use it. People are born into groups and die usually leaving a group behind; they function in groups in their work and leisure periods; they marry into groups, and join professional and hobby groups.

In establishing an institution of higher education, the state has provided a ready-made group system (see diagram 1 p. 23.) It can develop or decay, but cannot remain still, simply because it is a *living* system. Since tutors cannot escape this large group while they remain in office, they are well advised to try and comprehend the forces active within its boundaries, so they will add to rather than detract from or sabotage the large group system's purpose. Neglect, in my view, is an insidious form of sabotage, even though it may not be intended as such. The education worked for can only be achieved by staff and students relating to each other; the exploitation of group forces by the leader affects the functioning of the leadership as well as the membership zone. *Everyone* is part of this large group and what affects tutors will affect students for they all live and work within the same system. Although the tutors' and students' interests and functions are not identical they cannot operate successfully without co-operation with each other. Separated and strictly defined boundaries between them are highly undesirable, as undesirable and probably more so as the formation of factions A and B described earlier.

Tension, antipathetic to teaching and learning in institutions of higher education, often arises when staff and/or students become so angry at the rigid boundaries that confine them that they eventually revolt, destroy traditional boundaries and regroup themselves into angry cliques. These angry cliques feel persecuted by the greater system and withdraw from it. Alternatively, people become insecure because they think their own little piece of group territory is being taken over and the boundaries might yield to the invader, leaving them alone and undefended. This happened in a college where staff were suddenly asked, without discussion or preparation, to break up their usual fairly big teaching sessions (classes, lectures) into very small ones and to use 'modern' small group approaches within them. Teachers and students were confused by the boundary change, particularly as the leaders felt they could not discharge their new obligations properly, through a combination of ignorance, fear and resentment. Although the existence of groups is natural and ubiquitous, any imposed boundary change needs to be gradual if culture shock of leader and members is to be prevented.

Boundary types

(a) Boundary loss

Boundary loss denotes absence or vagueness of boundary, which results in confusion about group identity. The most common example of this is where neither the students nor the staff concerned appreciate the difference between, say, a tutorial and a seminar. They try to use both in the same manner, despite a difference in numbers or subject matter. The result is that people are not sure what the group's task is and why the course leader bothers to introduce two different academic structures if they are identical. Both settings frustrate the diverse needs of the learners. Another example of boundary loss can be found in the departmental troubles already discussed in this chapter. Faction A wanted the staff meeting to be training oriented, and faction B insisted it was a business meeting only. There were two different boundary perceptions, and no one would clarify or renegotiate, least of all the designated leader, the head of department. The leader abdicated his responsibilities as he could not face a confrontation in his group, and the consequence was group breakdown preceding the emergence of a new leader.

(b) Rigid boundary

A rigid boundary is exemplified by a teacher who runs his class in an authoritarian style, insists on absolute attendance, discipline and regular handing in of work. Everyone knows where they stand and written work is endlessly churned out. Any miscreants are punished or expelled from the group. No one can get into or out of the group without strict adherence to the accepted rules. No one can come near enough to the teacher to discuss possible modifications in his approach. Academic results may be very good if this teacher's methods fit in well with those of the examining board (another sub group system with a rigid boundary?) If the boundaries are unassailable because of the tutor's need to defend against the threat of 'progressive' methods, and he is in the minority among his colleagues, he may be sitting on a time bomb of student protest, and risking alienation from colleagues at a time when he will most need their support and guidance. On the other hand, rigidification of a boundary can ensure survival of the group in the face of external threats. When finals loom on the horizon, students willingly co-operate in tightening the group boundaries so as to help them get down to solid work.

(c) Boundary under stress

The following is an example of a boundary under stress. A tutor, supported by a few keen students, enjoyed a certain course unit which the authorities were trying to discontinue in favour of another unit which had already started, and which was proving popular and economical in terms of staff time. The two groups, one in the process of being phased in and the other out, were at war, and the border squabbles used up most of the available energy so that little work in either group was done. Safe boundaries which do not need to be defended are necessary if staff and students are to work together.

(d) Stable boundary

A stable boundary is one with no particular problems, but neither is there much creative activity within it owing to insufficient 'trading'.

(e) Flexibible boundary

A flexible boundary is the most satisfactory. It is flexible enough to allow influences from other groupings to penetrate, to receive 'visitors', and to send out 'ambassadors', yet there is no loss of group identity as a result. This two-way trade enriches the group's culture. An example is a staff dining club which maintains its own character despite occasionally inviting students to join in its sprees. It has an annual change of management committee, and encourages new recruits. It sends emissaries to student union banquets and parties on an exchange basis and sends members to other colleges' dining clubs as well as extending hospitality to them.

Groups as living systems

This early portion of the book is concerned with concepts and so an introduction to a systems theory approach to groups might clarify both the language and the assumptions which are liberally scattered throughout the text. Many tutors believe that handling a small, medium or large group involves applying new techniques to a series of random individuals, but in fact the most vital change required is a perceptual one. The tutor should begin to see and think and observe *holistically*. Using this new conceptual framework, what to do and say in the group, when and how, becomes comparatively easy. It is this profound attitudinal shift *inside* the tutor, rather than the adoption of isolated and frantic techniques, that makes for successful group work.

When her child cries, a mother interprets the cry in the light of her total understanding (ie she perceives it holistically) of the child's personality and history, as well as her own relationship with him. Any other adult in the vicinity, without this framework, hears only the cry and not its meaning. He is unsure what to do about it, or even how to understand it, so, if he has to cope, he resorts to desperate attempts at pacification — sweets, money, cuddles — to try and alleviate the distress. New students at university often feel very lost among a wide array of groups, from the very small to the enormous. Their intelligence alone is no longer sufficient to calm their fears about how to manage the new learning tasks, which bear little relation to earlier school work. Unrecognizable or unstated boundaries resulting from inadequate group tutorials/seminars confuse, bewilder and cause pain. This pain is sometimes expressed through work problems — the equivalent of the child's cry. Tutors need more than academic sweets to cope with this stress! If they themselves felt comfortable in various groups, and if they functioned expertly in their own staff groups, they would foster a sense of security in, and elicit high quality work from their students who would absorb from them this relaxed confidence concerning group settings. The child who is cut and bruised takes solace, ceases crying and carries on with life, not from the words, bandages and aspirins administered by his mother, but from the safety of their relationship and its protective, well defined boundaries. Identical assistance from any other adult source provides little comfort. Similarly, a feeling of being valued by the tutor within clearly defined academic boundaries spurs the learning process in groups. Comforting and confident relationships among members, fortified by the leader, are more relevant to the students' work than lists of study hints and exam tactics, which are mere academic bandages!

General systems theory has been characterized as a bold new development in human thought, though its central idea about the search for global concepts is not at all new. However, in recent years, a great number of complex fields previously unapproachable through classic science have been mapped out in systems terms and the literature is growing rapidly. Systems theory has evolved out of ideas about all reality being a collection of systems, about universal interrelatedness. Systems have been described as 'sets of elements standing in interaction'. (Miller, 1965.) A single system is always related to other systems, and it behaves according to a pattern; it operates on some quantity, which may be information, energy matter or a combination of these. (For example a jet engine converts certain chemicals into thrust.) In any system there is some input, an operating process and an output. This term 'system' indicates that an overall operational process is being examined, rather than a mere collection of isolated pieces. In terms of higher education let me take a classroom situation. In whatever way the class is managed, its existence represents a social system. Its inputs are related to the operational processes of the whole university. Students and their teachers enter and leave the classroom, materials and physical facilities are made available. Human relationships are regulated. This little social system is tied in with other systems — a course, a department, a faculty, the university and society — all of which affect the classroom system, to a greater or lesser extent, according to the ease with which information can cross the class's boundary. Within the boundary there is an intricate network of interactions and relationships composed of seating arrangements, status hierarchies, social differences, authority structures, different learning histories, abilities, and so on. Members of the class may be studied as individual systems, in dyads, or in small sub groups. Each of those bases for interaction are sub systems of the classroom.

Teachers are supposed to help students learn, and so they must attempt to sensitize them to information in the environment and within themselves. How the students process this information will to a large degree be fashioned by the tutor's example. If he thinks holistically they will too. When people are actively and dynamically related within an interpersonal situation (such as a classroom) their behaviour will tend to change as a result of that social system. Students may influence the teacher, but given his function and role within the system (especially during the early stages of its life), the students will adapt their behaviour and thinking modes to fit his, and thus try to build an atmosphere in which to ease communication. The tutor, in a group of whatever kind, is passing on to students far more than academic facts or opinions. He is offering them an example of how one person sees and experiences the world, manages his feelings and his thinking responses to the environment, assimilates knowledge, processes data, and how he succeeds or fails in making personal contact with fellow humans.

For the group to be effective, it is therefore vital that tutors study themselves as much as their subject. If they themselves can learn to operate at a high level of enjoyment, learning, and personal relating as a member of a group, then they are certain to make excellent group tutors. Tutor training programmes should offer opportunity for ongoing self-study groups with this aim, although this unit of training will tie in with other sub systems of tutor training. The total training system's external boundaries must overlap the boundaries of the tutors' day to day work, so that the one system trades with and is enriched by information from the other. This is one reason, over and above the practical and economic ones usually cited, that the in-service kind of training is often more fruitful than external short courses which are removed from the academic system (large group) to which any new learning about tutoring must be transplanted. Occasional training exchanges with colleagues in other academic systems, providing boundaries do not become obscured, can be extremely valuable as an exercise in cross-fertilization of ideas, but they are no substitute for regular monitoring of the tutoring work in its place of origin.

To return to the idea of systems thinking ('groups' being synonymous with 'social system'); most of us are accustomed to conceiving reality as a collection of parts, bits and pieces, entities, components and objects. As mere humans we are limited in our ability to deal with more than a few variables at a time, so we seek to make reality more comprehensible and less frightening by arbitrarily narrowing its parameters, dividing it into parts. We also live in a culture and use a language, both of which sanction the artificial subdivision of nature. We are taught from infancy to perceive the world as a collection of 'things', – components. Our education system divides rather than synthesizes knowledge. As the frontiers of knowledge broaden, the teaching and learning measures are supported by a scientific culture, much of which seeks truth in smaller and smaller segments, or hives off sub sections of knowledge into enclosed specialisms, with little room for intercourse with other specialisms. We are all continually assured that the first step toward understanding requires that we place finite limits or boundaries on the subject matter under consideration and study it in isolation from the whole of which it is but a part. This is the stuff of our culture, our language, our education, our deeply ingrained reinforced thought patterns. Is it any wonder many tutors are afraid to tackle groups holistically, to view them as human systems, within which individual systems and dyadic and other systems operate? What is being asked of them is a conceptual shift, and one with enormous implications. Of course, one can argue that by using such terms as 'systems' and 'sets' (and in human systems, 'small groups' 'large groups' and so on) we are again talking about units, things and parts – so there is no progression at all! This elucidates the constraints of our culture and language whenever we try to capture the essence of dynamic and ubiquitous interrelationships.

Perhaps Eastern thought, with the 'relationship thinking' rather than the 'thing thinking' of the West is more useful here. (Fortunately, many students are already interested in Eastern philosophy and have discussed it among themselves. Perhaps they can teach us about it, if we can let them cross our personal boundaries.) The concept of systems as sets of smaller wholes, and the notion of large wholes themselves can both be seen as parts and pieces, and demonstrate the limitations of atomistic thinking that characterize such perceptions. There is no new concept here. Rather, it is in the *interrelationships* of systems, the movement of forces within and between them, where the new ideas can be found. This is where tutors and their colleagues, and tutors and their students, must search for fresh insights into teaching and learning in groups. No man and no group is an island!

Reciprocal influence of the social system and its constituent members

The label 'tutor' denotes its wearer's personal involvement with colleagues and students, together with his academic engagement. His university world is made up of complex socio-academic organizations. (Social and academic transactions cannot be easily separated, as one set of transactions is but a facet of the other in college life, though different groups accentuate social or academic processes at different times.) He is leader at one time, led at another; giver, then receiver; he is at the top then at the base of a status hierarchy. His tutoring, which includes his own internal feelings, will be constantly impinged upon by these varied systems, which are not 'things' but groups of people with whom he cannot avoid interacting. As he learns his trade through introspection, experience and training, and as students through inspired tutoring learn theirs, both increase their control over their shared environment and over the tasks to be carried out in it. They all become more independent.

Attainment of independence does not mean that other people become superfluous; on the contrary, it shows an ever increasing willingness to extend one's *interdependence* with the environment in all directions. In the rather cold terminology of general systems theory such individuals and their institutional groups become open, self-correcting systems, within and among other open systems. The effective generation and management of interdependence is a skill each tutor must first develop, in himself and for himself, so that he may create open group systems in which students can learn it too. One cannot instruct a student about such matters; he must learn through his own experience of the open group systems made available by tutors. Tutors can be assisted to learn this 'openness and self correction' for themselves during inservice training groups. Interdependence within a system of human relationships engenders feelings of strength and security as opposed to the weakness and vulnerability authority-dependent people feel when the authority figures are removed or take their leave. The individuals so abandoned experience a loss of personal boundary and are therefore highly susceptible to new, possibly adverse, authoritarian influences. The educational, social and political implications are clear, and there are many gruesome historical instances of the authority-dependency tie operating in large closed social systems, involving totalitarian governments at either right or left ends of the political spectrum.

Many of the most important determinants of human behaviour lie outside the individual himself in the properties of the social systems of which he is a member. With these he must interact. By applying a systems approach we can see that these large institutions and organizations that make up society are themselves complex human systems which are potentially as amenable to understanding and change as the psychological system of the individual, with which we in our individual counselling and tutoring work are familiar. These social systems: classroom, department, university for instance, possess many of the same characteristics and problems as do individuals. Sometimes they are riven with conflict; they can mature or degenerate or even die. They go through developmental phases, as do persons; they undergo phases of creativity and stagnation. Often when severe problems arise it is the large group which requires diagnosis rather than the small group, or an individual student or tutor. Unfortunately, temporary human systems such as small teaching groups can be abused and exploited as a feeble expedient through which attempts are made to change behaviours and attitudes which really result from pathogenic factors in the permanent large system, (eg among the departmental, faculty, or total staff). For example, small group teaching is not a cure-all for student discontent or bad examination results.

In some circumstances the authorities may need to seek intervention from an external consultant who has access to all sub systems of a department or faculty in a way they do not. They need a person who is unbiased and who can therefore establish the necessary links between them. Tutors should always attempt to obtain sanction from the higher order systems in the academic hierarchy before instigating such new and potentially explosive activities. Otherwise they may encapsulate themselves within a rigid boundary, cut off from the rest of a suspicious institution, and bi-directional hostility reduces any possibility for improvement. Such has been the fate of many self-styled academic 'revolutionaries'.

If change is desired throughout the entire system or a large sub system, then the dyadic tutor-student contact must cease to be regarded as the end point in the development of tutor skills. The concept of student as learner must expand to include the learning group, the learning tutor, the learning department and the learning college. All large group members are in this respect students, and all should teach each other. In order to accomplish such an institutional level of development high ideals are not enough. The social learning systems in which tutors are prepared for their professional work must be improved. Tutors should be helped to understand themselves as members of social systems and equipped to design and apply tutoring strategies that reach far beyond one-to-one chats about personal problems, or delivering factual lectures to rows of unknown faces. These two tutoring settings are not unnecessary but they are by no means the essence of tutoring. Refusal to speculate about and eventually study the institution as a whole will ensure that although students may obtain the qualifications sought they will fail to improve the human systems into which the university will eventually eject them. The unsatisfactory condition of the greater society will perpetuate itself, unchanged and unchanging; a rebellious social system that is rebelled against. Gods and ideologies are endlessly and pointlessly erected and toppled. If we cannot send the most intelligent of our young population into the world ready to change systems, surely we have failed them and the society in which we all must live?

Summary

From this chapter we can group together three main sets of expertise required by the social systems oriented tutor:

1 The tutor should be able to isolate and analyze the effectiveness of communication routes (literal and metaphorical) within the various student and staff systems, and help broaden those channels, linking them to supra or sub systems. He thereby facilitates staff-student and staff-staff relations in many permutations, while ensuring that the course structures underpinning these relations are coherent. Along with his colleagues, he is an agent of departmental and even institutional change, where boundary problems and system-clogging require intervention.

2 To carry out these functions, competent human relations skills are vital. In twosomes, in groups and between groups the tutor fosters growth producing interpersonal relationships by sensitive management of others' feelings, and by his own personal example. He must therefore learn to be open to and to understand his own personality and the effect it has on other people. Mutual contemplation and shared introspection with other people is therefore an essential ingredient of any in-service training. This aspect of training, perhaps because of its initially embarrassing nature, has been universally ignored in teacher-training programmes. This serious omission has, in my view, contributed to many of our serious educational problems.

3 The tutor needs to thoroughly master the area of data processing; how to code, store, retrieve and communicate appropriate information to student systems. What is referred to here of course are the teaching skills, methods, and techniques which are taken so much for granted. These need regular overhaul as the varied social systems in which they are used alter and develop. The students who are members of these systems will express, over time, new needs in order to meet the demands and problems of the social system to which they must ultimately return and from which so many ivory-towered academics seek refuge.

Small group teaching in relation to the academic work: a modified Theme-Centred-Interactional (TCI) approach

Over-reliance on techniques

The working definition of tutoring cited in chapter 1 was that tutoring is a term which describes 'all those professional activities, attitudes and personal relationships which characterize all the teacher's dealings with all students'. The term is applicable to both teaching and non-teaching situations though the tutoring here described occurs at the academic end of the continuum discussed in chapter 1. Delivering a lecture, distributing notes, feeding subject data into a student group is only a very small portion of the tutoring process. The major part of group tutoring is assessing the group's mood and its readiness for or resistance to, the assimilation of new material, so as to plan how and when what sort of data to introduce. A *personal* approach has to be introduced into teaching for group tutoring to succeed. Some may argue that such assessment constitutes not 'tutoring' but teaching *method*. I prefer the active term 'tutoring' because 'methods' usually comprise a series of recommended techniques and as such are inanimate, divested of those interpersonal connotations which are the essence of good tutoring and without which learning is inhibited. Techniques can be very useful but must be used with discretion, and in conjunction with an understanding and appreciation by the tutor of the students' current psychological, social and academic preoccupations.

The application of small group teaching became very fashionable a few years ago when students claimed they preferred groups to large seminars or anonymous lectures. Many teachers and students failed to appreciate that the simple re-arrangement of people into small random units did not, of itself, improve learning capacity or lead to more productive staff/student relations. The results were disappointing for these groups represented only a new technique rather than a radical change of educational philosophy and policy. In fact, group work is altogether different to presenting formal lectures. It requires tremendous reorientation on the part of the tutor who must then train students to exploit this new environment, using fresh approaches to learning and discarding attitudes more appropriate to older-established teaching structures.

Over reliance on 'parent-child' approaches

Regrettably, a rather sentimental view of tutoring is perpetuated by many well-meaning, experienced senior tutors and tutor-trainers. This view stipulates that tender loving care will suffice in a group and that kindness is the highest virtue. Such a benevolent stance may appear on the surface to have much to commend it but we ought to remember that this shepherd-like figure is supposed to be educating and preparing intelligent young people for life, not protecting them from its vicissitudes. The philanthropic approach devalues the tutor's academic knowledge and teaching abilities, which tend to be regarded as an insignificant series of ritualized skills, easily duplicated for each new batch of students. I believe that the effective tutor should not be such a shepherd-like philanthropic figure. Genuine group tutoring is vigorous and exciting, full of opportunities to develop insight into the learning-and-teaching process, as well as into the tutor's own human relations potential. These two sets of insights are interdependent, for students' learning (as opposed to the memorizing of facts) flourishes in the rich soil of a personal tutor-student and tutor-group relationship that is confronting yet humorous; mutually critical, yet affectionate; well able to tolerate the inevitable troughs of gloom and fatigue which descend on most regular group meetings. The repetition of familiar techniques, irrespective of what the group and its members are doing, thinking and feeling is unhelpful and sometimes disastrous. Learning in a group will fade where there is absence of interpersonal commitment; where there is excessive passivity on the part of the learner; where roles are polarized, so that the teacher is 'wise parent' to the helpless student 'children'.

Values and norms about how teachers should behave and what attitudes students should take up towards staff are often passed on through generations of teachers and students via old-fashioned tutoring systems based on a cosy two-person parental model. The sudden introduction of group tutoring into such a deceptively supportive culture throws this role-playing into sharp relief and its ineffectiveness as a preparation for future social and professional intercourse is revealed. This contingency has led several institutions to retreat into their old-fashioned teaching procedures and to refuse to confront and analyze the limited learning possibilities generated by their dated, if comforting, tutoring structures. Paternalistic tutoring has its place; all students can benefit from parental assistance, now and then. However, paternalistic tutoring contacts must be dyadic, (ie they cater for couples). They take little account of peer support or shared study. In this situation roles are polarized: one person (the teacher) is perceived as, and behaves as though he were, wise and good (a veritable tower of strength) while the other (the student) is perceived as and behaves as if he were ignorant, confused and as dependent as a child. Such fixed roles are totally inappropriate to group work, however adapted they may be to dyadic relations. When called upon to practise group work, the difficulty with which many lecturers are faced is to stop relying upon an old set of security-inducing teaching premises. A transplanting of the pairing approach to a group is not possible, though many tutors try, and their groups fail to achieve work targets, or even survive, as a result.

Starting group work — fears of inadequacy

Great personal adjustment is required of the prospective group tutor and so he should not feel too alarmed by the discovery that despite this experience and goodwill, he still feels afraid in a group. Trainers and senior tutors should respect the fear of those new to group work and help them understand and share the origin of the fear rather than treating the anxiety as some sort of weakness deserving scorn. It is because many academics fear group work but are ashamed to reveal their fears that they rationalize away the need for this kind of experience and avoid investigating their group-teaching potential. 'Group-teaching is a rotten technique, too gimmicky' — how often have I heard remarks like that! Providing a tutor is prepared to change his own outlook and question sacred assumptions about his teaching, group work need not be frightening. But a teacher who is denying his anxiety about groups and warding off fears of professional inadequacy by rejecting the validity of group work will never find it interesting, nor will he develop the enthusiasm to master group leadership.

In a group, providing members are allowed to participate actively, the tutor is no longer dealing with the manifest and hidden, real and fantasized, verbal and non-verbal communication between two people only. Instead, he is exposing himself to a whole new field of forces. Feelings of vulnerability are to be expected and accepted. Group teaching is a complicated, difficult, (but rewarding) endeavour and the tutor requires not only benevolence and good will, but real expertise plus experience, like any other professional. He needs to understand the various levels of activity going on in the group simultaneously, so that he has more choice about how and when to intervene in the group's conversation. The three most important assets the tutor needs to develop are:

(a) The clear delineation of what the group has been set up to do and the extent to which the goals set can be achieved, (ie confidence about the boundaries).

(b) The detailed observation of latent group phenomena, (ie all those subtle communications and feelings in the group which are detectable just under the surface of the manifest content of what is being rationally discussed). In other words, the asset here is a 'third ear' and 'third eye', which 'scan' the group while the ordinary eyes and ears go about their usual teaching business.

(c) The ability to maintain an awareness of his own reactions to these phenomena and to process them quickly and accurately, so as to help him decide on group management from moment to moment and meeting to meeting.

Let us return to basics and ask, 'what is the difference between a small teaching group and any non-teaching group comprising similar numbers?' (Here I am including tutorials and seminars with a membership of between say, three and 16.) In terms of the group's raw material and developmental possibilities there is virtually none. Groups, like human individuals, share the raw material of intelligence, speech, capacity for emotion etc. Each group, like each person, is unique. All groups diversify, change, go through phases, regress, adapt and so on, in response to the internal and external fate which befalls them, just as individuals do. The major difference between a teaching group and any other group is that a teaching group has a designated central person who is responsible for identifying and understanding ordinary ubiquitous group processes, so as to harness them for the students' benefit. A skilful manipulation of group processes enhances learning; ignorance or unintentional abuse of them can restrict learning and can sometimes even destroy it. Group process can be de-mystified, and tutors helped to experience it themselves in their training groups. They can be taught some of the theory which shapes and organizes that experience. Groups are groups no matter what classificatory label is attached to them; there is nothing strange or mysterious about them (though conducting them is hard work and acquiring understanding of their operation takes time). This is despite what many self-appointed leaders of the group movement would have tutors believe.

Teaching groups can be unpredictable and sometimes unfathomable. Yet it is easy to accept that *individuals* have hidden depths and sometimes display unaccountable behaviour. It does not frighten us when our nearest and dearest do and say things we cannot explain. We shrug and say: 'that's human nature', 'people are funny', or 'that's typical of him'. Yet the dread many teachers feel concerning the workings of groups is out of all proportion to any terrors groups might actually hold. Once teachers can appreciate the way groups pervade every aspect of their daily lives and realize the commonality of group experience, perhaps group teaching might begin to be accepted for the very ordinary situation it is. As infants we learn in family groups; then in peer groups of young children, sharing our sandpit and nursery; in school groups later on; eventually in teenage 'gangs'. Why should adult learning be any different? Why should academic learning suddenly become an isolated business?

The necessity for self-examination by the group tutor

When a student group and their teacher are operating well, individuals experience validation from others of their feelings and attitudes, as well as their knowledge about the topic. Communication represents involvement of the participants, not an exchange of dead data. For data of any sort to live, it must be self-related: ie the students must experience an emotionally laden connection between the topic and themselves, their opinions, longings, fears; their politics, their ambitions, their values. The topic should have meaning in terms of their personal growth; it should challenge its direction, change its course, confirm or modify it. This is as true for mathematics as it is for poetry. This ideal can only be actualized by a teacher who is prepared to take on such emotional involvement.

The need to be aware of the group environment

How can a climate be fostered which would allow teacher and students to exchange fairly deep feelings and yet remain related to the subject under scrutiny? Knowledge can be acquired more readily by those who seek it when the learning environment is free from competitive anxiety; when the group has ceased avoiding the work by various unacknow-ledged 'games'; when there is no rival group preoccupation, such as anxiety about the teacher's attitude, the other students' imagined superiority, or the intellectual difficulties of the course itself. Obstruc-tions like these may have to be dealt with implicitly or explicitly, either between individuals or between the group and the tutor: the field can be cleared before knowledge is planted and eventually reaped. Unfortunately, many classroom techniques deal with the manifestations of such interferences by the use of discipline and/or extra work, or the behaviour is contemptuously ignored. Some tutors do not see it as their job to maintain student interest, or to discover why a group cannot get into subject matter which they find so absorbing. They maintain that any student who is not working must be lazy or unintelligent. Other tutors see group learning difficulties as the 'fault' of the member whose work is the most obviously hampered. There is no further examination of what is actually occurring in the group, between the 'casualty', the teacher and the other members of the group. The 'offending' student is often credited with a 'problem' and despatched to the counsellor or psychiatrist for 'help'. Occasionally this is the correct move to make, but it is often made more by luck than good judgment. In many other instances the student's difficulty is symptomatic of a *group* learning problem which, in the hands of a skilled tutor, could be sorted out in its place of origin, to the educational advantage of all members.

Even more distressing for some group tutors is the notion that they might pause when confronted with a 'problem' group and consider their own resistance to the teaching they are doing. The tutor may have previously quarrelled with a loved one, or had a ticking off from the head of department; he may be envious of his young carefree students who remind him of his former self, or he may be angry at having to teach this topic when his research interests lie elsewhere. He may be very shy and afraid of exposing himself to students and as a result over-prepares the subject. These peripheral matters can influence a group teaching venture in very significant ways; it pays the tutor to be aware of his own worries and fears as well as those of students. The students are not the only ones to have strong feelings about a course, college and teaching approach. It is not suggested that teachers should verbalize everything that goes through their mind when they are doing such mental stocktaking in preparation for a group, but an advance recognition by the tutor of his own feelings, particularly negative ones, is often enough to change his attitude and actions, which in turn will change his students' perceptions of him and hence their ability to work together. A psychologically inhibited tutor prohibits students from using the group freely; this blocks learning, which reduces student motivation and which further inhibits the already under-confident tutor — and so the vicious circle continues.

Feelings then are a crucial element of all learning processes, even though in group teaching they are not the 'official' theme to be explored. If group members' feelings of boredom, irritation, or work fatigue etc are understood as interferences with learning and are given respectful attention by the group and its leader, then a spirit of cooperation will grow. This enables students to share their learning and to teach one another; translating, clarifying, summarizing, lending and borrowing ideas and experimenting with concepts. This climate does not come about by accident. It is generated by a tutor who sees the academic subject as of paramount importance, but also as something which is only amenable to learning once obstacles to concentration and enthusiasm have been removed.

The work of Ruth Cohn

The Theme-Centred Interactional method, (hereinafter referred to as the TCI method) which was first studied and taught at the Workshop Institute for Living-Learning in New York City, provides a simple way of looking at how the topic, the teacher and the group processes can all be accorded the right amount of consideration. What follows is a simplification and derivation of Ruth Cohn's work (see Selected readings) as it applies (in my view) to small group teaching in the English higher education context. The method is holistic and humanistic and based on certain assumptions. For instance, that personal growth combined with education are facilitated when group members become more effective in using their autonomy (responsibility for self), and when they recognize and use, rather than struggle against, interdependence in the group. This is as true for the tutor as for his students. Each student needs to understand that he must rely on the teacher and his comrades in the group as well as on his own innate abilities for the acquisition of knowledge. He must take responsibility for himself and his learning, as well as for his activity/passivity level in the group. He must bear the positive and negative consequences of his own behaviour, academic stances, opinions and so forth, without using the group or the teacher to protect him from aspects of himself and his work, which he would rather disclaim. This is, of course, a sketch for 'group utopia', but these aspirations are important as they point the tutor in a definite direction. The tutor no longer relies on being vaguely 'nice' to the students. Indeed, the more he supports expression of his own and others' autonomy, the stronger, the more differentiated and confident are the contributions he can expect to come from the group. Merely being 'nice' can sometimes make students behave like sheep waiting for the good shepherd to feed his flock, with the right amount and kind of digestible academic tit-bits.

The TCI triangle and its globe

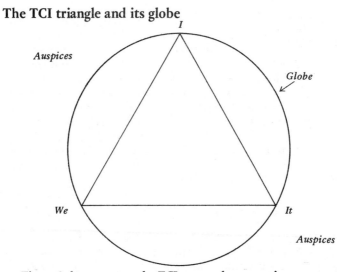

Figure 2 demonstrates the TCI approach to a seminar or tutorial:
a triangle within a globe.

The triangle illustrates the three basic factors which comprise all inter-actional groups:
1 The individual : *I*
2 The group : *We*
3 The theme : *It*

The globe
The globe charts the total environment, both material and psychological, in which the group meeting takes place. It includes such practicalities as the timing and location of the meeting. The globe incorporates such physical details as the presence or absence of desks, whether chairs are in a circle or in rows; whether the phone is allowed to interrupt pro-

ceedings or whether it is taken off the hook, whether the door is open or has an engaged sign on the outside, or whether refreshments are available or not. The globe also constitutes individual emotional states and the prevailing group mood as well as the leaders' current tensions.

Auspices
Unseen but influential factors external to the globe are known as auspices. These are the many determinants which affect the group but which are not present in the room, such as the implications of the group's relation to other groups on the same course and the teaching activity's meaning in terms of the staff rivalries in the department. Another auspice is the teacher's reputation, which reaches the students before he comes into contact with them. In addition, there are all the myths which surround any established course and which are handed down with elaborations from one year's students to the next. The status given to the meeting by other staff and the work's relation to assessment are two other auspices which it would be foolish to ignore.

The *I*, *we* and *it*
Within the globe, surrounded by its auspices, the individual psychological unit *I* must maintain a sense of uniqueness, yet deal with the *we* (ie group relatedness) of which *I* is a part and also manage the *it* (the topic under study.)

The theme
One problem many group tutors find is defining what a particular session with the students is for. The TCI method suggests using an active theme, which is spelled out clearly to all and to which all can respond freely. The theme is treated as common property to which the series of individuals (which includes the *I* that is the tutor) and the group-as-a-whole relates. The theme binds everyone together.

The tutor might view the tutorial as a way of helping individuals to discuss work problems, their difficulties in study, or comprehension of the subject, rather than looking at the subject itself. He may select a theme such as 'revising effectively'. In a seminar, where pursuit of knowledge is usually the understood *raison d'être*, a theme might be 'evaluating the theories of . . . (course subject)'. The gerund 'revising' and 'evaluating' directs everyone in the group towards a clear goal and can be referred to directly by any group participant or the tutor, when discussion strays. Discipline is shared; recourse to the theme is like recourse to the law. A theme with no such use of the verbal noun, eg 'Problems in revision', or 'The various theories of . . .' fails to remind the group that they are there to be effective, or to evaluate respectively. The language chosen to embody the theme must reflect a positive approach. The phrases 'evaluating' and 'revising effectively' are very personal; they cannot be viewed objectively, even though *what* is being revised or evaluated could in many instances be viewed in a rigorously scientific light. But to secure students' interest in the subject, no matter how objective it is, an active verb used in the stated theme encourages students to participate fully.

In a seminar as opposed to a tutorial, I have found that the group tutor tries to further an appreciation of the academic subject itself, but wants to use approaches other than the lecture method and hopes to produce discussion rather than a question-and-answer session. Certainly this is what many keen students demand. In an astrophysics seminar, then, we might select an academically-related theme such as 'travelling toward a black hole'. Such a theme, however like science fiction it may sound, immediately engages the students' intellectual curiosity and personal involvement, as they contemplate how they would feel, confronted by the boundaries of knowledge and a reversal of the physical laws they had always taken for granted. Similarly in a law seminar, where exactitude can be vital, a useful theme might be 'interviewing a client', which blends the personal element (feelings about self as an authority figure and one's management of interviewing techniques) with the professional (the importance of eliciting relevant and precise information). Sub themes could be introduced by the tutor according to the areas of law upon which he wishes to focus. Such themes assist learning in students and maintain their enthusiasm for the subject. The themes may also encourage debating skills, or arouse the students' curiosity about the subject in unanticipated directions. Theme-centerd groups can juggle with students' preconceived ideas, helping them to rearrange concepts and to look at them in different combinations. All these changes in the students' perception of the subject are achievements, but they do not replace the lecture, or the poring over books at home, or the exact laboratory experiments required for some courses. The group and its theme should be seen for what it is and its limitations recognized. Many academics feel that if they were any good they could do it all in a group, and this is not the case. Similarly, although methods of reducing formality and alienation between students in large classes and theatres do exist, teachers might also admit the impossibility of achieving in that setting what can be accomplished in a smaller one, where the students meet regularly and know and trust each other. In a tutorial, where numbers are often very small indeed, one of the auspices affecting the globe is the fact that the tutor is officially appointed to *help*. Great trust is then possible between teacher and students and student and students. Fairly profound examinations can be carried out by the students of the overall course unit and of their ability or inability to deal with the work effectively. In other instances however, the degree of intimacy provided by a tutorial (the regularity of close contact with others, the ever-present threat of unintended self-revelation), frightens many students (and teachers) who prefer a more anonymous atmosphere in a larger group setting. Different teaching structures satisfy different needs. The official role of helper in a small group situation frightens some tutors, as much as the demand to perform in traditional seminars intimidates some students. Auspices and individuals' reactions to them need to be considered.

Globe maintenance and the balancing function

In a group panicked into a silence (perhaps a silence resulting from people's fear of self exposure) the tutor, sensing the cause, would lay great emphasis in a counterbalancing way to the *it* part of the triangle, ie to the theme itself. If on the other hand the theme is already in the forefront but one or two *I*'s are finding it hard to be self-governing (ie to do what they want but fear to do) then the tutor would give his attention to these individuals, encouraging them to participate; helping them, with discretion and subtlety, to become more independent and confident in their opinions. If one person dominates, the tutor will enable that person to see his responsibilities to the whole group, either by assisting that individual to see his bossy behaviour, or by turning his attention to the *we* (the group as a social unit) and inviting 'the group' to comment on, question or defend the dominant student's views. Occasionally the group colludes with the dominant student because this absolves the other members from having to talk. Sometimes the tutor, grateful that at least someone is making a contribution, actually reinforces this student's behaviour! At such times the tutor would do better to turn his attention to the *we* of which he is a part. *We* has a responsibility to ensure productive interplay between people and *we* is responsible for the quality and level of discussion. The teacher who is using the TCI method, would at such a point in a tutorial or seminar draw the *we* attention to what is occurring, so that the group as a whole can alter the unsatisfactory pattern of group interaction. Different tutors will do this overtly or covertly according to their personal styles, which, if the students know them, will be easily understood. What is important here is not the content (words and actions) of the tutor's intervention but his recognition that the *we* corner of the *I we it* triangle is not functioning and needs his help.

The tutor's function in this method then is twofold. Firstly he structures the globe so far as this is within his power and ensures its stability, which is essential if the triangle within it is to remain stable. In practical terms this means he is consistent about time, location and furniture arrangements, as well as his own caring and hardworking attitude. As the students begin to feel safe in this regular, predictable setting, and used to the security of a clear and definite theme which they can understand and respond to, the tutor can then use his second set of skills for maximum benefit. These are his balancing operations which have already been described. He will concentrate on an individual, or the group-as-a-whole, or on the theme, depending on which requires his concern at any given moment. Once this second function is well established (though its actual execution should be unobtrusive) attention to the globe recedes and the *I we it* triangle comes into sharp focus. More intensive work at a more rapid pace can go on at this stage, whereas in the early meetings the building and consolidation of an atmosphere conducive to learning (the educational globe) is far more important than the triangle work. Premature pressure on the corners of the triangle, before they have become firmly supported by the walls of the globe, can cause them to collapse. If this happens, the tutor may begin again, learning from this unfortunate experience. There is no cause for alarm, self-reproach or abandonment of the project. A good deal of practice is required to master any of the group approaches described in this book, because the person using the theories and concepts described is far more crucial to group health than the theories themselves.

Timing

Timing of the tutor's interventions in tutorials and seminars is a very delicate matter. Undoubtedly most teachers intervene too much, even though their motives are impeccable. Intervening too early or too late has a stifling effect on the group. Neglect or over-protection of the individual prevents him from developing intellectual and social autonomy; excessive concentration on an academic topic when the group or individuals in the group require attention (eg if they are unable to comprehend the topic) reduces learning ability and can lead to boredom, irritation or fear of academic failure (which may connote personal failure). The balance between the *I we it* is permanently shifting. The tutor is like a man sailing a yacht. He is seldom still, moving his position all the time so as to ensure that his balancing manoeuvres not only keep the boat afloat, but also keep it moving forward.

Summary of TCI approach

Traditionally, academic teaching concentrated on the *it* (theme or topic) whereas counselling and therapy have concentrated on the *I* (individual), and the more recent group therapy movement on the *we-and-I* (the individual in relation to the group). The TCI method is based on a synthesis of psychoanalytic theory, group dynamics and group therapy and claims a primary interest in education.

A basic approach to seminars and tutorials

In my view, a teacher should not be required to do group therapy or counselling, but can realistically expect to develop, in time, a basic approach to seminars and tutorials which includes:
1 Sensitizing individual participants to recognize and own their autonomy. (*I* functioning.)
2 Helping students understand they are part of an entity and are therefore interdependent, and as a corporate entity can help or hinder the

group's work. The students need to accept group responsibility for group behaviour and not hand over custody to the tutor, who should refrain from accepting it. (*We* functioning.)

3 Clarifying the topic in such a way as to enliven students' interest (using a stimulating theme) and identifying the circumscribed area in which the learning he hopes for is realistically attainable. (*It* functioning.)

Any teaching atmosphere needs to be accepting and warm if anything other than the collective absorption of dead information is to take place. A tutor who is failing often produces a very depressed and passive group, even if they produce the 'correct' work. If the group climate is cool and restrictive, students will be working not on the declared theme, but on hidden themes connected with their hurt feelings, indignation, fear of a situation of rivalry, or terror of the complexity of the subject. If the teacher's personality is chilly and remote, however well designed the theme, students will relate to it only at a personally uninvolved level. It helps all groups a lot if the teacher responds in the early stages and encourages the students to respond to almost every statement made in the group, however momentous or trivial. He may add to a student's contribution, illustrate it, invite the others to amplify the point made. He may disagree with what is said but does so in a non-rejecting way. Thus he models acceptable group behaviour which students can imitate. All this detailed behaviour on the part of the tutor is designed to build and maintain a safe globe. It is essential that negative feelings are expressed openly too. Most group members find this extraordinarily difficult, and the holding back of hostility often halts a group's progress for weeks or even months. If the tutor can show by his acceptance of his own hostile impulses that he regards aggression as a normal component of living then students can admit negative feelings within the interpersonal transactions of the group. Negative feelings are most destructive when they are denied, hidden or converted into hypocritical statements or cruel innuendo. If the tutor's negative feelings are strong but hidden then the future of the group would seem limited.

The group tutor is very busy during a tutorial or seminar. He is watching and reacting all the time and observing his reactions. He selects from his own experiences, thoughts, feelings and knowledge of the topic, those items for open communication to the group or members of the group. For instance, if the group is becoming too factually orientated he may state his own feelings; in a pedantic argument about building houses, he may sense that political feelings need to be stirred up, the question of social responsibility examined. If the group is emotive to the point of self-indulgence and abandonment of the theme, the tutor might tactfully, jokingly, or firmly (depending on his personality) point this out. Or he may actively alter the balance of the triangle by bringing in some of his own academic expertise concerning the theme, or introducing the latest research report. 'Weight shifting' can be brought about by techniques in which the tutor already excels, such as summarizing, raising pertinent questions, playing devil's advocate, discreetly closing one sub theme and raising others. A sophisticated well-established group learns through latent processes to do this weight shifting itself. In a very successful TCI group the tutor is silent, though attentive, for much of the time.

Towards the end of a tutorial or seminar, if the group is mature and settled, the tutor can appeal to the group for discussion about and suggestions for future themes. If students feel that they have produced the topic, and that there is group approval for the theme, they will be more likely to invest in it, and the tutor can rest assured that it will be of abiding and genuine interest to the students. The teacher will use his own *I* (personal autonomy) to ensure that the themes are relevant to the course. Individual students may use their autonomy to disagree. The *we*, which includes the tutor, must sort out this conflict of interests. Therein lies one of the most exciting aspects of group tutoring.

I will end this chapter by suggesting one of my favourite themes to those readers who might wish to apply these ideas; that is 'participating in a seminar or tutorial'. Students always seem to enjoy this theme, as will the tutor, who can legitimately share his own feelings in an adult-to-adult manner, while gaining valuable information from the students about his teaching style and their learning needs.

Chapter 4

Three fundamental modes of group operation: student-to-tutor, group-to-tutor, and student-to-student

Small groups can be used in a variety of ways to help students learn. In this chapter, I shall endeavour to extricate three fundamental modes of operation from the welter of information obtained from the observation of *any* sort of teaching group. Separate or mixed, these three modes of operation are easily detectable no matter what the official purpose and structure of the meeting. Although the kind of group under review is a small group of students, these modalities can be applied to other groups, large and small, such as staff meetings, committees and total institutions. They can also be applied to the family group and larger social groupings and even larger organizations such as trade unions or industries. Naturally, the larger the group the more complex its internal organization, and hence the more sub grouping which will take place. The relationships of a group of sub groups to other groups of sub groups can often show the three patterns of group operation to be illustrated in these pages.

Once the teacher's interest in his group unit's functioning is aroused, he begins to observe and consider what the group members are trying to achieve, at a latent as well as manifest level; how they are responding to him and his authority; why and how they are building this particular social culture. He is now acting as a tutor and not merely as a mechanical information transmitter or translator. This is not to undervalue the information itself but to stress the need to investigate how information can best be given, received, worked on and assimilated. Different teachers employ different methods. Many tutors emancipate themselves and the group from the inhibiting presence of 'work' by introducing themes connected with current affairs to stimulate discussion and thus allow relationships to develop within the group. The friendly climate so created will bear fruit when 'work' does appear on the timetable! Other tutors have free and open discussion, but only within the limits of the course being studied. Yet others use games, questionnaires and role play, connected with the subject, to reduce interpersonal tensions. Conversely, some tutors think that 'work' should be accorded top priority in small groups and keep strictly to the academic subject matter. These strategies are matters of personal taste and different courses will impose different constraints on what a tutor might want to do in his group by virtue of the sheer volume of 'work' which the group meetings have to accommodate by a given deadline. Whatever the tutor decides to use his group for and whichever technique he uses to achieve this aim, he inevitably stands in some kind of *relation* to the group, though there may be significant shifts in these relations from time to time. These shifts of relative position can most simply be explained diagramatically. (See page 53.)

Boundaries

Before studying these three sets of tutor-student relations, it should be emphasized that whichever *set* predominates, it does not explain all that is happening in the group. The tutor should remind himself frequently about the boundaries within which his group operates. What rules and expectations has he set for his students? What is the group's exact purpose? Is the physical setting conducive to this group purpose? Do the students know if they are being assessed in this group, and is attendance compulsory? Do they understand how the tutor sees the occupation (the job) of the meeting? What are the limits to discussion and/or activity beyond which students and tutor ought not to stray? If these boundaries are seen, understood and accepted (with the provision that renegotiation is always possible) then the group has a good chance of survival. But beyond mere survival is group learning, a furthering of insight into the course subject. Learning in a small group never occurs in a vacuum but in a social network, so that how the student feels about the tutor and his own colleagues will affect the learning process.

Developmental phases

Tutors always need to monitor the group's developmental phase. The operational mode prevalent at any time can then be evaluated according to whether the group is new, confused and dependent; adolescent, rebellious, confronting and hearty; mature, stable and able to maintain and extend its own boundaries. It might even be a group which has outlived its usefulness, in which case the hollow structure within which equally hollow rituals are carried out can finally be dismantled.

Deployment of the three modes

The three modes to be discussed are 'student-to-tutor', 'group-to-tutor' and 'student-to-student'. Skilled group leaders often behave in a way which deliberately varies or combines these patterns so as to meet the learning needs of the group, from meeting to meeting and from one developmental phase to another. Staff unused to group work often

Operational Modes of Groups

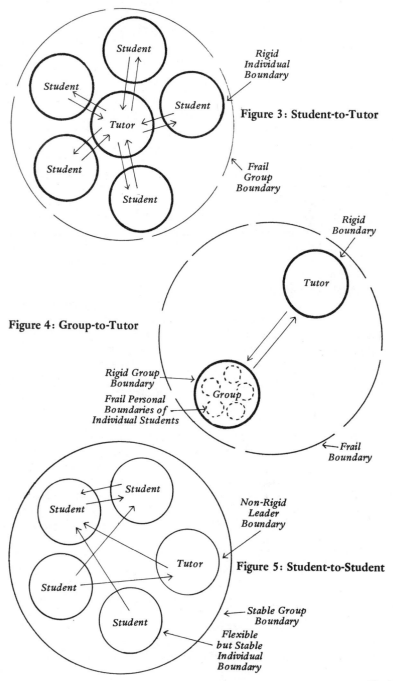

Figure 3: Student-to-Tutor

Rigid Individual Boundary

Frail Group Boundary

Figure 4: Group-to-Tutor

Rigid Boundary

Rigid Group Boundary

Frail Personal Boundaries of Individual Students

Frail Boundary

Figure 5: Student-to-Student

Non-Rigid Leader Boundary

Stable Group Boundary

Flexible but Stable Individual Boundary

complain about constantly unproductive and unchanging atmospheres in their groups, without realizing that the group is locked in one of these patterns. They are therefore unable to change the relation between the group and the teacher, so as to free the group members from this impasse.

The student-to-tutor group   (See Figure 3 p. 53)

Each individual is separately and primarily related to the tutor, so that an observer would witness a series of dialogues (and hence over time dyadic relationships between tutor and taught). The teacher is so pre-occupied with setting up a series of twosomes that he may often forget the notion of 'group' altogether. He sees not a group but a queue of individuals waiting their turn to interact with him. When one dyad (twosome) is in action he cannot see the rest of the queue. This group leader is often attempting a transposition of the individual tutorial to a group setting. When such a student-tutor relationship is deliberately contrived and carefully controlled, it can be extremely helpful to the group. Individual learning problems often require exclusive attention and this demonstrates clearly to the other students present that the teacher does not equate admission of difficulty with stupidity. Individual care apportioned to an underconfident student encourages him or her to show and share ideas and feelings and thoughts about the subject without being afraid of rejection. It is when this student-to-tutor mode goes unrecognized, and persists throughout the group's life that management problems arise for the group's leader. Participants in such a group (especially in the very early stages of a new, first-year group) tend to comply with, identify with and often unconsciously incorporate the tutor's ideas and are therefore heavily influenced by him. Many tutors fail to realize the extent of their influence over impressionable students and would not really want to be seen as so omnipotent. New, insecure students are in great need of authoritative figures who will protect and direct them at this exciting but stressful time, and often attribute superhuman powers to their tutors. As the group grows in confidence, such idealisation diminishes; peers become important; teachers appear mortal! As the group moves into this second phase, the dyadic bond is no longer always enough to keep the group together. The students may continue to come to the group meetings because they are obligatory, or they attend out of habit or fear of censure; but many will find this operational mode frustrating or even frightening. An ailing student-to-tutor group can often be diagnosed as suffering from a lack of corporate identity. The group's goals are perceived as the tutor's goals, not shared group goals, and so attainment only means 'placating teacher' rather than taking a personal pride in one's achievements. (Students' autonomy, in TCI terms, is actually denied them.) The students have little opportunity to converse with or get to know each other, and so any trust is between the tutor and each student, rather than between student and student. This makes for a highly competitive situation in which approval and concern and affection derive solely from the tutor. Those unsuccessfully competing for a dyadic encounter with the tutor may become depressed by this failure and loss of academic motivation may result.

If help and guidance and knowledge are seen to reside only in the official group leader, and this cultural norm is well established, students will fail to understand that other students in the group can help them over many work problems. But how could such a request for help ever be made in a group such as this? Even when a student appears to be learning well from the tutor, it is conceivable that much of the learning is superficial, attained via emulation of the tutor, rather than by gaining knowledge through his own efforts. A good tutor uses identification to encourage students but aims to inspire and not to indoctrinate them. If this manner of operation is pursued indefinitely, good examination results may follow in many cases. But chronic dependency on authority figures and a refusal to grow up and risk adulthood may also result. A good many students thrive academically in such groups only to fail dismally the following year when they are required to switch allegiances to a new tutor whose approach is different and who cannot hope to establish the same immediate degree of intimacy.

It follows that judging the effectiveness of a small group teaching policy in a given department involves a thoughtful estimate of students' subsequent behaviour and performance, as well as their current grades and ability to use their present group. Sudden changes of group climate can produce academic casualties of a severe kind. Dependency wishes and needs are not the sole prerogative of the neurotic personality; they exist in all of us. Tutors therefore have a responsibility to consider carefully the whole issue of student dependency, and to cultivate an awareness of the transitional problems (or advantages) occuring when students are forced to change groups. Although dependency to a degree is healthy and inevitable, tutors are advised to cultivate the art of weaning.

The group-to-tutor group   (See Figure 4 p. 53)

The leadership-membership relation is again dyadic, but this time the tutor perceives and reacts to the *whole group* as if it were one indivisible organism, distinct from himself. The group responds to him as if it were a single person. Newcomers to group work might recoil from this apparently bizarre idea. In an earlier chapter, though, I have tried to guide the reader toward conceptual formulations, which regard groups, large and small, as living systems. The human individual is a living system, made up of several interdependent sub systems, such as the cardiovascular, respiratory and renal system. Atrophy or disease or other alteration in one sub system will affect the others — so that a patient with a weak heart will develop breathing problems, and ultimately kidney trouble. As long as the interrelationship between these sub systems is maintained in a state of balance (for example a doctor will not prescribe a drug which aids one sub system and damages another, or if he does, an antidote will be given to counteract this unwanted side effect), then the total organism, the patient, will survive. Similarly the total group as a single unit must be enabled to live on, thanks to the tutor's injections of help, no matter what disturbances are located within and between its component parts (the students).

The concept of group-as-system is astoundingly simple, yet actually experiencing it *in vivo* for the first time can be a moving and memorable experience. People in the group who at one moment are viewed as static, discrete objects, are suddenly seen afresh as interrelated parts of a larger organism. The tutor watches the group's social context shaping or modifying the contributions of each member, and each member's contributions reciprocally determining the nature of that context from which the group's culture and its learning will eventually spring.

Many keen teachers have undergone a kind of conversion and owing to their newly discovered systems approach unfortunately sometimes lose sight of the ordinary needs of individuals in the group. It is essential to remember that a group is a living accretion of people and that the character of this accretion will be determined by the individual personalities and their proclivities. There are frequent occasions when individuals want to differentiate themselves from the mass and this needs to be respected. Others hide in the group's corporateness and never learn to stand up for their beliefs and opinions.

The group-to-tutor relationship is often seen when the tutor is charismatic and the students unite under his banner. He makes them feel special and chosen; they see themselves as his elect, his followers. All this is at an unconscious fantasy level, but the atmosphere in a group when this phenomenon is occurring is quite electric. The tutor, though he may not always be aware of it, is assessing the group with a view to the subsequent successful control of it. His thoughts tend towards 'the group is doing this'; 'the group is feeling that'; 'the group is working like so'. If he does give much thought to an individual's contributions in the group, his ensuing behaviour would suggest that he is relating to that student in a way that will re-establish and reinforce the student's loyalty to the group's norms and will bring his contribution into line with the group's general activity and discussion. In other words there is little opportunity for deviation from the group 'code'. Anyone brave enough to repeatedly express individuality would have to take on a very powerful leader and face the scorn of his fellow students. In this kind of group the rebel student can face a very arduous battle indeed and become quite depressed or embittered as a consequence. Other students, finding themselves in this unenviable position, will resort to sullen non-participation rather than fight. Those with original ideas about handling the subject matter in a different manner altogether will hardly get a look in. Such groups can work well, in much the same way that army battalions may enjoy high morale and a sense of camaraderie, derived from loyalty to the outfit and the 'heroic' leader. Many student groups are welded together by an ambivalent mixture of idolatry and fear of the powerful tutor. Bonds are strongest when such a group is in competition with another group; when the group unites with the tutor against a common enemy such as a head of department or college authorities; when certain political or artistic attitudes are shared. For some students such an experience is the high point of their university career; for others this kind of group functioning fills them with real terror, because they feel their own frail personal boundaries have been removed and they can find no sense of individual identity. In some cases the group-to-tutor group is highly successful, as when people unite to attain a common goal of academic excellence through corporate identification with a brilliant teacher/leader. However, some students are still in need of individual attention and a more parental response from their tutor, before becoming confident enough to work in a team of their peers.

The student-to-student group   (See Figure 5 p. 53)

The tutor does not see himself as a leader in the traditional sense, but more as a 'facilitator of communication' or an 'interpersonal enabler'. These somewhat clumsy terms borrowed from the personal growth movement do at least attempt to re-define the role of the 'boss' in the group, and to reduce hierarchical barriers between the tutor and his students. The group is conducted, rather than led, with the social culture of the group foremost in the tutor's mind. He is working on the assumption that students who can trust each other with their doubts and anxieties about the course, as well as their weak academic areas, can learn to teach and support one another inside and outside the group. It is also assumed that a 'democratic' group makes the tutor less frightening and more accessible, so that students will readily relate to him without feeling inferior or inadequate. The tutor appears to behave like the membership, but this is only superficially true because conducting this kind of group means positively encouraging interactions (whether personal or academic) *between* students. The tutor deflects attention away from himself and invites the group to take the major part of the responsibility for its own learning process. He assists them to define their own objectives and to work out means of attaining them. These tutors are sometimes mistakenly accused of laziness, as the group appears to be doing all the work, including sometimes the erecting of its own boundaries. This, of course, is the tutor's objective; he is trying to promote autonomous and yet interdependent learning, so that the logical result of the exercise would be his own redundancy. Looked at idealistically he is offering them a model of how to live as well as how to learn, helping them to explore and rely on their own innate strengths, and yet profit by group (social) belongingness. A mature student-to-student group can rotate or share the leadership and eventually manage without the tutor altogether.

A great disadvantage of this operational mode is the time factor. A tutor working this way will take a long time to assist a group in really understanding a piece of academic material, having refused to take the short cut by way of conveying its meaning directly. He prefers to facilitate their own discovery of the material's meaning, much as one allows a toddler to stagger about on uncertain and unbalanced legs when it would be much quicker to pick him up and carry him. Given the vast quantity of knowledge now available on almost all subjects, many tutors feel this slow student-to-student method of teaching would never get students past the elementary A B C stage of the subject.

Another legitimate criticism of this approach is that it avoids the very important issue of authority with which everyone must learn to deal if they are to be successful in family and professional life, let alone in dealings with police, bank managers, airport officials, and head-waiters. Many students will feel happy and comfortable, valued and able to value others in this group, but may never come into conflict with the leader, or indeed have any strong feelings for him at all, locating their emotional gratification in their fellows instead. Many group tutors who choose to conduct their groups in this way are terrified of hostility in their private and public life, and beneath the sound democratic principles on which they base their leadership behaviour there lurks a fear of showing their authority, or guilt at having been given such a powerful role. The student must eventually face a world in which authority figures and institutional systems will try to manipulate and control his daily existence. If he is to demand and obtain space and time to run his life the way he wants, he must be able to say no to Big Brother. If he has never learned to say no before, he will certainly not learn to say no in this benevolent kind of group. A liberal attitude to higher education is that it should prepare people for life and adulthood; this implies that resolving conflicts about authority should be on the curriculum, not avoided. Imagine a student who has just left a student-to-student group in his first year and, in his second, is pitched into a group-to-tutor group with an all-powerful leader, where very little democratic expression is allowed. How can he cope?

Summary

It would be quite unwise to suggest that any of these three patterns should be exclusively adopted by a tutor. Each has advantages and disadvantages. All groups, like all students, are unique and require differing degrees of attention, authority, patience, sympathy and confrontation in differing combinations at different times. If one of these three relationship patterns is fixed for all time, casualties are bound to follow. What an observer might find fascinating is the way in which all groups operate mainly in one of these three ways, even if the tutor has never thought about group process and leadership behaviour. The pattern is created, often unconsciously, by the leader and students respond by obeying the hidden rules about how to function in the group. The three patterns have been grossly over-simplified and in practice they are not as clearly identifiable as I have set them out. I have written this chapter on the basis of 'simplifying is clarifying'. Tutors might reflect a little upon their own group style. Probably they will find that they employ more than one modality, under different circumstances. Each tutor, though, will lean in a certain direction, and it is helpful to know one's own tendencies so that they can be checked when the situation requires it. The more conscious a tutor can become of how he is managing the group situation at any given moment, the freer he will be to change the pattern if it is failing to meet an individual's or the group's needs.

Let me give a few examples of how these patterns can be deliberately employed for students' benefit. In a group where there are disparate levels of academic ability and an important exam is due shortly, the tutor may be wise to employ a student-to-tutor model, giving individual care and supervision to each student, according to each student's personal need.

A complex course unit system can often severely isolate students, as well as reinforce academic specialism which can remove students from the mainstream thinking relevant to their subjects. In order to help these people keep in touch, socially and academically, perhaps the tutor could bring together students from many different units and run a student-to-student group, without worrying overmuch about achieving rapid intellectual absorption.

Often a group seems to be falling apart at the seams for no apparent reason, and the tutor, genuinely trying to make a success of it, despairs. It happens sometimes that the tutor is so busy with one particular student's problems, or is so over-conscientious with regard to the subject (the 'work') that he can no longer see the group as a whole social unit. Gradually the members begin to feel the loss of boundaries. The students pick up his confusion and uncertainty and sense, correctly, that they are not a group at all. It is at this point that the tutor might begin to rescue the situation by forgetting the academic goals *pro tem* and focusing on this group of students which appears somewhat hazy to him at the moment, shaping from the misty blur a distinct unit, in the group-to-tutor tradition. *Esprit de corps* is more important at this moment than any textbook or inspired teaching. The tutor himself must experience the group as a viable organism and must treat it as such before the members of the group are themselves able to accept it. A clear example needs to be set. It is more a matter of tutoring attitude than action which makes the difference. A tutor who can see his group work and leadership function clearly almost always keeps the most unpromising groups together. Similarly a confused and inconsistent tutor, however good his intentions, can fragment and scatter members of what could have been a tightly cohesive hard-working group.

Every group tutor, then, is a potential regulator. He must continually diagnose what operational mode is relevant for the survival and progress of that group and what mode might inadvertently sabotage it. We have seen how, once the boundaries are secured and the purpose of the group is clear to all, the tutor has great freedom of manoeuvre. He might choose to focus individual or group interest upon himself, or he may assist the group to explore its own resources for shared learning and discourage recourse to himself as the source of wisdom. He may choose to be the one who defines what the group norms and values should be, so that the students clearly understand what is to happen. Alternatively, he may choose to confine himself to monitoring the group system, as a mother might watch her children, without interference, unless dangers show themselves. He may see himself as a guardian of the group, securing the group's boundaries, negotiating, as the group's representative, with other group systems which interact with, or exert influence over, his own group system. Or, he may decide to hand over all internal group work, from delegation of responsibility and discipline to producing academic work, to the group itself. The point is, that understanding the group's functioning gives him a *choice* as to how to deploy his leadership skills. There is no 'right' or 'wrong' way. Tutors must teach in a manner which makes them and their students feel comfortable and academically motivated.

Chapter 5

Basic Assumption and Focal Conflict theory: implications for group teaching

Altering one's perspective from 'the student in the group' to 'the group of students' is a major feat; it indicates a move to a higher order of comprehension, when the lower order, that of individual tutoring, is complex enough. A major shift in perspective is imperative, however, for the grasping of social (ie group) phenomena. The individual in relation to the tutor and the academic subject is still just as important, but the physical, emotional, social and academic *context* in which the student approaches the subject and of which he and his fellows are constituent parts now looms into the foreground of the tutor's awareness. Through this contextual lens teaching/learning problems can be seen in a dramatic new light and the range of possible solutions widened, though the array of options offered by viewing students' behaviour in this way can initially produce much bewilderment. A student's behaviour is only truly intelligible after deciphering the operating process of his whole group. A diagnosis of his behaviour based on a 'lower order' of understanding (viewing him as an isolated unit) may turn out to be grossly inaccurate, as only a small section of the evidence was available to the tutor.

The work of Wilfred Bion

Dr Wilfred Bion, along with other army psychiatrists in World War II, contemplated treating the whole hospital large group as if it were a single patient. The individual military casualties were in hospital for rehabilitation purposes and had shown themselves to be quite incapable of functioning as society members in their roles as soldiers or as adult hospital patients. They constituted a sick group which needed treatment. However, the concept of the group as a unity was not, as many feared, a step towards reification — making groups into 'things' and thus depriving people of their individuality. The group, large or small, was not a mythical entity for Dr Bion, but a set of real functions carried out well or badly by an aggregate of individuals within boundaries, whether defined or vague. Dr Bion spent many years at the Tavistock Clinic working on his 'Basic Assumption' theory which is applicable to large groups such as the church and army, as well as to every small group, whether it meets for therapy or academic study or the building of a motor car. Of course it is easier to isolate group phenomena of a latent (unconscious or half conscious) sort in the 'pure' culture of a therapy group, where there is no occupation, such as studying Shakespeare or assembling a motor car, to obscure the researcher's view. This is one reason why some tutors think latent process has been invented by therapists and do not recognize it as a universal feature of groups. They have allowed their vision to be clouded by the academic subject they are teaching. I hope to blow away some of these clouds and show how essential is the appreciation of these hidden group processes.

There is an important common boundary between therapy and education, which is related to the students' or patients' self-awareness and interpersonal sensitivity. If both these qualities are developed by expert leadership, members' learning and psycho-social health, in both therapy and education groups are bound to follow. The difference between the two is merely one of emphasis. In therapy, group members learn to understand themselves and increase their knowledge of human psychology and social relations. In education a course is studied, and self-understanding along with social skills develop as by-products. In this chapter those aspects of Bion's work which apply to small group teaching will be looked at although their implications for psychotherapy will not. Readers should consider what follows to be a very diluted version of his work. It has undergone conceptual revision so as to extract its educational rather than its clinical relevance.

Bion's central idea is that in every group two groups are present, though not in a literal sense. In a student group, meeting for academic purposes, we would call them the 'study group' and the 'basic assumption' group respectively. The student group behaves as though there was another group in the room. One group talks conventionally and works hard; the other behaves irrationally, motivated by common unacknowledged psychological needs. They are of course one and the same group; but just as individuals can say one thing in all earnestness and go out and do completely the opposite, as if obeying an inner contradictory impulse, so can groups. I do not believe that anything so poetic as a 'group mind' exists, but there are shared hopes, fears and moods under the surface of the 'study group's' industrious veneer. When activated by one member's remark or action these latent preoccupations exert a powerful effect, both positive and/or negative, over the 'study group's' behaviour.

Study groups

The study group comprises members who co-operate as discrete individuals. Each student's interest is identified with the 'occupation' or 'theme' which is the official job the group has met to carry out. (For example, 'understanding free verse'.) The 'study group' constantly examines its findings and assesses its progress in a scientific spirit. The study group seeks knowledge, learns from experience and regularly applies itself to questions about how best to meet its academic targets. Unfortunately, groups which behave like this constantly are exceptionally rare, though often this study group is the only group that tutors dare see. A large amount of Bion's theory addresses itself to the difficult problem of why groups meeting for some kind of straightforward work, (such as the small teaching group) so often fail to perform in the sensible way just described, the way in which the members themselves and the group's tutor would like to transact their joint business. Even though highly effective group study is possible at times, on other occasions the group seems riddled with self-contradictory behaviour, unease, and ineffective attempts at work. Why should this be? Perhaps it has something to do with the presence of a 'basic assumption' group shadowing the study group.

Basic assumption groups

There are three kinds of basic assumption group: the dependency, the fight-flight, and the pairing group. These are only rough categories, as Bion himself readily admits. He recognizes that classification may have to be revised later or new categories added. This notion of basic assumption groups is for use as a conceptual guideline and is not meant to be regarded as dogma. Scientifically minded readers will feel understandably irked by the inexactitude of this chapter, but the newer group theories, like personal tutoring itself, labour under the difficulties common to all infant disciplines, that of linguistic limitation and crudity of conceptual formulation.

Basic assumption means the assumption in the group which is basic to its behaviour. It is what therapists call an 'as if' term — the group as a unit behaves *as if* such and such were the case. Basic assumptions here refer to *tacit* assumptions prevalent in the group, as opposed to those which are openly expressed and are concerned with the group's occupation. Although the activation of any of these three assumptions provide the basis for subsequent group behaviour, people are not conscious of them. Their existence can only be deduced from the overt behaviour of the group. The basic assumption group can threaten or even overthrow the work of the study group. Basic assumptions may lie quiescent or may simmer just below the suface of the manifest communications for some time. On other occasions basic assumptions erupt to the surface of the group, and the tutor finds himself at a loss; he tries to fathom just what is happening, why reason has inexplicably given way to chaos and why no learning is taking place.

From Bion's point of view there are three distinct emotional states of groups which give rise to three basic assumptions:

(1) *Basic assumption dependency* The essential aim of the basic assumption dependency group is to attain security through, and have its members protected by, one individual. It assumes that this is why the group has come together. The official work of academic study is experienced as an interference with the attempt to realize this (temporarily) more crucial ambition. Every basic assumption dependency group also has the survival of the group unit as its aim. Basic assumption dependency activity is seen most commonly in a new group of students, especially freshers; but it can also occur in relatively well-established groups, when for whatever external or internal reason the members' security within the group is threatened. Depending on the degree to which this basic assumption is operational, members act passively, as if they know nothing, are intellectually inadequate and are in need of spoon-feeding. Their behaviour implies that the tutor by contrast is omnipotent and omniscient. A group of new and eager students, waiting for instruction from a verbal, paternal and gentle teacher easily fits this picture. The students are temporarily (and often, alas, permanently) united by a common belief that if they sit long enough, the wise, good and clever teacher will produce all the answers, guaranteeing them a good degree and a rich all-round university experience. They act as if they do not need to give him adequate information about their personal, social and academic needs. They assume he knows everything and will plan the meetings and structure its activities in their interest. In this emotional state the group insists on simplicity; complexity cannot be borne. 'The tutor is able to solve all difficulties *if only we can force him to do so, by showing how helpless we are*' is the unconscious shared sentiment. The tutor is idealized and made into a god who will take good care of all his disciples. Often the tutor cruelly rejects this behaviour as it may remind him of his own denied dependency needs. However, he may be flattered and reassured of his own competence and agree to perpetuate the authority-dependency relationship for as long as the group wishes. Tutors might remember that students may also feel very resentful about being or wanting to be dependent. Which of these students' conflicting wishes should be supported by the tutor?

Since no tutor can become the paragon of virtue and wisdom demanded by students, he will inevitably arouse their disappointment and hostility. For some time the group members will blind themselves to his human frailties and will often resort to powerful manoeuvres designed to coerce him into taking proper care of them. A particular student, perhaps one who is shy, inarticulate, with a speech impediment or some other identifiable handicap, is frequently pushed by the group into even greater distress, in order to bring out the tutor's tender loving care, or, if there is mounting hostility to show him up as an 'unfeeling demon'. Although the group seems concerned for the distressed student, (and each member in any other context would see himself as genuinely sympathetic) in fact the underlying shared motive of the group is to use the student to force the tutor into the desired role of strong leader. As the original leader fails to meet these impossible expectations, he is sometimes abandoned and the group searches for alternative leaders. Ambitious group members offer themselves for the post, only to meet with the same fate. An interesting adaptation to the tutor's continued lack of omniscience often occurs in the student group. If he will not satisfy their demand for a deity, they will put his remembered words or written thoughts and ideas in place of his person. They will become 'holy words'. Many essays and exam papers provide evidence for this feature of group behaviour. Members who feel deserted by the leader often close ranks and 'snuggle up' like sheep huddled together for warmth. A cosy group atmosphere can develop which gives a temporary sense of safety. To challenge this artificial bonhomie, and insist instead on cerebral application or conflictual discussion, is seen as heresy and persecuted as such.

(2) *Basic assumption fight-flight* Fight and flight are to be understood as two sides of the same coin. The assumption here determining group activity is that the group must be preserved and that this can be done only by fighting or running away from someone or something. Action is the keynote here. 'We must *do* something!' For the duration of basic assumption operation the individual is of secondary importance to the preservation of the group. In battle or in flight the individual is totally forgotten, whereas at other times group members can be highly sensitive to an individual student's needs. In basic assumption dependency the weak person is valued for his ability to engage the concern of the tutor; in the fight-flight group there is no toleration of weakness. Consequently casualties can be expected and tutors need to be aware of this. The call for action requires a strong leader and, if the tutor declines the role, someone else must be found. He or she must be capable of mobilizing the group for attack or leading it in flight, and should be alert to the presence of enemies. A student with a chip on his shoulder can be very useful here, for if no enemies are clearly visible he will surely find one. If the tutor will not provide opportunities for flight or aggression he is ignored. In the fight-flight group, the fight may be with the syllabus, the lectures, the library, the labs or the leader. Basic assumption-fight activity may show up in an ideological argument about the subject itself, which is really a ruse to avoid the work with which the students are supposed to be employed and of which they are afraid. (The same argument, carried out legitimately by the study group rather than the basic assumption group, would be highly educational.) The flight aspect is demonstrated by the self-removal of the membership from the subject matter; either physically, in terms of lateness or absence, or behaviourally, in idle chat, constant attention to unnecessary detail (such as sharpening pencils and endlessly demanding book references or reading lists) and senseless objections to the academic

project suggested. Seminars are notorious for flight reactions; one student presents a prepared piece of work and the others leave him to it, not bothering to read up the material for themselves! Any teaching procedure that bores and excludes people will lead to flight reactions. It is easier to run away than confront the tutor about his method of handling the seminar.

How can group tutors reduce the opportunities for flight? Bion contends that the logical extension of fight-flight is panic. It would seem sensible therefore for the tutor to examine what is causing this pre-panic reaction in his students and find out if there is anything he can do about it. The anxiety which provokes a fight-flight reaction may have an obvious cause within the group, such as impending assessment, though the students do not consciously link up the prevailing mood and behaviour of the group with their fear. If the tutor can help them see this and give them permission to ventilate their fears directly, he may circumvent the panic which could ensue or from which one or two students might suffer in the exam hall itself. The fight-flight may be a reaction to an event external to the group — perhaps the impending end of the course or a rumour that the tutor is leaving. At other times the event can be group-specific — perhaps a relationship between the tutor and a particular student is highly charged in some sexual or aggressive or possessive way, which threatens the continuity of the group as a collection of co-equal members. Often the students sense a tutor's depression or apathy and panic because they believe that they have really been abandoned, that he is there in body but not in spirit. It is important to note that these causes, though they may be obvious to a detached observer, are causes to which the group and its leader are usually totally oblivious. Failure to deal with fight-flight means accepting a sometimes lengthy halt to the group's ability to do reasonable academic work. A fight-flight group is always brought about by frustration and, as in all basic assumption groups, instant gratification is demanded. Fight and flight are urgent group responses to crises; feeling stuck, not knowing whether to stay and fight or run away, is intolerable; action is needed, as it is the easy solution. The tutor needs to identify what the original common frustration is about but sometimes he will be unable to locate the source. He will instead temporarily resign himself to being firm, setting fairly rigid boundaries around the group — insisting on punctuality, handing in of work, sticking to the subject matter and so on. This may produce indignation, but it is also evidence of genuine caring: it reassures the members that no amount of fighting or running away is going to deter the tutor from getting the work done and maintaining the survival of the group. Many students will privately be thankful, while simultaneously publicly protesting about the way in which the tutor has become heavy handed as he protects them from their basic assumption activity. If the frustration has an obvious cause, the tutor enables the group to forego hasty action and helps them verbalize and think through the difficulty with him. The need to quarrel about an irrelevant matter or flee then disappears.

(3) *Basic assumption pairing* The assumption here is that the group has met for the purpose of bringing together two people who will somehow 'save' the group from its current predicament. Bion's idea is that symbolically, the pair will produce a child messiah, a saviour. The sex of the two people is immaterial; they are brought together for earnest discourse, and the rest of the group either shy away, as if ashamed and embarrassed at witnessing the act of procreation; or they watch eagerly with bated breath, not dreaming of interrupting such an important exchange.

Pairing frequently occurs in a student group when people are bored, angry or fearful and cannot handle these feelings themselves. A couple is 'elected' either to co-operate and find a solution, or each partner in the couple, acting as an advocate, represents the two different sides of whatever conflict is preoccupying the group. This could be likened to two armies saving lives by having two leaders volunteer for hand-to-hand combat (a classic example being Paris and Menelaus' dual in the Trojan war.) Many feelings can be experienced vicariously through the pair, without having to risk exposing one's own ideas and thoughts. Pairing behaviour often shows itself in the study group proper, although its driving force lies in the basic assumption group. (It is important to remember that the two groups are always intertwined.) This kind of pairing is not necessarily destructive. Students often learn vicariously as they watch the conflict of the two protagonists. Alternatively, the pair may join forces and inspire each other and the rest of the group to thoughts on the topic under study. There are similarities here with love-making. A couple's arguing and fighting is thrilling as well as frightening and is often a prelude to either happy sexual activity or violence in real life. Likewise, academic fights can be destructive or conducive to learning.

It is very common for pairing activity to occur between members in a group or on its boundary where the impact can still be felt. There may be growing sexual attraction between members, a member and the tutor, or a member and someone known by all in the social culture immediately at the edge of the group. This sexual bond may be nascent or very tenuous and the two people involved not even fully aware of it, but it may still be of sufficient import to mobilize wishes in the group for pairing activity. The pair finally elected will not necessarily be the pair sharing the sexual bond. The observant tutor ensures that pairing in the group is not allowed to ossify, leaving the couple concerned powerless to escape the functions that have been foisted on to them. On the other hand he promotes pairing when he has a willing couple, whose interaction may assist the group's learning. Ideally, everyone pairs with everyone else at different times in the study group. Basic assumption pairing though is primarily a way of coping with disappointment and failure. The group will be saved from its inherent shortcomings by the pair's 'messiah-child' — which of course must remain unborn, otherwise there is nothing left to hope for. Such a student group is characterized by anticipation and buoyancy: 'everything will be fine when we get into the second year'; 'when the new library is built'; 'when the spring comes'. The atmosphere is agreeable and lulling, but only because no one is allowed to raise the real issue of why insufficient work is being done. That would remind the others of harsher and more unpleasant reality and remove at a stroke their hopeful dream for the future. The tutor can often be seduced by this atmosphere and join in with the belief that things are not really so bad and collude with the students' wish to avoid work. The pair bond here is between tutor and group-as-a-whole. Both halves of the pair feel life and work would be fine if only the rest of the institution would conveniently leave them alone together. The pair resides in a fool's paradise, denying the reality outside the group's boundaries.

Summary and comments concerning basic assumption groups

The basic assumption groups are not distinct entities and blur into one another. They are operative at different times and occur at different levels of intensity; sometimes they are barely discernible and on other occasions they are blatant. Basic assumption activity and study group activity can go on at the same time; the study group and the basic assumption group are not mutually exclusive. The tutor has a special responsibility not to be inadvertently sucked into basic assumption activity — activity which can be challenged, managed, manipulated, borne, controlled or shown directly to the students who are involved in it. It is normal group behaviour and gives the tutor valuable clues about the degree of group preparedness or otherwise to accomplish work. When talking about basic assumptions in groups, we should realize that the picture is one of a study group suffused by, intruded into and supported by the basic assumption groups. The tutor is constantly lured away from completing the work function by powerful basic assumptions in the group (and sometimes in himself). The assumptions ruthlessly block effective group action because they are anonymous and no one individual takes responsibility for them. Both the study group and the basic assumption group are abstractions, merely useful ways of thinking about total group functioning.

Another idea of Bion's is that everyone has a tendency to engage in group activity in a characteristic way — this tendency Bion calls *valency*. Group leaders will find it useful to recognize which basic assumption activity attracts them most. Tutors almost certainly play a part in actually 'fixing' a group at the basic assumption functioning level with which they themselves are most comfortable. For instance, I have to admit my own enjoyment of hectic fight-flight activity. What effect will my fight-flight valency have on a group of tutor-trainees or students in group therapy, who are moving naturally towards or away from that same basic assumption activity? Do I unwittingly lead them back to my own preferred territory, because I know I teach and treat better when there is a battle going on? Is this fair or right? Battles may be good for me but are they good for the group?

The tutor with a dependency valency will probably be seen by his students as trustworthy and highly dependable; the fight-flight tutor as courageous and bold in his teaching style and expositions of the academic subject; the pairing tutor is probably creative, or the one sought out for the purposes of intimate confession. He may prefer counselling type work with individuals, tending to avoid group situations. A good deal of this discussion on the significance for tutors of some of Bion's work is speculative and awaits much-needed research, particularly in a tutor-student rather than therapist-patient or trainer-trainee situation. Leader management of basic assumption groups now needs examining in the light of *educational* objectives.

In Bion's work and in the work of H Ezriel and Dorothy Stock Whitaker, (outlined later on in this chapter) there is a tendency to analyze much of what happens in groups as 'defensiveness' or 'group avoidance'. Insufficient emphasis is given to realistic dependency needs, natural productive pairing, ordinary dispute ('fight'), and understandable boredom (so-called 'flight'). These authors do admit that large portions of group behaviour can be left well alone and accepted at their surface value, but their advanced researches have been made in clinical settings, often with very ill patients, where the defensive processes which stifle group progress must be studied in detail for the therapeutic benefit of the patient and the survival of his treatment group. Their research has of necessity concentrated on the negative effects of latent group activity. A vast amount of pioneering work in groups was carried out not with patients, but with training groups of clergy, social workers and doctors. A body of knowledge was also accumulated from selection-recruitment procedures during wartime. The results of these investigations have been heavily applied to therapy but hardly at all to education. Few teaching groups collapse completely, and few students break down. But the group phenomena are the same as those which occur in therapy, in training groups, in industry and in HM Forces, though perhaps different in degree, in intensity and leader exploitation. In chapter 7, which discusses leadership, I shall take a less pessimistic standpoint and look at the more positive significance of group processes and how the tutor might utilize his understanding of them.

I shall now briefly examine the theories of two writers who have envisaged the group as a total living system and whose work finds echoes in Bion's.

The work of D Stock Whitaker and H Ezriel

The focal conflict

This manner of analyzing a tutorial, seminar or other small group can be extremely useful after the event, when the tutor tries to gain an overview of the session and formulate some kind of pattern from the disparate contributions that were made. It does not explain all the group's activity (no simple formula could do that) but it does help the tutor to conceptualize latent group process (those currents and cross currents which one can almost feel and touch in a group, but which are secreted beneath or within the academic discussion itself). A focal conflict would not show itself as blatantly as I shall explain it, but would be picked up by the tutor's 'third ear' or 'third eye' as he went about his usual teaching procedures in the group. Those readers who find the notion of 'touching and feeling of cross-currents' as preposterous, might consider their own experience. Have they never walked into a room and known instantly and with certainty that people had been talking about them before their arrival? That is the kind of atmosphere or cross-current which tutors, with training, experience and some natural aptitude, can reduce to something far more exact and usable in their teaching groups. Perhaps the reader has sat on a committee and has become convinced that in half an hour a showdown between factions A and B was inevitable; or at a dinner party that John Smith and David Green were spoiling for a fight and that Mrs Green was not unconnected with it — even though no evidence for such hostility was to be found, as everyone was behaving with extreme decorum. Such intuitions mean that the observer has, in seconds, seen, heard, and automatically processed a whole set of minute and subtle intra-group communications, to which for some reason he is already sensitized. Perhaps he has hidden designs on Mrs Green!

In focal conflict theory, the diverse contributions made by the various group participants in one single meeting are seen as contributing towards the gradual building up and final expression of a single 'group focal conflict'. It can be represented schematically as follows:

Group Focal Conflict

Disturbing Motive
(usually some wish or hope)

Reactive Motive
(usually some inhibiting feeling
such as fear, guilt or shame)

Group Solution
(usually some implicitly shared agreement
or perception which deals with the
disturbing and reactive motives and
the reality situation)

It is essential to remember that group activity is generated at many levels. The 'focal conflict' is an example of *latent* group process, in that the group meets for some kind of tutorial or seminar work and not deliberately to produce such conflicts. However, they happen none the less, interwoven between the threads of manifest communications. The wish or hope of the group or the majority of its members (disturbing motive) is not necessarily deeply buried in the minds of the group participants; but for the moment this wish, though operative, is latent, as manifest attention may be occupied in assimilating educational matters. The reactive motive is probably even further away from the surface and the students may experience vague discomfort only. The group solution is arrived at without any conscious thought at all. Let me give an example which may illustrate the above diagram. One aspect of the work is particularly obscure and none of the students has really mastered it. The wish (disturbing motive) is for the tutor to forget about participation and 'democracy' and give them some straight-forward clarification of the concepts he has been trying to make them see for themselves. The reactive motive is the shame at letting the tutor down and/or fear of his disapproval or even rejection. One group solution (compromise) is to ask him for yet more references and books around the subject; another may be to conspire together to divert his attention from the subject altogether and add fuel to his enthusiasm for another subject in which they too can produce sparks, allowing the whole group to enjoy itself.

This scheme, though deceptively simple, has important academic implications for tutors. Considering the case cited above, we can see that the focal conflict's solution protected the tutor from realizing the inadequacy of his teaching in a certain area. Let us now look at the more 'personal' angle. In a tutorial, where the students only ever group together for this special meeting, there may be a real hope of making contact and even friendships with others, so the 'disturbing motive' is the wish to disclose as much as possible about oneself and to promote reciprocal self-disclosure in others. Even with a permissive easy-going tutor present, these wishes provoke parallel fears; fears of rejection, fears of being responded to angrily, of being scrutinized and deemed unworthy by the others; fear of invading others' privacy or being in turn invaded; fear that everyone will turn out to be far more clever and more fascinating than one's dull self. The group's solution may be to drift into a discussion apparently by sheer accident, about *other people*, — how secretive they are, how they hide beneath masks of social convention, class, profession, etc and what might happen if they, 'the people', actually dared to be more themselves. There may be an intellectualized solution even more remote from, but still connected with the disturbing motive, such as talk about how capitalist society alienates people. This discussion may have intrinsic academic merits, but could just as easily be conducted in the coffee bar. A shrewd tutor, in touch with this focal conflict, would enable members gently and gradually to become more intimate with each other, perhaps by disclosing things about himself and so setting an example. If he understands the disturbing motive, and deems it a healthy group-wish, he can ensure it is gratified.

Some focal conflict solutions can be quite dramatic. A group may be furious with a tutor and really want to confront him (disturbing motive). They fear he is too vulnerable to withstand their anger or that he will retaliate in some way — (reactive motive). The temporary solution is to stay away on the day of the wished-for confrontation and the surprised tutor finds he has no group members that morning. These solutions are not consciously thought out or discussed, they just happen. It may be called latent group process or unconscious communication but it is not magic and it is not my imagination; it really happens, as many tutors will testify, tutors who have never heard of a focal conflict.

From my many conversations with hundreds of individual students, I know that the fear of criticism or ridicule from peers and/or tutor dominates most of their group behaviour, as well as the shame about having such fears at all. They imagine they are the only students who feel that way, yet manage to enlist the co-operation of all the others in bringing about a group solution to common conflicts. The issues could not have been settled better had they called a special meeting to discuss them openly. Typically, in seminars, students will 'agree' not to ask awkward questions of, or even look at, the person presenting a short talk and, in exchange, the same treatment is accorded to them when it is their turn. The tutor meanwhile despairs of ever instigating any discussion and imagines his group is just bored and unstimulated by the subject. In fact they are entrenched in focal conflict solution. They may also be colluding to avoid competitiveness of any sort, thus solving a conflict between wanting the approval of the tutor but not wishing to excite the envy of their colleagues. They agree to be equally average students and no one is allowed to shine. Often a group will explore a whole series of solutions, or compromises, before hitting on one that is capable of reducing the gap between hope and fear to a manageable size.

Certain emergency solutions are transient because they give rise to other disturbing and reactive motives which in turn must be dealt with. We can imagine the anti-learning impact of a permanently imposed solution; it may solve the conflict, but it can ruin the work. The ardent research worker, watching a group over a series of weeks through a one-way screen, would become intoxicated by the emergence of a complicated series of focal conflict patterns, in all manner of hierarchical sequences. For the tutor who is only just beginning to open himself to group process all that he requires at this stage is an appreciation of the basic principles of focal conflict theory, as I have here sketched out. I should stress that my account in no way does justice to the breadth and scope of this method of analysis for the purposes for which it was intended, principally group psychotherapy; I am merely adopting ideas from the theory which might help tutors see their groups with fresh eyes. In general, the more the tutor is able to nurture the development of real trust (which includes an ability to express negative feelings between students and students and students and himself) the less likely is a focal conflict, and is first adopted solution, to root itself in the group culture. In an ideal context the two sides of the focal conflict, the hope and the fear, can actually be spoken about. Usually though, the tutor must content himself with an identification of it, followed by skilled management. Where there is little trust (as in a short life group, or a group with a population that varies from week to week, or where the tutor will not allow any other interaction than that which concerns the subject) the hopes and fears are often displaced outside the group and the tutor can easily neglect these concerns. For example, complaints about bad cafeteria services, poor quality food, alienating concrete-jungle campuses and so on may have more to do with the particular group in which the feelings are being expressed than with the institution itself. Such remarks indicate that students are commencing a feasibility test, working out whether or not this group is safe enough to begin work on focal conflicts. Many groups are forced to abandon their emotional level altogether and act in an exclusively rational way. The result is often a dull, if 'correct' exchange of information. The tutor should be able to help the students move from indirect expression of hopes and fears to more direct ones; solutions can then be arrived at more openly and with more satisfaction all around. This in turn builds up more trust and encourages even more direct expression of feelings and tighter emotional bonds within the group. An ascending spiral of increasingly sophisticated solutions is set in motion by a really competent tutor. The group quickly learns to identify, and resolve its own conflicts. The way is then cleared for concentration upon the academic task to hand, without interference from unresolved conflicts.

Required, avoided and calamitous relationships

Dr Ezriel's work at the Tavistock Clinic is also of interest to the tutor, but does not translate easily to the educational setting unless it is drastically simplified and re-arranged. What I am here discussing is a principal idea derived from his writing, but I make no attempt to summarize the work itself, or to transplant the complexities of the theory or the strict therapeutic techniques which arise out of it. The techniques would be quite disastrous for teaching purposes; nonetheless the three-tiered structure of one of his central ideas about group functioning is not totally dissimilar from the notion of focal conflict and should be considered.

Ezriel reminds us that the disconnected thoughts, feelings and actions of people in a group belong together dynamically — they are meaningfully related within the boundary of the group and spring from a common group well. In a teaching group this would be happening in addition to and in combination with academic work. One member's remark, behaviour or pervasive mood can 'click' with other members who, because of the 'common pool', share certain preoccupations, over and above their strictly individual and personal concerns. As more members join this 'cause', the matter or mood begins to almost dominate the group and other work (the group's official occupation) slows up or becomes diverted, or is confused with the half-conscious or unconscious group movement. All this can prove disconcerting for the tutor, who cannot see why the students are not following what to him are unexceptional aspects of the subject, which ought not to create difficulties.

Once this atmosphere is established, Ezriel predicts a series of *required*, *avoided* and *calamitous* relationships. If the tutor were able to observe another tutor's group, he would see (according to this theory) that the group tries to create (once the 'clicking' has occurred) a certain style of behaviour among its members, directed particularly at the tutor — (this model is clearly a group-to-tutor way of looking at groups). This is the *required* relationship — it is required by the group, whatever pattern of relationship the tutor may try to engineer. A battle of wills may be waged to see whose requirements, the tutor's or the group's, are to be met. The group's requirements are fought very hard for, because it is motivated by the fear that, unless this relationship is quickly and firmly rooted a worse fate and a more frightening relationship might develop. This is the *avoided* relationship. It is avoided because its logical outcome would sooner or later be a *calamitous* relationship.

A very obvious academic example can be found in a group of students overworked by a dedicated specialist in a highly esoteric field. The work he is giving them is over-coloured by his own research interests and too advanced for them at this stage in their undergraduate career. He expects them to produce work for seminars which is extremely difficult for them. But they do not revolt because the *required* relationship is one of propitiation and obedience. They *avoid* having to express anger towards their leader. The students would like to object bitterly to this unfair treatment, but such a relationship, while totally justifiable, could be *calamitous*. Students are highly sensitive to teachers' personality quirks — they do after all see them regularly in a very intimate atmosphere. They may well appreciate that here is a man in love with his work who has very little else to bolster his self-esteem. He takes it for granted that the passion he feels for his subject should be felt by every other student. An assault on this tutor could upset him a great deal; students fear that he may crumble under their aggression or that his obvious disappointment would produce unbearable group guilt. They may snigger about his eccentricities once away from his seminar and enter it with trepidation, expecting to understand little of what he is trying to teach them, but they will maintain a propitiatory relationship at all times rather than risk a calamity that probably none of them has really thought about, but of which all are aware, in that secret area of unspoken group knowledge and communication.

Summary of chapter 5

I have borrowed, modified and tried to elucidate three sets of group theories which might open paths to understanding for tutors. Each set has been put into a melting pot and reforged into constructs which are simple and usable for tutors attempting to understand latent group activity. I should emphasize that tutors are not advised to concentrate exclusively on group processes like these; when work is going well and tutor and students are getting out of the group more or less what they came for, such theories may be safely and happily ignored. Their primary value is in helping tutors to think about why a group may be persistently malfunctioning, despite constant ploys to put it right. A different vantage point can be of assistance, though theories alone are insufficient to meet the tutor's needs in this respect. Group training for tutors, during which they might experience and discuss group behaviour and have it analyzed by a trainer, and where there is also a forum for group case discussion is very important. Although it might be time-consuming, its repercussions for the standard of group teaching throughout the college will ensure that it is not time wasted. Students will benefit personally and this should be reflected in the quality of academic work. Effective group tutoring would reduce absenteeism, many psychosomatic ailments, seminar phobia, feelings of social isolation and academic inferiority all of which may otherwise lead many students to counselling and psychiatric services.

Chapter 6

Major processes
within the small group

Process

Process thinking like *system thinking* is a habit to be cultivated by the
tutor as preparation for successful group work. There is nothing esoteric about it and it is gradually acquired once his resistance to new
ways of thinking and learning is overcome. A book like this can only
guide the reader toward the observation and management of group
process, each group and tutor being unique so that standardized explanations and recommendations are inadequate for helping him to deal in
detail with a specific group. If the reader firmly believes that 'group
process' is something other people, probably social scientists, observe
during *their* teaching activities, and that process thinking is a habit he
(or she) can well do without, let me offer him a rapid mental exercise
to carry out to demonstrate the degree to which he is already aware of
process, even if he feels unsure of how to organize or apply this knowledge. This exercise should initiate the reader into process thinking, by
helping him see how process is shaped by factors with which he is already very familiar.

Process-shapers
Think of any small group recently taught. Do not logically and sequen-
tially reconstruct what was said and done or strive to recall the details
of the topics studied. Instead, accord precedence to people's level and
quality of participation, their overall proclivity or reluctance to work
and your own feelings about the group's functioning. Now ask yourself
the following questions:

(1) *How does group composition enhance or diminish the propensity
for work?* How many members were there, and of what age and sex?
How did their innate ability and past academic experiences compare?
How many students were 'open' and eager to share their ideas with
others and how many were 'closed', unwilling for the moment to risk
revealing their own personalities and knowledge? Now apply all these
categories to yourself as the influential leader — how motivated, secretive, clever, confident, able and outgoing were you?

(2) *In what ways do boundaries facilitate or restrict group contributions?* Before asking the questions, I will redefine boundaries. Boundaries are literal or metaphorical series of perimeters inside one another, which we can picture as shrinking and expanding constraints. Within these, the group and its leader must collaborate if they are to survive as a group. Now for the questions: What were the 'entry requirements', fulfilled by your students, to the group? Was the locational boundary a help or hindrance? How was the physical space within the boundary designed and used and for what desired effect? What was the temporal boundary within which the group assumed corporate identity and was this time the result of planning, convenience or accident? What were the agreed or imposed structural boundaries, (for example the advance academic preparation) or set procedures (such as the presentation of papers in turn?) Were the structural boundaries facilitative or obstructive?

(3) *How do I lead?* Were you possessive of leadership; did you share it, abdicate it, delegate it, rotate it, ignore it, or bequeath it to another member?

(4) *Is the group's atmosphere an accident?* Was the group industrious, perverse, bored, restless, clinging, or hostile? What steps did you, and perhaps others, take to alter or maintain the group mood?

(5) *Does a group generate its own culture?* What invisible rules and codes of conduct were obeyed in your group; were there any identifiable shared values and behaviours which you had not deliberately introduced?

I am sure that most tutor readers can make some kind of reply — probably rich and lengthy replies — to all of these questions and many others I could have posed. All the questions above related to factors which closely connect with group process and/or part processes. Alas, processes do not conveniently run in parallel lines for easy identification. They activate each other, combine and diverge, strengthen and weaken each other and often each part process is but one facet of another. We are therefore watching constant *movement* as we monitor group processes; we are not seeing a static array of *things*, easily categorized, for the group mystery finally to be solved. (The much abused term 'group dynamics' embraces this concept of fluid process). Nonetheless if we are to appreciate the importance of processes, and if we are to teach others about them, we must attempt a hypothetical isolation of them, however limited the value of such conceptualization to which such codification can lead. Like love and happiness, or pain and loss, group processes are not concrete entities, but result from ever shifting emotional states *between* people and defy satisfying definition. The recognition and subjective experience of love is evidence enough for the person concerned of its true existence. Similarly, I cannot 'prove' the fact of group processes, but will try to illustrate some of them in the same cumbersome way one strains to capture the essence of love for a bewildered listener. Scientists have justifiable cause to groan when called upon to witness the inexactitude and terminological impoverishment of workers in this comparatively new field. Sifting a group for suitably encapsulated phenomena to which a name can then be ascribed is a hopeless task. We can mine an inexhaustable supply of process jewels, but their gleam is bewitchingly different each time we gaze upon them. Group work is vastly more complicated by a major fact which, when faced and respected, makes group management very much easier. All group processes, whether manifest or latent, occur over time and space, between and among people and are never fixed. Process happens within boundaries which themselves can be subject to change.

Processes and parts of process are sometimes influenced by events external to the boundaries and are also nurtured by psychic events inside individual persons who interact within these boundaries. Here, the earlier analogy of the group as a mine of jewels breaks down. Processes are not frozen, heated, compressed into solidarity, secreted motionless in a timeless dark awaiting detection. They are not fossilized. On the contrary, they undergo rapid mutations, sometimes from second to second, exploding into everyone's attention, fading, running underground, and bubbling up to the surface of an interaction once more. Processes alter, replicate, display turbulance and quiescence, engulf people, exclude them, frighten them, cheer them up. Surprisingly few tutors are aware of these powerful forces, so conditioned are they by their academic milieu, to the meticulous appraisal of exclusively cerebral activity, or the written word. They are prevented by their own blindness from the recognition that group process can cripple a student's efforts to participate in serious work and paralyze all attempts at verbal inclusion in the group. Conversely, properly fostered and controlled, process can raise the level and speed of learning appreciably. Can we afford to be disdainful then, relegating group process to the stature of a plaything beloved of social scientists?

A word now about 'process' and 'part process' as terms. The connection between them is the same as that which links 'the Seminar' (capital 'S' — relating to the scope of a whole term's work for a prescribed set of individuals), and 'seminar' (small 's' — relating to a single meeting and constituent part of the Seminar). The two are interdependent and cannot exist alone except by linguistic convention.

Process shapers in the teaching group

To ground total process and part processes and show that they are not just products of a febrile imagination, we require material and non material boundaries — a physical and psychological 'laboratory' in which they can be generated for observational purposes. A seminar or tutorial is ideal. We must have people (in this case students) among and between whom the processes can pass and by whom they can be influenced. The group's occupation (whether a lab experiment, a revision session or discussion of essays) is another moulder of processes, as well as, on occasions, a repository for some of them, as we shall see later. The boundaries, the group members and the work-occupation itself are like bricks and process is the cement. If the house falls down because the cement is not sticking the bricks together, or if windows and doors become so clogged with cement that no air can get in or out, then the builder (tutor) is in dire trouble! This handy analogy should not be extended too far, however. People are not inanimate objects, but human agents who give birth to processes; maintaining them, controlling them, driving them towards fusion with other processes. People are the recipients and mediators of processes and are affected or even conditioned by them. From this we begin to see, that what group members bring with them to the group, in addition to what is already there will have an inestimable effect on all future group processes. Both the tutor and the students bring to the group a wealth of anticipation, fantasy, and personal history. These attributes will colour and be coloured by the group's processes.

Anticipation All members have hopes, expectations and fears about the group before the first meeting even if these discomforting impulses are suppressed or minimized to make them more emotionally manageable. The strength of these anticipations and the degree to which they enter into the participants' conscious and unconscious group contributions and behaviour will shape reciprocally the way other people struggle with their anticipatory hopes and anxieties.

Fantasy Similarly, everyone brings a fantasy, often hard to contradict even when the tutor repeatedly states the correct facts. The leader is God perhaps, or that this is a place where one is intellectually massacred, or that this course is the most difficult/easy ever invented, and that the other students are the most stupid/intelligent ever accepted in a university. Assumptions are often associated with the fantasy, such as 'if I am academically bright the teacher will love me', with its corollary, 'if I don't understand the work I will be seen as dumb and worthless.' Each participant's anticipations and fantasies have evolved as products of his singular life-experience.

Personal history All members of this new group have had previous experience of all manner of formal/informal, natural/institutional, professional/social groups, and by now possess a range of group behaviours. They will therefore respond to the new situation idiosyncratically. Each has his own feelings about authority, sharing, intimacy, co-operation and rivalry. Individuals differ in their willingness to articulate and their degree of social confidence. Before the group has physically come together the stage has already been set for a real life drama, and some of the main themes, if not the precise plot, have already been written.

There are other behind the scenes 'givens' which distinguish the director-tutor from the student actors, and they can exert such power-ful force on the group-play that they should never be ignored, although they often are. The student is in the group for a short period, whereas the tutor probably runs a series of small group meetings or another version of it every year. His principal commitment is to the subject, to research, to the institution, or to teaching as a vocation. The student, on the other hand, is more oriented towards self, to what he can gain from this transient period through rapid gratification of his intellectual, social and psychological needs. His attitude might therefore be urgent and impatient (however restrained his actual behaviour). This contrast in tutor and student approaches to the group is important and while by no means obligatory, it can sometimes be discussed openly in an appropriately organized small group. (To contrive an infiltration into the occupation of an otherwise stable working group to discuss this matter would be reckless.) For the student, this group is often more important as a social than as an academic context whereas the tutor probably sees his own social context as his home and friends, and to some extent colleagues. The tutor sees successful socializing in the group as a means to an end (competent teaching), rather than as a sometimes painful and hopeless end in itself, as it is for so many stuu-dents. If they cannot manage the social transactions, even basic ones such as speaking, misery and loss of motivation follow. The tutor can pass on knowledge without first having to win a popularity poll but sometimes he assumes, incorrectly that students bestow as low a priority on successful social skills as he does.

Students often have relationships with each other outside the group and quickly develop quite pronounced attitudes to the course and the college. In many cases they may have inherited from previous students a whole mythology about the new tutor: his habits, foibles and eccen-tricities. Once again we find that new groups are subject to a set of conditions (auspices in TCI terms) that formerly we may not have noticed. These conditions strongly determine how processes may grow. We can understand how easily they spring up, for the instant a group comes together, even if none of the members have met before, all the dynamic potential is there. A familiar example is a big football match. The stadium is full, the crowd expectant; the grass is groomed and lines newly painted white; the ritual songs have been sung. The players have been arduously training for weeks, and are now finalizing preparations in the dressing room. What remains is for the game to be played and for the spectators to play their part; in other words, for process to occur. In groups, process, whether manifest or latent, is *always present*. It can be ignored, denied or censored, but it will never go away. Some processes can be happily left alone for they are congruent with the group's occupation; others are neglected at the group's peril for success-ful work, or even group survival may depend on their being creatively exploited. Fortunately processes are amenable to manipulation, conversion, accentuation and inhibition by skilled intervention.

The Foulkesian perspective of group process

This chapter and the next (which are interconnected) contain my own rather drastic revisions of the ideas of the late S H Foulkes, the founder of Group Analysis. His work does not require reinterpretation in its own therapeutic context, but as it stands, it would not transpose easily to group tutoring. However there are conceptual nuggets buried in his work which tutors could convert into valuable educational coinage, and I have tried to attract prospectors by digging over the top soil of his writings to bring the more obvious riches into the sunlight. I hope that my professional colleagues and my ex-trainers, with whom I share in my work a group analytic orientation, will not be too shocked at what I have done.

I am certain that Dr Foulkes would agree that much understanding of group process is gained by learning to see the obvious, (just as Freud admitted teaching us that which all nursery governesses of his period already knew with regard to infantile sexuality). In groups we must sensitize ourselves to processes which we have known about all our lives, but have forgotten or traded in for an excessive reliance on language or the written word. Resurrection and retraining of our very real sixth sense, the sense that picks up interpersonal process, is more useful to tutors than weeks in the library studying the mammoth and sometimes obscure literature on group work. I shall here use Foulkes' terminology as well as my own, often hybrid, terms. 'The object of this exercise is to show the need for new words and phrases to describe the *tutor's* approach, not the therapist's, or trainer's or sociologist's. Many group analytic concepts are not wholly relevant to the tutor, but many contain specific elements which are essential to his work. In these circumstances I have produced similar terms to the original concept from which the element has been extracted and have tried to describe their significance in the educational setting. Readers who will subsequently go to another source to explore these ideas further will become confused unless they realize what I am doing to Foulkes' work in these chapters and why.

Resistance and resonance as basic forces in the group

Group processes of whatever sort have a tendency in teaching groups to show themselves in *resistance* or *resonance* to learning. Resonance indicates a co-ordinated wish to learn which reverberates like a hum around the group. The students may say after such a group, 'I really got a buzz out of that session today', or 'I don't know what happened, the seminar just took off somehow, and we zoomed through the work'. The resonance to learning is possible because of a deeper resonance between members at a personal level, to which they are almost always completely impervious; plus, of course, the absence or successful management of resistance, usually by the tutor. Many tutors I know deal with resistance by intuitive methods gained through long experience and then assume the happy result to be purely fortuitous.

In general terms, we can think of resonance and resistance as being opposed to each other. Competent group leadership necessitates the mobilization of resonance and the reduction of resistance. I will return to this matter of facilitating resonance in the next chapter and will here look a little more closely at some of the part processes which promote resistance. Group resistance (deliberate or unconscious) is not to be confused with collective laziness or unwillingness. Group life has a profound effect on the feelings and actions of members. In the same way family life is a specialized group profoundly affecting its members. Its inbuilt assumptions, role allocations, shared values and prejudices fashion mother's, father's and child's study attitudes, career motivation, and eventual professional performance.*These personality characteristics of family members are not exclusively determined by innate talent and ability*. Similarly in group life: a student can be highly resistant to any learning one term, and yet shoot ahead the next. This dramatic reversal may be related to which group he finds himself in, rather than to his intellectual aptitudes.

Resistance and its source Resistance has many sources. After some general remarks about resistance I shall confine myself and the reader to a glimpse of how process and part processes which can be grouped together as *interpersonal distortion* bring it about.

Individual resistances

Firstly, we should realize that not all the resistance in a group emanates from purely *interpersonal* transactions. Many students and/or the tutor himself bring to the group their own inherent resistances, though in their conscious thoughts they may desire mastery of the subject. These personal resistances can be exaggerated or reduced depending upon the 'dovetail effect'. That is whether or not their own private resistances 'lock' with a prevailing group resistance, so that both are reinforced. An individual's resistance might be revealed by a total inability to be told anything, either by his fellows or the tutor. He feels that if he needs telling, he is weak; raising queries is equated with submission. He keeps up a pretence to himself and others that he is following and is in command of the material. Unfortunately, in many instances, the other students follow suit and a group resistance grips the learning situation. A common individual resistance is to the academic material itself. The old is in the way of the new; old fixed ways of reading, writing, planning essays, marshalling data will not be given up. This position can be seen as a defensive one, taken up to ward off the fear of unlearning, the vital prelude to relearning. The boundariless chaos about his own person — let alone the group, which the student fears might result from the unlearning process, only serves to make him cling determindly to old patterns of study. This resistance is particularly virulent and infectious when a group is faced with a teacher using group approaches poorly understood by both him and the students. They try to placate him with the styles and standards that always pleased the headmaster. If the group members are new to the institution and unsure about these new pressures, they may band together in defiance of any unfamiliar teaching methods and plead for set tasks identical to those which they received at school. The result is resistance stemming from a very natural fear of changing one's whole philosophical perspective with regard to the subject, never mind the adjustment to new study habits. This is the same resistance that many teachers face when they begin to feel pressed into group tutoring; they cast about for all kinds of sane, sensible, and valid reasons for perpetuating the *status quo*. If the tutor is the victim of his own resistance to group tutoring, with its demands for a change in philosophy, he cannot hope to free the students from their resistance to small group learning. The terror in student and staff alike may be the same: 'at least this is the study/ teaching perspective I know; if I tried the new way, would I be any good? Would I lose the esteem of my colleagues, look a fool, and then maybe find myself unable to return to the safe position I had abandoned?' Some students can be helped greatly by having before them a model (either another student, if group process permits, or a tutor), who demonstrates his readiness to change. He is willing to experiment with new and unexpected facets of the subject itself and to try new ways of co-operating on the work project with other participants in the group. He shows his preparedness to face uncertainty and doubt in the interests of new learning. The person modelling, if he carries any weight in the group, will encourage imitation by the others.

Most students want to gain face, not lose it, and some will keep face even at the high cost of learning. Their willingness to sacrifice knowledge (become resistant) is explained by the fact that their goals in the group are not ranked hierarchically in the same way as those that the tutor has for them. The tutor probably does not have the preservation of self-esteem on his agenda at all, whereas for the student it often has top priority. If the tutor was able to produce a climate in which high marks for adventurous work was equated with 'face', half his teaching problems would be over. Unfortunately many students are confronted with a choice of keeping face or risking new learning. They usually choose the former, and while avoiding risks they produce dull if adequate work.

Generalized resistances
Group resistance is at its most insidious when it has the gloss of co-

operation. It is not unknown for massive collusion to set in and for tutor and students to 'agree' to a safe and orthodox programme, without experimentation. Such a group can be cosy and harmonious and may even produce good examination results. These exam results may in turn reflect an archaic assessment system which rewards memory rather than learning and 'party line' thinking in preference to originality. The resistance here is not confined within the boundaries of the group but extends into the entire institution, permeating all its official academic procedures and its social relations. This collusive resistance is most likely to occur when the tutors are terrified of any expression or hint of hostility, irritation, or frustration in their groups. So afraid are they of negative reactions that they go out of their way to elicit exclusively positive ones. The outcome is learning paralysis. On an institutional scale, resistance to new educational approaches and denial of healthy intergroup conflict results in excessive conservatism and a tight embracing of traditional values, which closes any possibility of natural rebellion or public debate which are essential pre-requisites for the college's development.

Interpersonal distortions

(a) Transfer

I shall now return to a discussion of how sub groups of participants, a participant and the leader and sometimes the whole group membership insist on perceiving one another wrongly. All kinds of consequences follow, usually inimical to efficient study. Some learning can still take place despite interpersonal distortions, but it would not reflect the group's true capabilities. One of the major distortions in any group, (indeed in any two-way relationship) is that induced by *transfer*. (This has similarities to the psychoanalytic concept of transference, but is not the same, for in psychoanalysis, transference has a very strict meaning compared to the wider application used here.) Students as well as the tutor will respond to the new small group more or less as they have elsewhere in the past. The prospect of joining a new group will reactivate memories of old group experiences. The anticipatory images of the new group thus conjured up are replete with old dreads and hopes. No one really comes *tabula rasa* to a new group. Each person will negotiate the group situation in a way that is typical for him. He *transfers* old ways of coping to the present circumstances. If the new situation and constellation of relationships within it do not look the same, he tries, albeit unconsciously, to make it look the same and force it into a recognizable pattern. He may for instance transfer his fear and hatred of the powerful, ambitious and exacting aspects of his otherwise loved parents to the tutor, to whom he attributes these qualities, without waiting to see if he really possesses them. This is an example of unconscious transferring.

At a conscious level the student sincerely believes he is making an objective evaluation of the tutor's personality. Conscious transfer is easier to deal with, for the student can choose to change his transferring behaviours as they are subject to his will. If he transfers the expectation that he will be academically mollycoddled as at school or home, he may be disappointed. As he can clearly see his transfer distortion, he can correct it and make a new start from a new vantage point. It is the unconscious or half-conscious transfer distortion by the student that is dangerous to his learning facility. He insists on transferring to other students and teachers properties belonging to a past situation and to other people and compulsively reacts to those around him in his present situation as if they were someone else from the past. He will go to extraordinary lengths to bring about the repetition of previous experience. For instance, a student may persistently 'forget' to hand work in and, when the tutor finally approaches him on the matter complains that he is being victimized, just like 'at school' or 'at home'. He forces the tutor into the role of persecutor.

In a new group where everyone is consciously and unconsciously transferring past experiences to the present, a whole tapestry of erroneous perceptions are interwoven with all the other more accurate perceptions. Not all transferring behaviour is negative; people make personal attachments and resolutions to work hard, after very short acquaintances with other members of the group. In this case, transferring of positive characteristics to fellow group members might have occurred. When there is instant rapport between student and tutor, it may be that the tutor is seen as a 'father protector' to the group and is assumed to be wonderful and worth pleasing, as was his prototype, the student's real father. In the early stages of the group, allegiances, enmities and all associations in between these polarities are made on the basis of very flimsy evidence. They are made on the basis of transfer assumptions, the less entrenched of which are eventually tested against harsh reality and corrections in mutual perceptions are then made. The more free ranging the verbal and non verbal exchanges allowed in the group, and the more opportunities for 'reality checks' that are provided, the faster will be the group's adaptation to undistorted reality and the quicker they will immerse themselves in genuine work and authentic social relationships. If the tutor hurtles through a list of items, not pausing to allow reflection, asking 'closed' questions and demanding instant answers, giving out books and reference lists, holding dyadic conversations which the others dare not interrupt, keeping himself and everyone else frantically busy, then the group members may get stuck with their first transferred picture of the group and never dare to find out what it is really like and what one might be able to do in it. More important, they will not learn how one might be able to do it all differently this time, with better results, and less need for resistive coping strategies than in previous groups.

A classic example of how people bring their histories to the group, and then often become trapped in them, can be seen in the meeting where everyone regularly adopts the same seat. This can happen through consensus and may be evidence that the mature group has worked out its social patterning and is content with it. However, it is more likely to mean the following: Mary expects to be picked on for being silent, so she hides in a corner and pulls at her fringe nervously, as if to curtain herself off from the rest of the gathering; John sits opposite the tutor confident of an intellectural battle; Ann huddles next to him, either to avoid being seen or to have him shield her; Jack sits scribbling, eyes focused on his notepad all the time to avoid having to look at anyone who might want to get close to him. Jean wears tight jeans, puts on eye-shadow and lipstick and sits in the most obvious place, as she feels that otherwise no one will notice she is a woman as well as an 'egghead'. There are dozens of other examples which any tutor could quote. It is worrying when, after months in the group, nothing has changed for these members. Jean is more interested in the tutor as a man than in his subject; Mary has said three sentences in as many months; Jack has still not looked at or laughed with anyone, and John monotonously hogs the meeting. Saddest of all is that they have almost certainly always related and learned, in a limited capacity, very much like this in former groups of different kinds and will continue to do so.

What about the tutor? Does he transfer images, first handed down to him in childhood, of the omniscient, paternal, all-responsible teacher to the present situation? How will he cope with having to surrender the traditional pedagogic role which he has been taught to revere and instead share time, power and responsibility with the group? Does he sit halfway on his desk, symbolizing his partial readiness to change and simultaneous clinging to a familiar (transferred) teaching style? Does he feel obliged to 'give' all the time, feeding in information in accordance with his transferred image of himself as teacher, rather than learning to operate as a catalytic agent in the group? If he can cope with these transferring problems, managing the uncertainty involved in any transition to a new *modus operandi*, then the students may dare to do the same.

(b) Displacement

A second means by which interpersonal distortion comes about is *displacement*; moving a bit of oneself, one's uncomfortable feelings, or one's unwanted psychological accoutrements, and dumping them on something or somebody else. Individuals do this to one another and often the whole group, acting in concert as if it were one organism, does it to the institution, to the course or to the tutor. The widespread acceptance of displaced 'personal property', without realization of what is happening, can inhibit group development quite seriously. Often people can hardly recognize themselves or each other, so loaded down are they with each other's mental baggage, which they have adopted over time. Let me give some examples. Probably the most usual displacement is the collusive group displacement of anxieties on to the work. A new, rather frightened, group, a group with a 'sticky' atmosphere and hidden conflicts which people want to steer clear of, or a group conducted by a very nervous tutor will often 'agree' to keep at bay emotional expression, in order to avoid all hostilities. They generally keep the peace by 'working hard'. Often disproportionate academic anxieties or excessive preoccupation with peripheral work come to the fore. Obsessions with minor details about presentation or preparation of writing require endless advice, reassurance and comfort. These requests often have more to do with prohibited feelings, the original source of insecurity, than with the work itself. No amount of tackling artificially created work queries will satisfy the students' demands for paternal guidance. The tutor is frequently the root cause of this kind of difficulty. The students are sensing and responding to his personal teaching problems. Anxiety congeals around the work rather than the person of the tutor who is too vulnerable to be directly challenged or whose goodwill must be bought at all costs. A change in leadership behaviour as a result of insight into this piece of group process will put matters right.

Individual displacement may occur when a student displaces his concealed shyness and passivity, which he normally struggles against and is ashamed of, on to another student who epitomises these qualities, and whom he then protects. This can be helpful to begin with, especially to the protected student, whose feelings appear to be recognized and understood at long last. However, if such relations continue indefinitely, the overtly shy student is shielded from ever having to develop autonomous action, or from accepting responsibility for the effects his withdrawal has on other group members. Meanwhile the guardian is placed in a position of strength and dependability which bolsters his self-esteem, but his confidence relies upon the 'weaker' student's wish to lean upon him. This is a very straightforward example and it can be seen that little or no harm results from this very ordinary kind of displacement, even if it is not very growth-promoting for the people involved.

Envy can be a great stimulus to learning; it can help a student to compete or copy in a non destructive fashion. Unfortunately, if the student *displaces* his ambition, his wish to please the teacher, and his need to dominate others with academic superiority, (all sentiments of which his 'better self' disapproves) on to another successful student (whose motives in working hard cause him no conflict), then difficulties arise. The envious student attacks and tries to spoil the unwanted aspects of his own personality which he sees in the tranquil student. He cannot learn from the more successful man, for co-operation with him would be tantamount to an admission of his own ambitions which

87

he is trying to disown. None of this is thought out consciously by the envious student, but this inability to co-operate happens in groups all the time, and is a displacement phenomenon easily discernible to a perceptive tutor.

Foulkes has likened the group to a hall of mirrors in which parts of ourselves are reflected and counter-reflected; we see facets of ourselves in others and others see themselves in us. We sometimes admire and cherish others and learn from them because they seem to represent our better selves; we distrust and confront or ignore parts of other people which 'mirror' the darker corners of our own personality. It is when group members deny and disown parts of themselves, (for example, failing to realize that the attitude adopted by the member next to them, which they are challenging vehemently, is actually an attitude they themselves secretly espouse) that attempts to work become fraught with tension. Tension evolving purely from academic debate is exciting and productive; chronic tension resulting from various interlocking mutual displacements, which are not understood by the displacers or the receivers, can be quite destructive to the group's occupation because they never lead to resolution, or agreements to differ. An ostensibly academic debate which persists long after others have need of it; a lab experiment, the technical approach to which several students 'rationally' but endlessly argue over is often heavily laden with interpersonal displacement of this kind, requiring some active intervention by the tutor if the circular argument or abortive experiment is to be curtailed in favour of a group learning situation with a more hopeful outcome. The tutor cannot ban displacement activity, but can avoid consolidating it and may also wish to change the course of a discussion to break up such process.

The tutor must examine very carefully his own tendency to displacement, if he is to maintain enough objectivity *vis-a-vis* his group to assess those displacement behaviours which are counterproductive to learning. Tutors may sadistically attack students who mirror unwanted parts of their own personalities. One tutor I knew personally, a male who was generally well liked and successful at work, was particularly strict with a sickly, rather depressed looking youth, who cowered whenever anyone in the group spoke to him. Eventually the tutor saw that this student represented his own self of 20 years ago and that that self was not, as he had thought, dead and buried. On the contrary that self still clamoured for expression in his marital situation. He forced himself to stand up to his wife and adolescent children, even though his real urge was to yield; to go to bed and plead illness and/or fatigue, and to get himself nursed. Sensing that the tutor approved of their behaviour, the group made a scapegoat of this student who represented the defeatist in them all (including the tutor who wanted to eliminate the sickly boy inside of himself). The student was thereby driven deeper into passivity and withdrawal. Eventually he deserted (or was deserted by) the group, producing a medical certificate which said he was suffering from the protracted effects of glandular fever.

Other tutors give special care and attention to students who portray under-developed aspects of themselves or who remind them of a significant person in their lives. A male science tutor of my acquaintance had only one girl in his tutorial group. Both her christian name, and rather commonsense down-to-earth temperament was the same as his own mother's. She had been a clever woman who had surrendered her education for domesticity and the bringing up of seven children. She had gone out to work to help put our tutor through university and he had been grateful, yet guilt ridden about it. He promulgated fairly strong views on women's liberation and took a great interest in this girl, who subsequently became quite embarrassed by his attentions as the other male students seemed jealous. They hated not only the blatant sexual discrimination against them, irrespective of academic merit, but also the fact that competition with the leader for the favours of the only girl in the group was a non-starter. They were bound to lose, and any tokens of competition (so my speculations about their fantasies went) might affect the assessment of their work. The girl politely but firmly sought out the tutor privately and asked him to stop behaving this way. He was very hurt, but eventually saw how he had both transferred feelings about his mother to his student and then displaced on to her the guilt-induced ambitions he cherished for his mother, if he could but put the clock back. When the female student had first appeared, it looked as though his wish had come true. Here was his mother, a perky clever apple-cheeked north country lass of 19! At the time all emotional connections between his mother and the student had escaped his notice.

(c) Splitting

The tutor may displace by *splitting*. For example, one group of students is labelled by him as 'good' and another as 'bad'. There may be some truth in the allegation that one group is working better than the other, but re-routing *all* good atributes in one direction and *all* bad in another is damaging. It intensifies the idealisation of one group (which a detached observer would realize is nowhere near as perfect as the tutor makes out), and increases the tutor's despair and contempt when he reviews the other. Our detached observer may see a psychological link between the two groups. One group *has* to be experienced as totally useless (though in fact it is just 'difficult') so that the other may be perceived as flawless. If the observer could show the tutor some of the faults in the perfect group, or help him see signs of change in the hopeless one, the tutor may then be usefully confronted with his need for a 'showpiece' group, the price of which is another redundant ineffective group.

A very good example of splitting displacement can be seen in chapter 9, where a case study of a law teachers' training seminar is presented. In the early meetings, conceptual clarity, accurate definition of all language employed, ruthless examination of facts, dismissal of any vagueness, or untested ideas was the cherished norm. Feeling, moods, allusions, analogy and metaphor were regarded as inferior, inadmissable, valueless and academically not respectable. The adherence to scientific thinking was the result of disowning anxieties about enforced intimacy with each other. The splitting displacement came about by members collectively making reason and intellect a god, and emotion or intuitive thinking the very devil. It was the fear about beginning to let the two mingle, the fear that the devil might destroy the god, leaving group members abandoned and afraid, which drove a wedge between the lawyer participants representing pure reason, and myself representing raw feeling. (In fact, of course, the lawyers were as capable of raw feeling as I was of pure reason.) But the displacement and splitting process type-cast us in ways that wrecked real co-operation for weeks, even though at a conscious level we remained grown-up intelligent people trying to work together.

(d) Scapegoating, pairing, stereotyping and blaming as part processes of displacement

Massive displacement occurs in the group when certain taboos prohibit the direct challenging of the tutor. The taboos are arrived at through unconscious group consensus or because the leader of the group makes the taboos apparent by his behaviour. Some other person has to be elected to receive the group's accumulated uncomfortable feelings. Should the tutor realize himself to be the real target for these displaced feelings, he would be horrified. Rescuing a scapegoat is an important part of the tutoring function and often necessitates him showing his readiness to accept direct hostility. Other 'elections' are rigged all the time. The rebel student can speak on behalf of the others and also be punished for *their* rebellion. In Bion's work, we have already seen how a silent member can be elected to do the task of 'wringing the tutor's heart', so as to perpetuate the meeting of dependency demands. Pairs are often selected as solvers of a group problem or as repositories for two sides of a group conflict. The pair is left to fight it out while others passively watch their own passions being tossed across the mini stage they have erected. What matters here, is that group roles such as 'leader's victim', 'rebel', 'silent member', 'group clown' and 'dominant member' can become so stereotyped and permanent that the group as a whole cannot tolerate any change in these fixed positions. Everyone's 'reputation' has stuck fast. Therefore, the clown can never show his seriousness, the aggressor can never show tenderness, the silent one must not speak and the victim must eternally ask for more punishment. The tutor has lost his freedom of movement and his capacity to direct events; he is squeezed between all these cardboard characters, who, were it not for him would not come together or opt for and assign roles to each other. This state of affairs is undoubtedly his responsibility: it is no use blaming the students for being a 'bad group'. The group leader must never allow roles to become entrenched like this.

Displacement, however its part processes combine to produce it, is not always kept within the group's boundaries. Business may well proceed satisfactorily within the group itself and all the unwanted, disowned feelings are projected upwards or outwards, beyond the boundaries, so that hostilities within the group seem to have disappeared altogether. Leader and led may conspire to blame the course, the head of department, the economic situation or educational philosophy for all manner of problems and frustrations which ought ideally to be sorted out in the group. The apportioning of blame elsewhere, preferably to a place or person so far away, in terms of status and accessibility, that nothing can be done about it, is a ready-made solution to many group problems. If that which is being blamed and displaced on to can be a system of thought, a political system, or bureaucratic machine, or something equally intangible and remote, so much the better. This kind of massive displacement makes for group solidarity, but creates a high resistance to any possibility of wider institutional change. People settle down comfortably, safe in the knowledge that all problems are 'their' fault, and 'we' are the goodies and 'they' are the baddies. This happens in groups of 'converted' tutors, (possibly some readers of this book!) who see the unconverted as reactionary, unhelpful and even persecutory. It becomes impossible to see colleagues' distaste for personal tutoring as deeply buried resistance, based on a fear of personal change, because all the spleen and bitterness of those personal tutors struggling to have their views heard is displaced on to the 'uninterested' teachers, who are then experienced as savage attackers, 'out to do us down'. Many traditional teachers of great integrity simply do not understand the newer ideas in tutoring because no one has told them, and they are defensive as a result of being blamed so much. Some are just very afraid of the personal change that is being asked of them and are in need of greater support from enlightened colleagues, as opposed to confrontation by a militant in-group who demand instant acceptance of their ideas. Psychological resistances, unlike physical ones, can never be overcome by this kind of force. Some resistances, it must be acknowledged, will never be overcome at all, as motivation is absent rather than buried.

Communication and feedback

Having inspected two blocks of process, transfer and displacement, I now want to look at two more generalized processes — communication and feedback. As always, we must respect the degree to which feelings engender process. Without positive and negative feelings, happy, sad, hopeful and fearful, exciting and dreary, there would be no process at all. There would only be a collection of intellects, a computers' convention met to assimilate data and regurgitate the right answers at the end. Where people work together there is feeling; where there is feeling, — its inhibition expression and exchange, there is group process. Process is inevitable and can make or mar learning. A recognition of processes as they occur spontaneously in groups is the first step taken by a tutor in coming to grips with group work. He does not need to make processes happen, though he may need to interfere with them; what he needs at this stage is to watch them being spun all around him and to avoid becoming entangled by them!

The most easily discernible process is of course *communication*. So unintentional. Dress, facial expression, posture, silence, and fidgeting or manner of communication, not only the information that is communicated. The group, aided by its leader, establishes a common zone, in which all members can participate at various levels, the level of data exchange being only one. Why that particular piece of academic or other information is being selected, at this time, and why it is being transmitted to that other person or persons, may have repercussions which will echo in the group for weeks to come, and significantly effect the group's learning potential. Within this communicational matrix group members develop their own verbal physical and academic language, a kind of group shorthand which regular membership enables them to decipher. All the happenings within the group boundaries during a meeting of its members are tied to different types of signals whether to each other or to the leader; they may be deliberate or quite unintentional. Dress, facial expression, posture, silence, and fidgeting or gestures say a great deal as do nailbiting, blushing, avoiding or demanding eye contact, losing notes, producing too many, sighing, yawning, etc. These are all communications which can be understood at different levels depending on how the expression communicated is combined with other parts of group process. A yawn can indicate individual fatigue or a late night, or the student may be telling the tutor something about his teaching style on behalf of the whole group. The group may talk fitfully or frenetically, or may seem to be in an hilarious mood more ready for a holiday than hard work, or may appear gloomy and preoccupied despite the fact that individually and separately, in their private lives, they are quite content. They are therefore communicating something important about the group system at the present moment within special boundaries and under a specific group conductor. Much communication is unknowing, and it is for the tutor to decode inadvertent messages which might signal distress or eargerness to learn more in a member or members.

Linked to communication is *feedback*. All people in new groups, unless they are desperately ill, will show some as yet undefined interest in each other and will feel an urge to make contact. Over time they begin to interact, communicate and form tentative positive and negative attachments which in turn produce a series of communicational wave bands on which members can broadcast to one another. This is the feedback network. How a person feels he has been received by another will determine what and how he transmits next time. His subsequent message then influences what others will choose to reveal about themselves to him.

People meet one another for the first time, and at first there is hesitant reaction, interest and contact. Then there is the stage of interaction, self revelation and distinct relationships. Consequent upon elaborate feedback (broadcasting) procedures, people modify their early impression of others and decide how much they will disclose about themselves and how intimate they can afford to become. The group is no longer a random assortment of individuals — it has now an indelible character of its own. The more openings that are created for the feedback of information, feelings and ideas, the greater is the potential for group intimacy, trust and sharing, and the more opportunities for better learning and closer attachments. Many new tutors assume, incorrectly, that they are the only ones qualified to give feedback to the students, and the only legitimate message to broadcast is approval or disapproval. This is how they were taught, and they cannot see the point in allowing students to circle round each other, assess one another, indulge their curiosity about one another, and strengthen group ties on the basis of accurate perceptions of one another. The tutor may regard all this as a waste of time until he sees from experience that groups whose members elect to share the work load, laugh and make friendships, fight and compete, learn better, faster and more lastingly. The students learn other values too, which may be of just as much value to their future lives as the academic qualification they obtain.

Many tutors, while encouraging feedback in their groups, suddenly find themselves encouraging feedback in their families, their partners, colleagues and bosses. They are amazed to find chasms crossed, barriers pulled down and inhibitions loosened, with trust beginning to develop where suspicion and the urge to withdraw for self protection lurked before. Feedback must be approved by the leader, or even asked for and demonstrated by him. In a group where members feel the atmosphere does not really permit feedback, they may well resort to seeking it secretly and non verbally, thereby increasing their susceptibility to interpersonal distortion. A good tutor, by giving them a chance to offer one another feedback over their work, can promote an atmosphere conducive to further feedback at a more self revelatory level. He might remember the importance of them getting to know him too, rather than transferring to him outdated images marked 'authority'. If he as 'the boss' cannot give or take feedback, how can they ever share his authority and cultivate their own, especially if their school experience has taught them to revere the 'teacher' and do as they are told. Students need permission to be themselves and positive help to personally meet one another in an academic setting, for they have probably spent their school career being conditioned to control natural social impulses. This is not a healthy model for higher education or for adulthood in today's often asocial world.

In the next chapter I will concentrate on the desirable behaviour and attitude of the tutor and must therefore refer again to these processes which he encounters. I will try to show how he can draw out or accentuate those processes which are in harmony with his educational objectives.

Chapter 7

Leadership requirements in group teaching

The impact of a small group on students is significantly different to that of the lecture, formal class or the one-to-one tutorial. The tutor should identify the special properties of groups and exploit them for the benefit of the participants. The leader's activity is intimately bound up with the interpersonal conditions he provides; both will elicit responses from students, who will in turn, through both deliberate and unwitting feedback, alter and sculpt the designated leader's counter responses. Some tutors undergo incipient panic reactions as it slowly dawns on them that their own feelings and behaviour are governed by forces in the group, as well as by their own will. Group work usually arouses more fear in leaders than any other teaching approach. Tutors are often distressed to discover that direct application of other teaching methods to the group situation fails to counteract this natural anxiety. In many cases it is the academic goals themselves that are imported from other teaching settings. It may not be possible to reach these goals, at least in their current form, in a small group. As the tutoring means change so too must the ends worked for. The group cannot duplicate for students the lab, the field trip, private study, or note-taking; group work is a precious addition to the tutor's repetoire not a substitution for other teaching structures or a short cut to quick results.

In this chapter, some of the differences between small group and other types of teaching will be explored to help the reader understand the changes required of him if he is to undertake this work. Tutors can cope and can survive in a group without absorbing the concept of social system already discussed; they may relate well to each individual student. But if they cannot conceive of the group as a total organism and take account of group transfer, displacement, climate, resistance, shared values and the other group-specific features already examined, then they are lessening the group's learning potential. Banishing group process to the periphery of the tutor's awareness forces him, against his better judgment, to be a controlling didactic teacher who has to *manage* rather than *conduct* the group — as if it were a class of desk-bound school children. This style stifles the emergence of creative, innovative teaching and offers to the student only one learning role, that of the dependent receptive child. Some group members welcome this, with its secure school-like familiarity, while others restively kick against it, unable to pinpoint their frustration exactly but well aware that their adult selves are not being allowed a look in.

The maturational benefits to the members of a well conducted small group experience are very great. Undoubtedly the adoption of competent group work represents one of the most valuable preventive steps we can take in our institutions with regard to student mental health. A team of well trained, seasoned group tutors can donate far more to students' well-being than psychiatrists and counsellors trying to 'treat' students who complain of shyness, social ineptitude, inability to be assertive and phobias connected with public speaking. These complaints can be symptoms of personality problems not attributable to the institution at all (this is where therapy is properly applied) but often they have been intensified by, or have even originated in, the teacher-student relationship, or lack of it. This point has already been made earlier in the text, but is so central to my thesis that good group tutoring makes for maturity as well as good degrees, that I stress it here once again. Argument about whether one-to-one academic tutoring or group work is more worthwhile is sterile, for both modes create different experiences for tutor and student and each will have their personal bias for dyadic or group relating. Irrespective of his preferences the competent personal tutor will slip easily from a counselling type of role to that of an individual academic tutor and again to that of group tutorial convenor or seminar leader, making the necessary personal and technical adjustments as he goes along. This book has not been written to justify the view that group work is superior to all other staff-student contact; it has been written because group tutoring is probably the least understood and certainly the least documented part of the tutor's work, and the one which seems to harbour the most suspicions, doubts and anxieties.

A comparison of group and individual tutoring approaches

What then might an accomplished tutor offer students in a small group that he cannot make available in the formal class or during a cosy office *tête-à-tête*?

Consider the tutor's exhilaration, renewed motivation, confidence and relief when a withdrawn student finally manages to blurt out his own fervent opinion, or finally bring together for public consumption a cogent argument which impresses his colleagues. Think about the risks that had to be taken by that student. Consider how the tutor must have assisted the others to have enabled this student to declare himself eventually. The tutor had perhaps demonstrated risk taking behaviour by taking risks himself, or he may have helped the student by shutting up when he longed to pontificate and impress the group. He may have patiently constructed the group ethic that risk taking is praiseworthy and personally profitable and useful to the group's endeavours. This social, academic and personal improvement may not have been possible for the student in any other setting.

In the dyadic (one-to-one) relationship there is no doubt who is the seeker and who is the giver. In a group, students understandably anticipate a similar role allocation, for they bring with them no real history of collaborative learning and help-seeking from colleagues. The designated group leader must teach students how to relate, not only to the academic material itself but also to the group resources which reside in and between its members. Students are not telepathic in this matter. Few students look forward to a future of social or professional isolation. If they are to become productive society members they must learn how to pool every group's resources with others for the maximizing of data collection, analysis and interpretation. Now that we live in a world of diversification, co-operation among groups of specialists is a vital part of most professionals' lives; a good degree is only a small part of the qualifications essential for jobs today. This is where many graduates fall short. I have watched many students in teaching groups, *in vivo* and on videotape, and their misery about their lack of communication skills in groups is only too apparent. The contrast between their group behaviour and their individual spontaneity afterwards is striking. Students should therefore be trained to use a group, just as teachers need assistance to see what group tutoring is about. It is not surprising that leadership in group teaching poses problems, for most academics translate individual techniques, attitudes and aspirations to the group situation, experiencing only limited success. Students likewise repeat school patterns of passive learning behaviour as no alternatives have been offered to them. In a one-to-one tutorial, or in a classroom, students know how to behave; they have had a long training at school. Whereas small groups can produce much anxiety — anxiety which has very little to do with the work.

When individual tutoring is successful the student believes his teacher to be on his side and can monopolize his total attention. In the group though, with its shifting alliances and its web of personal intrigue (competition, jealousy, intimidation), all the protective guarantees have disappeared and the student as well as the tutor is faced with a bewildering set of circumstances and feelings. In addition, a way must be found to share the teacher! The first lesson a group tutor must learn then, is that simulating the one-to-one relationship in a group setting will not solve his leadership problems.

The group as a social system

If he is able to sacrifice this vain hope, the tutor will begin to heed the 'group-as-a-whole'. With regard to his group, he starts to experience what in existential language would be called an *I-it* relationship, rather than the more personal *I-thou* interaction of the twosome. This *I-it* stage engenders anxiety at first, owing to the emotional distance created between the tutor and his students, whom he now sees not so much as discrete individuals but rather as a coagulated human mass called 'group'. The personal attachments, intense discussions, conflicts, affections and rivalries which burst into life whenever people meet in a group, do so *between* members — the tutor no longer being the single focus for students' feelings and attitudes. The effective tutor monitors these interactions, reinforcing those which promote cohesion and trust, but he refrains from intruding uninvited into inter-member relationships. The leader has a lonely position, for he must console himself with the honour bestowed upon him by his official status, of watching, nurturing and preserving the *whole* group; he is deprived of constant contact with each individual. Too much intimate involvement in the membership region would prevent him from carrying out this system observation. Feelings of exclusion from the group, particularly when an exciting academic issue is at stake, are upsetting for a tutor who, till now, has taken teaching to mean giving his knowledge direct to grateful students. Seemingly superfluous, robbed of his professionalism, he longs to regain control, and so sometimes defiantly lectures to the group. The art of group tutoring lies in disseminating knowledge in new ways, not, as sometimes despondent tutors think, in just throwing away academic responsibility. Intellectual excellence still counts. Only tutors of inferior standard use the group teaching structure as a means to hide their own ignorance.

In a one-to-one tutorial the tutor usually takes a pride in the student's progress and sees his own efforts and talents reflected in the student's work. In a successful small group, where everyone learns at different times in a variety of ways from lots of sources, the tutor may be hard pressed to find much correspondence between the interventions he makes in the group (or the number of times he has desisted from intervening) and the learning or personal growth of any particular member. Unless he is comfortable with 'system-thinking', he will never learn when to congratulate himself on his process management, or other leadership abilities, without which learning would have been minimal and growth at a standstill. Any good teaching he may do, and any learning that eventually happens, seem on occasions to be two ends of a very long chain of events in which his contributions to the group are interwoven with everyone else's and he cannot work out who should take credit (or blame) for what. A tutor bent on the design and preservation of a group milieu in which all this complex personal social and academic learning can occur in a reciprocal manner must defer the traditional teacher gratifications — the 'right' answers, good essays, respect and admiration. He has in exchange the more long term and infinitely more satisfying reward of a mature group of individuals studying co-operatively and dealing with authority issues together, in preparation for a world that is waiting in some desperation for effective team members and self-directed leaders. The successful group tutor is responsible for the upkeep of a social climate in which late adolescents, especially vulnerable to influences which may damage their self-esteem, can receive the authenticating force of their peers. If everyone could be promised that subjective experience in higher education, I am sure the student drop out rate would decline dramatically.

In-service training for group leaders

This 'consensual validation' as Foulkes has called it, is just as essential for tutors. They should feel able to rely on the support and insight of their experienced fellow teachers, their peers, who will help them learn *tutoring*, just as teachers assist students to adapt to their jobs as *learners*. Regrettably many tutors deprived of group support from colleagues do not understand the merits of group tutoring and hence cannot assist students to see the merits either. Any tutoring *must* be backed up by in-service training and/or regular departmental staff meetings so that this ethic of mutual help can be maintained.

'The corrective experience' in groups

If the tutor deals deftly with inter-group communications of the manifest and latent sort he will contribute to a series of what group analysts call 'corrective experiences'. The student with unhappy memories of previous groups will *elicit* from comrades in a well conducted new group responses quite different from those which his inner fears led him to expect. If this is happening to several members at once the group will consolidate its progress; these 'corrective emotional experiences' will promote *trust* which will stimulate further risk taking behaviour. More advanced 'corrections' will be attempted all the time. The tutor begins to undergo similar uplifting feelings himself. His anticipated failure, his worst imaginings about himself as a tutor are 'corrected' by the evidence of success before him. This positive shaping of one another's feelings, (coldly described as positive feedback) is probably the most intoxicating experience a group tutor will ever have and, in my view, leaves other more easily obtained teaching rewards very much in the shade.

Managing the major processes

Previous chapters on the small group have established that the overall responsibility of the tutor is to promote resonance and reduce resistance to learning. He will operate in such a way that transfer, displacement and other interpersonal distortions do not solidify, leaving members and himself with rigid roles and functions to perform. In the group he will ensure that communication does not become blocked, or ritualized; he realizes that a good many students, although willing to work, are nevertheless prepared to resist learning if maladaptive behaviour can alleviate non academic anxieties. If the group is allowed to polarize around its strongest members (including the tutor) the others will withdraw their emotional investment (motivation) from the learning enterprise and reconcile themselves to second class status. If the tutor dwells on his self-oriented needs, (for example, deluding himself that he is teaching well, when really he is demonstrating his intellectual superiority); if he revels in his own authority, enjoying his position of privilege in relation to individual students, then a group climate can result which is sullen and rebellious, deceptively obedient or plain bored. The tutor must not exclude students from problem solving activity or from interpersonal relating, which is a healthy social inclination; he should not use the group as a platform for showing off his own prowess and then expect the students to admire and imitate. This demand to copy inhibits the development of their own unique if embryonic intellectual powers and prevents them from building up their group into a safe and supportive forum, peopled by trustworthy fellows, who might cooperate in collective learning so that *all* can share pride in mastering the subject. A collective sense of achievement is a spur to greater learning feats; submission to a resented authority is an inhibiting factor.

The leader's function in the early group meetings

Therapeutic expertise is not demanded of the tutor but he should find his own 'style' of enabling people in the group to feel relaxed enough to talk. At an early stage in a group's meetings, perhaps this can be done by introducing some controversial, exciting aspect of the subject concerned, without too much pressure on academic output. A heated discussion, communal laughter, with the tutor showing that he intends to resist the school-master role, can guide the early group process in a direction conducive to shared learning. Once the principles of group discussion and collective responsibility are learned they will be adhered to quite automatically, even when intensive 'work' with defined objectives and deadlines is asked of the membership.

The first meeting is of paramount importance, determining the future developmental possibilities of the group. From the conductor's point of view such details as time arrival, clothes worn, physical posture adopted, inadvertent non verbal communication, light, furniture arrangements provided, all matter greatly. They inform students just how seriously or casually this tutor regards this group meeting; just how interested or bored he is by the whole affair and just how much he is prepared to care for them and their work. Neglect of these factors increases the likelihood of resistance; consistent careful attention to them will help towards learning resonance – that all important 'it's good to be here, let's get cracking' feeling, in which the whole group becomes immersed despite their individual woes and problems outside the group. Learning will be enriched also, if students realize that the tutor is making concentrated efforts to understand their idiosyncratic approach to study so as to help them widen and improve them, rather than assuming that they will copy his own working style.

It is crucial that students do not have familiar props removed too suddenly – whether these props are redundant study techniques, or standardized and outmoded responses to the social (group) situation or to authority figures. We all need to feel we belong, know the ropes, know how to behave without making fools of ourselves. Fears about starting work with a new tutor in a new group are real and predictable and should be respected. Students feel greatly relieved to meet with a tutor who clearly understands their apprehensions. He is able to tolerate their adherence to old academic routines, while he gradually introduces them to the rewarding new notion of interdependency and mutual support in the group. These students are more prone to work than those who are highly anxious, having been urged prematurely to change their ways. A high anxiety level causes missed meetings, lateness, and an astonishing incidence of colds and flu.

It is not always necessary to discuss these issues of 'newness' and the need to find transitional behaviours and work techniques with the students. It is the manner in which the tutor receives and handles their contributions and/or non contributions, the way in which he subtly reinforces group-appropriate behaviours and declines to be seduced into leadership behaviour he does not want, which imbues students with calm and enables them to recognize that this is a relaxed and supportive environment (globe) in which learning is a common experience and not something that is competed for. Here, learning is enjoyed not suffered, and the rewards therefrom come from the body of the group, the experience of belonging. A sense of belonging is often scorned as sentimental but belonging is as vital to life as food and air. This is why in group literature, across the whole spectrum of group disciplines, the concept of group cohesiveness is ubiquitous, even though different names may be substituted for it. Cohesiveness is the technical term for a sense of belonging in a group. (In the army it would be called *esprit de corps*.) It is as fundamental to the growth of the group as is the mother-child bond to an infant. A deprived group and a deprived baby will not necessarily perish but without an early exposure to cohesiveness and attachment respectively, both organisms, unless several 'corrective emotional experiences' are implanted, will merely enact the motions of living and learning. Any opportunity for real communication will be missed, rejected, not recognized or (as is alarmingly common in students) hoped for but circumvented so as to avoid disappointment. It is safer not to be involved. Teaching a robot like group is a depressing experience. It is often illuminating to look at the tutor's private reactions to belonging and to trusting others as his own personality difficulties may be adversely affecting the group's propensity for cohesiveness.

The importance of group composition and the need for selection

One should bear in mind that really unlucky tutors can get landed with six 'silent' members, or a particular mix of personalities that even an inspired group analyst would find impossible to cohese. Therapists can select their group patients; tutors cannot. This raises an important issue about allocating students to groups. While it is impossible to handpick a group, care might be taken at a staff meeting to put students in groups where they stand a reasonable change of relating to the others. For example, one male might experience additional adjustment problems to the group if membership comprises seven women and a female tutor. Students from other countries are often pleased to find that another member of the group comes from their part of the world. A mature student, worried about age differences, may be glad to find someone else of his own age. Whenever possible, all the tutors who are to teach in these groups should be brought together beforehand to discuss the selection of students. It is risky if not counter-productive to place four or five 'quiet' students in the group of a tutor famous for his solitary pursuits, introspection and monosyllabic utterances. The course may not allow much leeway for selection but the concept and desirability of selection should not be dropped for adequate matching of the tutor to the general temperament of the group can make all the difference. New tutors are particularly vulnerable to anxieties about group leadership and extra care should be taken when allocating students to their groups. Co-leadership can prove invaluable to new tutors and no loss of manpower is incurred if two groups representing the same course amalgamate. An 'old hand' and a new tutor can teach one another a good deal by observing each other's style, especially if their personalities contrast or complement one another's. Clearly co-leading must be done voluntarily and with good will and honesty between the partners, otherwise the group will be treated to a regular staff brawl, which, though perhaps entertaining will not help the learning!

Boundary maintenance

It is the tutor's obvious responsibility to erect and perpetuate the group's boundaries for cohesiveness can only develop within a safe boundary. (A boundary is simply a perimeter, any line which distinguishes 'us' from 'them', 'inside' from 'outside'.) The tutor delineates what is academically achievable within the group; if he misjudges this, students will be subjected to enormous strain and the tutor made to feel a failure; he may find himself annoyed with the 'unachieving' students. He will to a greater or lesser degree define the overall content, the specific subject matter and the way in which group members will converge upon it. It is not true, as many suppose, that the more obscure and casual the group organization the more successful it will be. As has been said before, lack of boundaries is as restrictive to group growth as tight inflexible ones. On occasions, boundaries may have to be secured by the tutor or group members; at other times they may be relaxed to accommodate emergent process or new learning patterns. In times of 'civil war' in the group they may have to be re-negotiated altogether! Students must be shown what is permissable, how much or little freedom there is for interpersonal manoeuvres, for confrontation with tutor and others. They must know why and when they are being assessed and what the limits and range of possible behaviours and work production are.

The tutor's behaviour attitude and comments in the first few meetings should induce a feeling of security in students, so that they understand roughly what is acceptable and unacceptable and the extent to which they themselves can influence group interactions and decisions within the boundaries. Many meetings I have attended are so lacking in boundaries that work is impeded and invaded by the latent group process which, when analyzed, shows that group members are subconsciously milling about looking for or even desperately inventing boundaries around the ragged edged group; it is as if they do not belong, but as castaways they must find a way of accommodating this new uneasy situation. Their energy is so concentrated upon survival strategies there is little left for learning. Many of these students will have witnessed the tutor giving lectures, enjoyed a drink with him in the bar or will have sat on committees with him. Some will have had private dealings with him in a personal crisis. They like him so why are there boundary problems in the group? They and he must understand that although the tutor is the same person in each of these contexts, the nature of each calls forth a particular facet of his expertise — in short a different set of boundaries. If the teacher is clear about his function in the group and does not confuse it with his other roles and duties elsewhere, then the students will learn group-appropriate responses too, which will help them put aside concerns extraneous to the group, as the tutor must, and instead apply themselves to the here-and-now of the work. Too many well-meaning tutors conduct a group as though they were still in the pub, or as if they were counsellors, lecturers, or loving fathers or mothers.

Modelling

One of the tutor's vital functions in the early stages of a group is providing an example of desirable group behaviour: how to use license but keep within the boundaries; how to pool ideas; how to argue one's point without demolishing the other person's confidence; how to reward positive contributions; how to let others get a word in edgeways. Students will copy the tutor's behaviour. Imitation is a potent initiator of group process as several of the case studies in this book show. Later, the tutor will encourage and assist individual students to develop their own participatory styles, but at first students will look to the tutor for an example of the 'right' behaviour. Should he deal with his own anxiety about the new group by modelling an exclusive emphasis on information transmission, students will follow suit and this pattern may set in for the entire duration of that course. I know of many seminars and 'intimiate' tutorials where, at the end of the term, no one has even worked out what to call the tutor, who ends up not being addressed by name at all! He is still perceived as 'one of them', the staff. Even if he is liked and respected he is still an 'alien'! The group may have cohesed well, but may have done so by a process of uniting against a common threat — the tutor. Thus, when they turn up together, as comrades, to the group session, he may well correctly perceive them as a group with a corporate identity, but he himself is excluded and expelled to the very edge of the group's boundary by them. He experiences them as close to each other but distant from himself, as if he is teaching through a telephone and understandably feels somewhat rejected.

Interdependence

The chief factor which produces cohesiveness is interdependence. Students arrive in the group holding the false belief that power, responsibility, knowledge and decision-making rest with the official leader: the tutor. All dependency needs, psychological and academic, are beamed upon him, not each other and it is the tutor's job to change this state of affairs. If he resists the role being thrust upon him the students must begin to take some control of the group themselves within the boundaries set by the designated leader. Left to take total control, as a result of dereliction of duty by the leader, the group is more likely to collapse altogether, or the few members who remain will fight earnestly for power to the detriment of work.

The competent tutor does not refuse leadership; he discharges it in a less traditional manner. He shares and delegates leadership functions among the membership and teaches them, concurrent with the subject, how to creatively exploit the power that is now theirs, (albeit within the limits that he has prescribed.)

If the tutor refuses to dominate and control all the proceedings, and at the same time, refuses to deny that he is leader in the group, members themselves eventually learn through him and his behaviour how to recognize, understand and alter group processes and how to promote mutuality and interdependence. Members originally unable to talk begin to feel trapped in that role and want to escape, to become more verbal. One or two other students may be manipulating group interactions with ease because in the very early stages they were the only ones brave enough to speak. The tutor, desperate for an active 'hard working' group is in danger of reinforcing this pattern, by responding to the dominant members to whom he feels grateful and abandoning the quiet ones. He rationalizes this by maintaining that it is wrong to persecute the shy people; that they are happier left alone.

The tutor who can resist such temptation and who has patiently cultivated a 'this is your group as much as mine' ethic, will be rewarded when the quiet members, tired of being pushed about, assert themselves at last. Sometimes the tutor will have to encourage these developments by inviting the more reluctant members to confront and dispute with the more dominant ones. In acting thus, rather than handling these overbearing students himself, he is saying to the quiet people: 'your opinion matters to me'; 'I value you as members of this group'; 'I believe you can exercise your rights too and I approve of your so doing'. All these messages can be conveyed by hand gestures or an enquiring expression. Before he can execute such a simple but potent act, the tutor must be sensitive to the overall group process or he will fail to see the need for intervention; instead he will busy himself in fluent discourse with the monopolizing talkers.

The group conductor

Foulkes refers to the leader as *conductor*. This term stresses the qualitative difference between conventional leadership and the group management advocated here. Conducting a group well, even while sitting quietly, is an exhausting business. The conductor is watching and translating all that is happening on the manifest and latent level and noting his own reactions to those observations. He has to work out how capable the group is of resolving its academic or process problems, given time and approval by him, how much he should intercede, interrupt, support individuals, confront others, refer to the occupation or allow them to veer away from it so they can deal with process matters obstructing the work. What the tutor does *not* do and say is often as important, if not more so, as what he does initiate and say. This is particularly true if the group have prepared the work in advance so that no further structure need be introduced by the leader and the members are free to have open discussion, or if it is a tutorial in which there is usually little task setting by the tutor anyway. The freer the group is from structural impediments such as question sheets, reading aloud, galloping through a tutor's crowded agenda of topics, the more rein can be given to process, which will increase the likelihood that interdependence will develop. However, students come to university for a degree and work must be completed; they are not on the campus only to develop social awareness, leadership potential and good citizenship.

Ideally, the tutor knows how much 'work' should be undertaken and when and how it should be inserted into the proceedings; he exerts or withdraws academic pressure in relation to the amount of resonance available. He understands that a tutorial group presents very different tutoring questions to that of a formal seminar; perhaps different priorities can be accorded to group occupation and process in each setting, even though both are small groups. The general trend which I have found is to use the small tutorial in a more process-oriented way so that the tutor is released from the demand for rapid academic 'results'. In the seminar, the process underlying the attempts at work is only tampered with when it interferes with the group's ability to coalesce around the topic. Otherwise, process is of secondary interest. It is vital that students should be made aware of the purpose of any group meeting. Not surprisingly, they tend to assume that all groups are the same and so become puzzled, impatient and confused when their manner of participation in one group is not regarded as appropriate in another. When the tutor also has group boundaries confused in his own mind, everyone begins to think that perhaps small group teaching was not such a good idea after all! The advantage of the lecture and traditional class is that they possess well established boundaries and everyone's role and function is clear; people are not uncertain about what is expected of them. On the other hand, the dominant students in the lecture *always* tend to control events and the quiet ones *always* tend to be speechless. The teacher remains undisputed leader and is deprived of more intimate aquaintance with his students' needs, as well as more understanding of his own personality traits, which affect his own teaching, learning and personal growth.

Conducting a small group, therefore, necessitates a certain amount of objectivity and emotional distance — which is not the same thing as disinterest. The tutor must observe the group-as-a-whole, while also participating in dyadic and multiperson interactions. He is involved in current communications but can stand back far enough to link thematically what is being said to earlier events in the group's history; he can see too how these communications are moving steadily toward a shared and repeated group preoccupation, a focal conflict perhaps. He can also watch the group's specific occupation progress and judge when the right time will be to force it into the foreground, thus attacking resistance head on; when to let it fade into the background *pro tem*, in order to permit the group members to struggle with the group process themselves, hopefully to a state of resonance. If he does not maintain distance he will enmesh himself so much with the ongoing process that he will lose his monitoring and management function altogether. When this happens his group will yield to chaos, or he will have to exercise the depressing option of rescuing the group by authoritarian methods which at least re-establishes some boundaries and smoothes out some of the chaos. Then the tutor must begin again to foster the right kind of climate and guide students away from their perceptions of him as patriarch. New tutors, keen to adopt modern teaching approaches, often fall into this trap of joining their own groups as members, giving up their conducting role along with the unwanted authoritarian stereotype.

The conductor is a catalytic agent. He puts the group in the centre of his attention and not himself. He sees himself as an instrument to be used by members for their learning, both academic and personal, (always inseperable in a small group context) rather than as an instructor. He may usefully instruct from time to time, as a deliberate *technique* but not as a *role*. He applies the technique only when the group is amenable to it. Whenever possible he lets the group speak. He brings out rather than suppresses agreements and disagreements, work related or personal, (though almost invariably they are combined). He activates what is latent and might benefit from manifest expression. He encourages contributions from all members and often gives theirs precedence over his own. The extent to which he is catalytic and receptive will depend upon the aims and objectives he has laid down for the group.

Again many tutors would see the tutorial as a place where the catalyzing function is of paramount importance and the seminar as one in which he has a more didactic role to perform. The catalyzing work here is an essential precondition for subject-related discussion, but not an end in itself. It must be weighed along with academic input, and the correct measures of both estimated carefully. The group conductor in either situation treats participants as equal adults, even though they perform different functions than he does in the group. He exerts an important influence by his own example, setting a pattern of desirable behaviour and work attitude, rather than preaching directly to the group congregation. He promotes toleration of individual differences by his behaviour and is seen by the membership to respect and reward understanding and insight into the work. He values and expects the students to value independent thinking and voluntary verbalization, frankness, an open mind for new experience and an ability to appreciate other people's ideas.

Almost everyone in education, both teachers and taught, seem to cringe in embarrassment at the thought of saying 'well done' to one another. When deserved, such praise is crucial to individuals if they are to persevere in complex learning. I am often saddened when students enthuse to me about a popular tutor who has never been told by anyone in his group how stimulating his seminars are: likewise, many students producing B+ essays are told only how to make it an A next time! The tutor must conquer his own reserve in this matter if he is to help students encourage one another.

107

Resistance and resonance — the balancing function

The conductor is an integrator and an analyzer. By cultivating reson-ance the group becomes more and more integrated as a social system. Analyzing the resistances and managing them successfully re-channels those energies absorbed by resistance into the opposite process of group integration. The more integrated the group, the more resilient it will be to all manner of internal and external pressures and the more able to face complicated and profound aspects of the subject itself. Cohesiveness makes for a 'together we'll do it somehow' feeling; group disruptive forces are repelled at the outset and identified immediately by the group as interfering with the work. An un-cohesed or segregated group will welcome disruptive forces, from within or from outside the boundary and will recruit them as agents of resistance or further segre-gation.

The individual or the group: which has priority?

Tutors often view themselves as beleaguered generals mediating in a war of 'the individual *versus* the group'. Constant doubts and anxieties are expressed about which should take precedence. Foulke's conductor would prefer the formula 'individual *in* the group' because this allows the group's conductor to deploy his skills like a photographer. He focuses his lens: first on the individual, then on the group context which adds definition to the person, then on the middle-distance — in other words on the relationship of the individual *to* the group. The tutor controls the lens and chooses the composition — that is he inter-prets what he sees before him, but it is the students who are the sub-stantive pictorial elements.

Authority requirements and decrescendo leadership

It has already been stressed that in new groups the membership regard the tutor as absolute leader. This, however is what he wishes to avoid as a long term eventuality. He therefore accepts his elevated position initially and uses the authority transferred to it by the students, to wean them from this need for total guidance. He frees himself from the continuous temptation to play a godlike role, to satisfy his private needs, or to take this transfer phenomenon as an accurate reflection of his innate power and strength. If he shares their fantasy of him he may find himself intimidated by the leadership role, for no one could live up to these impossible expectations. Nevertheless many tutors try and of course fail; while others' fear of commencing small group work can be traced to this cause. When tutors stop acceding to imaginary obliga-tions to be all wise, omniscient and all powerful, the task of group tutoring is viewed in a new light; making mistakes is finally acknowledged to be an intrinsic part of learning how to teach, not a sin to be punished. Many tutors entertain private fantasies about what constitutes good group work; living up to these and meeting students' transferred demands for dependency drives many to feelings of gross inadequacy which are needless. Repeated struggles to attain impossible objectives leads to disappointment, anxiety and depression — experiences which are very common among academic staff, though they may strive valiantly to contain or disguise them.

This illustrates once again that staff support groups, in which work experiences can be shared, should be scheduled as an integral part of the tutor's job and not regarded as an added luxury for those lucky enough to find a little free time. The group's initial dependence on the tutor places him in a position from which he can radiate a sense of much needed security, which emanates from the authority that members have transferred to him! He accepts this position temporarily, in order to be able to liquidate it later on, (for he could not wean the group from something which had not previously been established). If there is no authority around which to coalesce at the outset, the group members feel uncertain and suspicious about the boundaries. This naturally reduces effective functioning. As the group becomes cohesive, and there is less need for an authority figure, the conductor invites what Foulkes calls a 'decrescendo move' from the original leadership stance. He does this not by standing down, which would be an unexpected and panic-inducing jolt for the group, but by passively 'allowing it to happen', letting the group at its own pace bring him down to earth, demoting him to the status of mortal. The move is from leader of the group, to leader *in* the group. The leader's authority, while still available, is put in storage for group emergencies and the group's own authority comes to the fore. A skilful decrescendo is brought about without anyone in the group knowing about it! The idealization of the leader in a healthy group will fade gradually and naturally — the mature tutor merely helps this process along, without suffering wounded vanity. His active involvement at the inception of the group is imperative, or else the group feels too lost and afraid to begin the inauguration of interpersonal transactions.

Contrary to the popular view, a strong leader, in whose judgment and authority members have confidence, creates the very conditions in which group codes and standards can be safely tested and tentatively questioned. A new group brings together random personalities who collide in an atmosphere of high emotional tension; without the protection of a judicial father (or mother) figure whose authority is respected, such a situation is experienced by many students as emotionally unmanageable. The tutor who tries to divest himself of leadership too soon may well be viewed as weak or incompetent by the students. This generates feelings of unsafety and enables the more vociferous and perhaps bullying members to take control straight away, subjugating the others. Unless the tutor first accepts the leadership role, (distinguishing in his own mind real leadership from the mantle he is being asked to wear), his subsequent contributions and demands will not carry the required weight and his personal example will not bring about the degree of respect required to stimulate the students to emulate his behaviour. They will interpret his premature informality as careless teaching and his unwillingness to dominate as indifference or cowardice. In an ideal group three distinct but interrelating processes can be observed after just a few meetings. There is first a comfortable social adjustment to fellow members (as opposed to formal courtesy); there is then a settling down to the work without waiting for this to be instigated by the conductor; thirdly there is a lessening of dependence on the tutor-conductor.

The tutor's personality

The group tutor impresses students with his character as well as with his store of knowledge. This has obvious repercussions for individual personal tutoring. When students have problems and personal crises, they will find it easier to approach a tutor who has already disclosed much of his temperament and attitudes in a group than a distant lecturer with whom there has been little personal contact and who is still on the receiving end of all the students' fantasies about authority. The group tutor has been 'reality tested' and in the troubled student's mind is already stamped 'approachable' or 'unapproachable'. If trust and feelings of safety have grown in the group's culture, the student will already see the tutor as a safe and trustworthy person to whom personal problems can be confided when the group meeting is over. Pastoral tutoring networks are practically useless, no matter how well organized, if they do not in some way tie in with the students' day to day academic relationships.

Conductor receptivity

By this time the reader may find himself quaking at the prospect of running what used to be a 'simple' tutorial and suddenly having to ask, 'what are the group's basic assumptions and its focal conflicts? What developmental phase has it reached and how is the climate today? Are the boundaries in order? Who is displacing what onto whom? Am I aware of my own feelings, and keeping the correct distance? How do I do all this and teach nuclear physics too?' The concept of free-floating attention may calm the reader a little. The tutor does not have to strenuously hunt for evidence to fit the group theories he has learned, for while isolating one piece of process, he will miss another and also fail to concentrate properly on the group's official occupation. Free-floating attention means being *alert* to group processes, always receptive to them — they leap unbidden onto his deliberately cleared 'radar screen'; free-floating attention operates like a scanner, while the tutor goes about his ordinary academic duties. This demands the adoption of a novel, more passive, wait-and-see attitude. The tutor is used to actively pursuing knowledge, whereas in group work he must wait for data to impinge upon him, must allow himself to be penetrated by processes before translating them. He does not need to arm himself with a list of questions, such as those listed above, whenever he enters a teaching group. Such questions soak up his attention and blunt his perceptual apparatus. Simply 'seeing' process though, is not sufficient for successful group management. Some theories about it are needed if the tutor is to forge this insight into practical tutoring skills. On the other hand, recourse to clever theories and technologies without this vision will not remedy a sick group. A convenient denial that unsavoury concepts like authority, dependency, rivalry and other group phenomena exist and a substitution of vague notions such as 'caring' is no way to deal with group difficulties either. It is a combination of theoretical understanding, insight into group process, and group experience that will bring about the desired results.

Summary

The following list summarizes those basic changes and adjustments required of the tutor embarking upon group work, which have been referred to in this and preceding chapters.

(1) He gives up the conviction that group tutoring is no different from other teaching situations and ceases to transfer to the group his tutoring style or behaviour from other environments.

(2) He begins to concentrate upon the group as a whole system rather than merely a collection of separate and random individuals.

(3) He erects and maintains stable but flexible group boundaries, and is aware of the effects of student selection.

(4) He models desired group behaviour for the members.

(5) He takes advantage of the role of strong leader at the outset but makes strenuous efforts to resist colluding with the group's continued demands for protection and authority when such qualities are redundant.

(6) He plays down his own leadership behaviour and gradually invites the group authority to take over.

(7) He promotes cohesiveness, reinforcing any inclinations toward interdependency.

(8) He 'conducts' rather than 'leads' the group, minimizing resistance and maximizing resonance.

(9) He is a participant-observer in the group, always aware of the changing distance between himself and the system.

(10) He watches and diagnoses the various group processes in order to help him conduct more usefully.

A fitting conclusion to this chapter is a quotation from Foulkes' *Therapeutic Group Analysis*. (See Selected readings). Addressed to group therapists, it holds equal meaning for tutors and no conceptual revision is needed.

'The spirit in which these groups are conducted and the qualities required on the part of the conductor have an essential affinity to education according to the concepts of a democratic way of life and for good world citizenship. We have mentioned what are the essential preconditions in the therapist and shown that his qualifications correspond to a desirable type of leader in a democratic community. He must be reasonably secure and reality-prone in his own person. He must have outgrown and be immune against the temptation however strong, to play God, and to use his group for his own satisfaction . . . He loves and respects the group and his aim is to make its members self-responsible individuals. He wants to replace submission by co-operation on equal terms between equals. In spite of his emotional sensitivity he has self-confidence, which comes from modesty, and the courage to lead, which springs from his social responsibility.

When all is said, there will remain a nucleus, not at present further reducible by science, more nearly expressed perhaps by art and religion, bound up with his own personality, a primary rapport (charisma Max Weber called it) based on love, respect and faith. Without these, he cannot awaken nor bind the spell of what the poet called "the old enchantment" '. *(Foulkes, 1964:65)*

Case Studies

Chapter 8

An inter-departmental tutor training group, with consultant-conductor

This is an account of eight one-and-a-half hour inter-departmental staff meetings conducted by myself, at University College, London, using mainly a group analytic (Foulkesian) approach. The sessions took place on a weekly basis throughout a spring term in the afternoon. At that time I was still new to the institution (this was my first training venture in my new post), and not acquainted with many of the lecturers. Open invitations were sent to all the academic staff, asking them to make contact with me if they were interested in joining a seminar on staff/student relationships. To my knowledge, there was no established tradition of in-service training for tutors, and I expected that seminar participants would have only a very limited or non-existent acquaintance with psycho-dynamic and group-analytic theory.

I was a little anxious about the prospect of working with men and women of diverse and advanced intellects and finding a way of bringing them together into a cohesive group. I realized that some of them would have a lot of teaching experience and quite senior positions in the hierarchy and that the self-disclosure cultivated in these kinds of groups might seem disturbing at first. Fear that expertise and authority may be undermined is a very common worry among academic trainees. It is often expressed by a complete avoidance of any group involvement, but more commonly by a verbal rejection of 'all this new fangled group stuff' from within the group ranks. Older staff, wondering if some of their educational philosophy seems dated, are understandably afraid of being shown up in a bad light in contrast to younger, more with-it colleagues, whilst the younger staff are afraid of exposing their lack of experience. Bearing in mind all these possible deterrents to new learning, I decided upon simple but fairly rigid boundaries for the group:

(1) Attendance would be voluntary and self-selecting.

(2) The group would be limited to eight sessions in the first instance and advertized as such, so that doubters would not feel they were signing on for life. Ending by contract would ensure that if the group lost several members, loyalists remaining would not feel

responsible for the group's termination.

(3) Participants would be told briefly and explicitly how I saw my role in the group. The purpose of this would be to reduce a little of the tension with which all new groups are imbued. In this case the tension would be exaggerated because members would have to struggle with what to them was unorthodox leadership behaviour. I reckoned that too little or too much explanation and clarification at this stage would result in flight or dependency respectively of quite an extreme kind; this basic assumption activity could require at least eight sessions to achieve resolution and the group's overt occupation ('looking at staff student relationships') could be expunged. The degree to which dependency needs could be met without hampering the development of group process too much would have to be constantly monitored.

(4) Wherever possible I would use academic language and/or plain English; group-analytic terminology would be avoided. I hoped that this self-imposed rule would help me understand better how the group participants thought as university teachers and by what alchemy such thoughts were converted into tutoring practice. I also wanted to protect them from loss of self-esteem and from the irritability and hostility which jargonistic exhibitions usually arouse.

(5) I would always be conscious of the limited time available to us and would therefore dissuade members from long cerebral debates (in which most academics excel) about group dynamics. The hope was that by a modelling process they would absorb a style of leadership from me, more or less unconsciously, which could be carried over with their own personal modifications, into their own tutorials and their dealings with students.

(6) In our eight sessions, I would focus on the material they produced spontaneously in connection with their interactions with students and student groups. If this seminar were to be beneficial, then their here-and-now experiences in my group comprising real and reported events, the pooling of learning resources, the giving of support to each other would rub off on the group members leaving them enthused enough to tackle their own group tutoring with fresh vigour and new insight.

Owing to the constraints of participants' time tables, my own availability, and doubtless a lot of unconscious resistance on some people's part, the 20 interested teachers eventually whittled down to seven. One young chemical engineer withdrew after the first session, leaving a steady membership of six. There were three geographers, (environmental, sociological and ecological) a microbiologist, a lawyer and an electrical engineer. There were three of each sex. Approximate ages ranged from 25 to 50. One member had been at the university for only one term and this was his first teaching job; another senior tutor had been at the college for more than 20 years.

Session 1

We all sat in a circle around a coffee table in my room which I had made as welcoming but unobtrusive as possible. The phone was disconnected, and care was taken to provide comfortable seating and adequate but not glaring light. Refreshments were not provided so as to discourage the chit chat and disruption this would create. I was trying to convey through the room, (which was always arranged in advance for the meeting), 'We are here to work, but let's work in comfort'. I started off by introducing myself and stating the title of the seminar, the times at which we would meet and when the group would terminate. I then explained briefly that I would not be composing agendas, but was happy to provide background reading and references if needed. The idea was that they themselves should find a way of approaching the group's theme and would learn mainly from each other. I would occasionally comment on the subject in hand or the manner in which the group was tackling it. I made it clear that I respected their teaching expertise and their knowledge of students; I tried to acknowledge that I had much to learn from them, but that my training and experience in group work might be a valuable contribution to our endeavour too. Then I ceased speaking and there was an awkward silence. Members introduced themselves to each other with some self-consciousness. There was much comparing of tutorial procedures, teaching methods, hierarchical systems in the various departments which they each represented. After this, individuals began to recount a little of their career histories and their attitudes to the higher education system in Britain. There was a good deal of nervous but well-intentioned laughter as educational and professional jokes were traded; to my relief there was no silent member.

Half-way through the session, the group became very industrious and work-oriented; it was decided to formulate a plan which would ensure they studied the subject properly. After much earnest and complicated talk, three aspirations for what they might get out of the group became apparent. I clarified these to the group members by way of a summary of their preceding discussion. Different people were asking for:

(a) discussion about the philosophy and politics of higher education, and, subsumed under that heading, the role and activities of the personal (ie pastoral as opposed to academic) tutor.
(b) A study and comparison of known tutoring systems and teaching methods in order to make a decision about which are the most effective.
(c) A discussion of 'nitty-gritty' case material.

The teachers then looked with dismay at the impossible demands they had set for themselves. Again they struggled to define what they might actually use this first meeting for and what they could realistically be expected to accomplish. This was a training group and not a therapy group so I did not interpret the obvious hostility to me — (their frustration was mounting moment by moment). Instead I related the situation they were in to their own students, who in group tutorials all want different things and have different interests; how could they as teachers meet all these needs? In any case, if the teacher gives instruction all the time, never offering an opportunity for free debate about the tutorial's function, how can he discover what the students needs are *vis-à-vis* the academic subject?

A discussion about the agonies and rewards of small group teaching ensued, and there was much sharing of the stress that this kind of teaching produces.

I concluded the session by saying how I appreciated the impossibility of everyone having just what they wanted here, but that as a group they would have to find a way of dividing the cake between them so that it was satisfying to all, and that no one starved.

Session 2

Almost the entire session was used to talk about the job of the leader in a small group tutorial. They all found it difficult to promote an atmosphere of trust and togetherness amongst their students, or to get them to interact with each other rather than placating the teacher. Student absenteeism from tutorials, and the reasons for this, was examined. (This was an interesting topic as we had an absentee in this group who was never mentioned!) I felt the group was complaining about my unsupportive leadership and their ensuing confusion; they were angrily striving to make me rescue them by my giving a lecture on how to use group techniques. I refrained from verbalizing this observation and from providing the lecture.

Soon the hostility rose to the surface, no longer concealed by discussions of other student groups. The displacement ceased, and polite, icy, well-articulated dissent was expressed directly. What on earth was this group for? Was it a study group? If so, they could get down to reading the research data and various educational treatises — if only I would be a proper leader and give them the information. Or was it one of those crazy 'encounter' things where, as one member put it, 'you get a junior teacher to tweak a professor's nose so he can be intimate with him'. This anecdote, which related to a real event, created simultaneous hilarity and alarm; the temperature in the room shot up immediately, and everyone became very anxious indeed. Work effectively ceased, so I reiterated the group's purpose, giving a reassuring 'speech' about how our learning might be enhanced when we trust each other enough to be more honest with our feelings. I then made it very clear, through the medium of a joke, that there would be no pillow-bashing and no nose-tweaking here.

The temperature dropped and I then made public the private frustration people were feeling. I added that while I understood their respect for rigorous study, this group, depending on their emotional willingness, might eventually have something different to offer its members, a new way of learning/teaching, not one more set of techniques to add to their already extensive collection. Perhaps learning was not an exclusive function of the intellect; perhaps we could explore experiential ways to learn. They were puzzled and divided about this. Some seized the point; some understood it but appeared afraid of its implications; others were clearly muddled. There was then a request for 'something solid' on leadership, which reflected their anger with me and their anxiety about what psychological tricks I might be playing. I could have exposed the absurdity of this fantasy of me as a potent and malicious Svengali, but instead I circulated a paper by Fritz Redl, in an attempt to gratify some of their dependency needs. (*Group Emotion and Leadership* — see Selected readings).

Session 3

This meeting was brisk and business-like. Redl's paper was dispensed with, as containing too much 'jargon', though it was considered 'interesting' and 'thought provoking'. Members had obviously enjoyed reading about 10 separate styles of leadership, and identifying themselves and colleagues with the various types.

One of the academics, with the eager permission of the others then presented a case history. The subject was a female student under going pre-exam panic who had failed to improve despite lengthy academic coaching and much reassurance from several members of the staff. There followed a long group examination of the different strategies which might be applied in the handling of this student. Eventually, after I had been biting my tongue so as not to intervene and direct events, the group began to look at why the tutor reporting the case could not ask the student about her personal life. This gave rise to a most fruitful discussion about where teaching ends and counselling starts; everyone shared similar experiences of their own, and tried to explain where they personally drew the line and what the limits of their professional expertise were. The consensus at the end of the discussion was that maybe this student should be referred to me for counselling, but only after the tutor concerned had done a bit more work with her in preparation. The tutor felt relieved and supported at the end of the session and said she would continue to work with the girl, but felt very nervous about it, and would report back next week (which she subsequently did, revealing just how sensitive and helpful she could be, once freed from her previous inhibitions about 'counselling').

The session ended as usual at 5.30 prompt, but this time and at the end of each subsequent session, I was invited to join the members in the common room bar for drinks. I accepted gratefully, but made a mental note to keep the boundary between bar and group uppermost in my mind, so as to prevent leakage and dissipation of group material. In the bar I insisted, albeit lightly, that we talked of matters extraneous to the group.

Session 4

Redl's paper was raised again. One or two tutors were curious about the terminology, which always seemed to be connected with love or sex; they found this difficult to reconcile with teaching! The subject was dropped like the proverbial hot potato and reluctantly I let it go, sensing it would return to the fore when the group was better able to assimilate that kind of controversial material. The substitute topic, manufactured hastily, was examinations and assessment.

The argument clearly reflected the rivalry that had been slowly brewing in the group between what became known as the 'trendies' (the artists) and the 'traditionalists' (the scientists). I worked hard to create a balance. I allowed hostilities to be openly expressed in the hope that group participants would *subjectively* experience that anger is quite manageable if it is out in the open, but that blocked anger makes for blocking of learning. On the other hand, I very much wanted to avoid antagonism so polarized that we might end up with two irreconcilable groups. I felt that each faction needed help to look at what the other might have to offer. As I suspected that the more traditional teachers viewed me as a trendy, I gave slightly more emphasis to the desirability of limit setting and authoritiveness in teaching late adolescents. This was admittedly a bit of deviousness on my part, to avoid an 'in' and 'out' group situation, but I also believed in what I was saying, else I would have found some other way to contain the hostilities.

Throughout the session I was careful not to take sides; this was comparitively easy, as I could genuinely sympathize with both factions. Though temperamentally some of these teachers were very different and used very diverse educational models in their work, they each had illuminating views on staff/student relationships, all of which eventually came to be valued by the group's members as contributions to its total store of knowledge. Over several sessions it became clear that participants were incorporating amended versions of other people's ideas into their own educational philosophy (I suspect without even being aware of it).

The end of this, the fourth meeting, was quite tense. I was feeling rather helpless, as the problem seemed to be that some were willing, able and eager to work faster and at a more self-revelatory level, whilst others were unconsciously fighting hard to keep the group from increasing its pace or depth and claimed to be content with the *status quo*. Neither side would yield. All I felt I could do was to leave them as a group, to work out the conflict for themselves over a period of time, and not to impose my own aspirations upon them.

Session 5

The arts/science split became even more pronounced. There was much heated debate about progressive versus traditional methods of teaching, and this quarrel infiltrated the protracted discussion which followed about small group teaching. The disagreement, ostensibly about teaching methods, became so intense and feelings were running so high that I ventured to comment on the dynamics of *this* group, in what I hoped appeared a relaxed non-critical manner. I felt that too weighty a pronouncement at this stage might be experienced by members as an authoritarian intrusion and evidence of my disapproval. I therefore commented casually on how some of the difficulties they were recounting, such as their tutorials and their students' resistance to learning, might be about students' jealousy, competition and rivalry, in relation both to one another and to themselves, the teachers. I said that when powerful forces like this are ignored by teacher and taught, no wonder learning is stressful or that some students feel upset and leave. This remark was hotly challenged by some tutors who denied that any of their students could possibly have such uncivilized impulses towards one another — really they were all very friendly! One or two of the group members protested on my behalf, maintaining that maybe I had a point and that they ought to think about it. The group was definitely split on this issue too. On this occasion I persisted doggedly, and pointed out how normal and ordinary rivalry and competition was — after all, I said innocently, it was going on all the time in *this* group and we were all still alive and well, and even drinking together afterwards! Perhaps then, 'negative' feelings were not necessarily destructive? There were a few shocked responses to the suggestion that we in this group could be so 'childish' or 'nasty', but my translation for them of our group process had been correctly timed for the session concluded with a very open discussion about the rifts within this group. Such a topic would not previously have been admissable. The geographers hastened to assure the rest of us that all was not rosy in the geography department and that their modern ideas had by no means solved all their problems. The scientists were at pains to share with us the experimental teaching projects that were being planned in their department; their old fashioned reputation was quite unfounded. The arts people admitted some of the weaknesses they had discovered in being over-permissive; they now recognized the need for different approaches and methods to different academic subjects. Perhaps there were several ways of teaching, they ventured, not just a 'right' and a 'wrong' way.

As the job of personal tutor had cropped up time and again over the past two sessions, and as group members had had an intensely emotional session this time, I circulated a paper of my own on personal tutoring as optional background reading. This offered the opportunity for more cerebral activity next session, if group participants so desired. The end of the day drink in the bar was particularly friendly on this occasion, with members fighting to buy their round first and members of opposing camps sitting next to one another.

Session 6

Interest and approval of my paper was expressed, much to my relief and edification. In the paper I had mentioned that some students found the climate of some higher educational institutions arid, that is, not conducive to personal growth and development. The group picked this up in terms of their experience of college life and their need for job satisfaction if they were to teach well. There was much talk about how teachers ought to co-operate and support one another instead of competing for jobs and prestige, or getting bogged down in the publish-or-perish ethic. The shared view seemed to be 'If we are going to help students, we must first help ourselves'. At a deeper level, I felt this talk represented a resolution of last week's conflict between the faculties and the crystallization at last of solidarity within the group.

Later in the meeting, the whole group became sluggish and uninspired, though good-natured jokes abounded. I decided not to chivvy them but to wait patiently. Suddenly one tutor came right out with her annoyance about me, but it was the most pleasant confrontation I could have wished for. It was, I felt, a mature, woman-to-woman, 'now look here, let's get this straight shall we?' approach. Although she thought I was an inadequate chairperson, she was beginning to understand, she said, what I was 'really up to', but it frightened her a bit and she demanded that I offer more structure and teach them rather more directly. She seemed pleased to be able to get these cross feelings off her chest at last. I reminded the whole group that they were free to decide how they wanted to work, and they then agreed it was time to re-define the group's function. To my delight, no one dreamt of consulting me or making demands on me, instead they decided as a team to work out a plan of action. One member was duly elected to present a short talk the following week which everyone would then 'get their teeth into'. In view of the interest expressed in institutional problems I arranged to circulate Isobel Menzie's paper on *A Case Study on The Functioning of Social Systems as a Defence against Anxiety*. (see Selected readings).

Session 7

One of the tutors presented a short informed talk on 'Tutors and Professionalism' which dwelt on the rather more intimate transactions which go on between teachers and taught but which are rarely talked about. He concentrated upon twin subjects. The first was the intellectual affinity (along with the sharing of political and social values) that weld teachers and students together or divide them. Secondly he talked about the undertow of sexual feelings (attraction and repulsion irrespective of age, gender etc) which again draws teachers and students together or prevents them from working harmoniously. The sexual aspect this time elicited an enthusiastic response, and was vehemently discussed. The sexual conduct of academics was considered, as well as their own and students' sexual fantasies; hidden sexual manipulation between staff and students in the classroom was also examined. I was surprised that this group could grapple with such very personal material at this stage. Many of them talked freely about their own attitudes, biases, prejudices and sexual feelings toward students, though some were more reticent than others. I intervened little except to occasionally underline how always, at some level, such feelings and fantasies are operative, affecting academic transactions. (I felt it would be too anxiety-provoking to point out sexual overtones in our own group.) Learning can be accelerated or hindered, depending on how these powerful, non-rational, non-academic, non-intellectual reactions between staff and students are managed. I felt that much insight had been gained by many and that this had been a productive session.

Session 8

The previous topic — sex — was continued via a less emotive discourse on what constitutes an acceptable degree of intimacy between teacher and taught. The general feeling was that too much or too little was not helpful; every teacher must work out his or her own optimal distance at which he or she could best and most responsibly function. It was unanimously agreed that no stereotype of a good tutor existed — each person must work out his or her own definition of the tutoring role. All agreed they needed colleagues' help, to talk through such delicate and personal matters as we had touched upon here, and so some in-service training or regular get together of the staff was essential.

Everyone then recalled the earlier sessions. There were several giggling admissions about how awful the group had felt at first, and how dreadfully inscrutable and unhelpful they had found me at the outset.

Summary

This has been a sketchy, heavily edited, and perhaps unconsciously censored version of what actually occurred. I believe it to have been a reasonably successful venture, although ideally I would have preferred to work with this group for at least another term. Whatever benefits accrued to members were largely due to their openness, keenness, and preparedness to tolerate the frustration inherent in the group-analytic approach, an approach they had never heard of.

If as the conductor I had allowed the group to become too experiential (process oriented) or too academically slanted I am sure it would have failed; throughout I tried to balance these two aspects. There was a good deal of rich process material which my therapist-self longed to bring into play, but this would have been inappropriate to a time-limited training group. Much was left unspoken and unworked through and will now never see the light of day. The group cohesed enough for work to be done, work of a rather different order than that in which these academics are already proficient. It was hardly a mighty achievement, but my hope is that short but productive experiences like this might encourage trainees to take up further training options of a more profound and long lasting kind. I believe very firmly in the desirability of sampler sessions like these to generate interest and create a demand for further training. It is quite unfair to forceably baptise tutors in the deep and unknown waters of group-analytically flavoured training before they even know what it involves.

Trainers must respect the wariness tutors feel when invited to work in a new modality. They must also be prepared to meet hostile and dependent barriers in the training group without becoming personally offended and distressed by what is predictable group resistance to new learning. Giving up accepted view-points about teaching is extraordinarily painful for trainees and they will work hard to hold on to familiar habits. I have found that the tougher the resistance, the harder the group conductor must work — but the wider, deeper and more permanent is the new learning, when and if it happens.

Chapter 9

A departmental tutor training group, with consultant-conductor

When a request came from University college's law school to organize some meetings for lecturers I gladly but nervously accepted. I had worked with lawyers before, though not in a training capacity, and I was keenly aware of the communication gulf that often appears between their specialized discipline and my own. This is because law exalts the universe of fact and psycho-dynamic work the universe of feeling. The mutual discovery of a common boundary is a prerequisite for any joint learning. I knew from my experience of training counsellors in groups that serious difficulties could arise when all the members shared the same profession, in particular the propensity of members to reinforce one another's defences against insight and new ideas. Participants in these groups often succeed in resisting a new conductor's teaching influence by making quite unconscious gestures of solidarity against the new invader who threatens to usurp the already established group norms. The shared discipline enjoyed by all but the leader rests on a foundation of common attitudes and values, which can be used as boundary constrictors. This gives members a sense of security as they huddle together behind rigid boundaries from which the conductor is excluded, even though physically present. Somewhat optimistically though, I held fast to my belief that these bonds might also bind participants together supportively; that because of this 'safety in numbers', they might dare to take emotional risks and hence work faster.

Over lunch with Simon, who was initiating this project, we talked about possible themes for these meetings. The maximum time available was seven one-and-a-half hour sessions over a term. In view of this we decided upon the same title as the one reported in chapter 8, 'Staff student relationships'. As this was a first training venture in that school it seemed sensible to offer meetings which the lecturers could make use of more or less as they wished. The interest so far expressed had ranged from group teaching to counselling 'problem' students; attending to one would deprive some of the staff of learning about the other. Full justice could not be accorded to both, so we agreed on this open-ended title and left the group to interpret it, from week to week, with respect to its own changing needs.

My own objective in the group was not to teach members better teaching techniques, nor to teach members how to 'counsel' students; neither did I see it just as a social or public-relations activity, nor yet as a simple information exchange. I wanted these lecturers (only one member had the official title 'tutor') to take responsibility for their own learning situation and to choose their own subject matter within the confines of the boundaries I had already set. I made it plain at the first meeting that I would not be leading the discussion in the traditional sense, but I would follow the group rather than lead it, offering my thoughts and comments in the wake of their contributions from time to time. My reasons for doing this, I explained, were two-fold. First, this method ensured that members had the opportunity to explore issues in the staff/student relations area with which they themselves were preoccupied, rather than being forced to adhere to my agenda. Second, in delegating responsibility for group functioning to the group itself, I was freer to observe the group-as-a-whole's operations and the interpersonal relations occurring within its boundaries which could be useful to their deliberations. I felt it proper to make a more exact statement than usual at the inception of this group, owing to the nature of the members' teaching subject which I wanted to show my respect for by making 'legally acceptable' statements. This noble sentiment proved quite useless, for reasons which will become apparent as I examine the group's resistance later. Whatever I had said and however long I had taken to say it would not have made any difference at this early phase of group development. By the end of our seven sessions we had together found some common ground on which we could peaceably confer, but there was no time left to take this hard-earned progress any further.

I did not, of course, plan to use my observations in a purely psychotherapeutic manner as this was not a treatment group. But group process and interpersonal transactions which are oblivious to the people making them are not restricted to the therapy group. I hoped to illustrate live group process to these teachers, a process which they were creating and maintaining, in order to help them see how these currents and cross-currents were similarly repeated in their own teaching groups.

Membership of this group consisted of four men and two women, all in their twenties or thirties; all Oxbridge graduates, working together in a day-to-day academic setting which was competitive and demanding for staff and students alike. They taught within the context of an efficiently organized personal tutoring system. They all knew each other at a professional level within the school but Simon was the only participant with whom I had had prior contact.

Before I recount the sessions, I would like to outline my approach for the benefit of trainers. My conducting technique was pitched half-way between that of a group-analytic therapist and a small group teacher. Psycho-dynamic interventions were made only sparingly, so as to further the group's exploration of topics raised by members or to unblock a communication problem. They were never used to treat individual's personal anxieties which were not related to the group's occupation or to reveal private psychological conflicts. Such interpretations would have constituted an intolerable invasion of privacy and transgression of the boundaries. My didactic input was small and highly selective. I preferred that, given the short time we had, participants should help one another realize what they already knew rather than that I should bombard them with new material.

Two other boundary issues should be noted. First, as the instigator of the group, Simon was placed in the unenviable position of having to face split loyalties; to his comrades in the law faculty and to myself. This made for tensions in the group which were never openly admitted. His discomfort was very obvious to me and I felt unable to relieve him of a sense of responsibility for the group's outcome. At the same time I felt pressured to put on a 'good show' so as not to let him down. In some respects we were perceived by the rest of the membership as partners or co-leaders, and often in the early stages he and I seemed to be adopting polarized attitudes as if competing for dominance. Both of us were acting as though the group would succeed if only we could be left in peace to do it our own way. Fortunately at the end of the sessions, Simon and I had found a common wavelength which I personally found a rewarding experience. In many ways this was one of the most trying groups I have conducted, yet at the end, though the work was certainly incomplete, I was positively aglow with good feelings towards every member, and the emotional leave-taking of the group caused a great wrench.

The second problem, which was linked to the first, was that the group assembled each week in Simon's room. On one occasion he forgot about the group and held a student party there; on another, I was brought in to the room to witness an impressively led tutorial which was just coming to an end. This underlined to the others the special relationship obtaining between Simon and I. I felt it impolite to reorganize his chairs and lighting, and thus I was severely hampered from ensuring the correct physical environment, which in my own office would have been stabilized. As the conductor, it was a salutory experience for me to lose control over one important aspect of my work. No great harm came of it, but if the resistance I shall describe had intensified, then boundary incidents like the students' party could have increased, leaving the group homeless and demoralized. As it was, a new and comfortable home was found for us. (However, I know of colleagues who have run groups in corridors or gardens after failing to cope with boundary incidents.) One can argue that this was an accident, not an incident, and that the substitution of a party for the group was quite fortuitous, though I reckon that unconscious sabotage was at work. Had the meetings been held in my room, such an event would not have happened, or if it had, my own unconscious mind would have been the culprit! The reason for meeting in the law school was that I wished to display readiness to come to their own territory, but this concession was of dubious value. On the whole, to convene a group on strange premises would seem helpful only if the conductor knows the host well enough to be able to dictate the conditions under which the group will operate without giving offence.

Session 1

Content

Simon introduced everyone to me, using both my names. Thereafter, I took the liberty of using first names only. In a longer term group I would have promoted discussion on the subject of names, but here I opted to set an example of informality, without asking permission. In group work with time limits some corners have to be cut and this was one of them. Many training groups collapse because the conductor is so painstakingly considerate and slow. In the anxiety to avoid hurt feelings, all feelings are censored and work grinds to a standstill, or members leave out of boredom. Alternatively, the group finally achieves cohesiveness only to find that time has run out and there is no work to show for it. Needless to say, the same applies to some small group teaching!

I explained how I proposed to conduct the proceedings, (as outlined previously). This was received politely, and then totally by-passed. I was assailed by questions about my student counselling work. Which department were my clients from? What did they think of the law school? What is the best way for a teacher to handle the lazy, aggressive, shy student? I answered some of the questions directly in order to avoid the impression that I was remote and uncaring; others I deflected, hoping the group would pool their feelings and experiences about such matters. A good many stereotyped student/teacher problems came up for discussion and finally I suggested that, as unfortunately no panacea for the management of these problems existed, perhaps it would be more instructive to discuss real examples, so that the unique circumstances of one such case could be investigated in depth. This too was ignored at first, and the courteous but insistent demand for handy hints on student problems continued, with mounting frustration at the eventual realization that I did not, after all, have any simple answers.

Then a debate about streaming began, a procedure which everyone in varying degrees appeared to endorse. The spotlight had been angrily taken away from myself, as I was clearly 'undeserving'. For a time Simon was in the leadership role.

Towards the end of the session my remarks about case study presentation were remembered and Allan offered to bring us live material to look at next week.

Process
Irritation mounted steadily as it became apparent that conventional leadership was not on offer. The open-ended nature of the structure I had laid down seemed new and frightening for them. Urgent efforts were made to allay these fears by searching for practical answers to practical problems. The streaming topic seemed to provide a safe region for their elegant discourse, which reduced feelings of insecurity. This non-argument (for in principle they all agreed) about the need for accurate classification of students reflected the group's need to know where they stood in relation to me and the 'education system' I was foisting upon them. I did not share this interpretation of the situation with them, as they were already suspicious and worried. Their anticipation of criticism was attested to by their frequent questions to me about their faculty's reputation in the rest of the college and how their school's lecturers might compare with others. I chose on this occasion to remain silent despite my tumultuous feelings.

Conductor activity
I tried to tone down the anxiety level by responding directly to some of the questions, and by acknowledging with them that our 'languages' were rather different and that we would need time to adjust to one another. However, I refrained from too much mothering, which would have been infantalizing, and perhaps would have been damaging. I hoped they could endure the stress in order to teach a deeper psychological understanding of staff/student relationships by understanding their own in this group.

Impression
The mutual reinforcement of members' resistance to this kind of group work was already obvious. Resistance is natural in all group training work, but the intensity of this resistance, *en bloc*, was virtually palpable. The group members showed themselves to be highly intelligent, fluent, well read and capable of extraordinary linguistic gymnastics.

Session 2

Content
Allan gave us an account of his interactions with a female student whom he thought was very unpleasant. He feared I might accuse him of making value judgements and was prepared to be convinced that she was 'mentally disturbed'. He said 'I am prepared to be corrected in this matter!' The student concerned was 24 but acted younger; trailed around after Allan and a colleague, visiting their rooms and monopolizing them at social gatherings. She had a boyfriend in tow whom she treated with disdain. In seminars she always produced legal red herrings, and argued with Allan and other teachers over irrelevant issues. She

complained that the law is unfair. Allan said he was becoming progressively annoyed and felt the whole seminar group, 'which are an immature lot anyway' was being ruined by her behaviour.

This time, the others joined in and asked him questions about the girl, wrestling with his account to see what the teaching difficulty was really about. Allan explained about her chronic protestations in seminars and how he was endlessly driven to justify what he was saying, while the other students took a non-participatory ring side seat. Then the lawyers, with a little prompting from me, discussed ways of including the other students in these battles, rather than having Allan collude with her attempts to lock him in a self-perpetuating twosome. Allan felt she perceived herself as attractive and a bit superior, but the rest of our group considered whether this could be a compensatory activity and that perhaps she really saw herself as dull and unattractive. Her infuriating behaviour might be the only way of commanding attention. There was insufficient evidence to answer this but everyone sympathized with Allan, as everyone had confronted students like this themselves in the past. There was much relief that in this group it was quite permissable to express negative feelings about students. We managed to help Allan see that some of his fear about having things out with her on a more personal level was to do with his fear that he would be treated in the same way as her boyfriend. We considered how he had talked with her, over a period of months, about a great many subjects, in the classroom and at social functions in the department. Yet not once had he felt safe enough to tackle her about her disruptive behaviour in class, or his own frustration. He seemed to feel this would be somehow 'ungentlemanly'.

This issue caused some anxiety in the teacher group as a shared taboo seemed to exist on facing students with their own behaviour, or telling students about the teacher's own personal feelings. A change of teacher was suggested, and the possibility of sending her to a psychiatrist or counsellor, but no one took up these suggestions very seriously. I tried to explore how Allan and the others appeared unable to deal with these kinds of delicate matters with students, because of their lack of inner certainty. The lawyers operated from the premise that there were 'right' and 'wrong' questions to ask students. It seemed unthinkable to muddle along with 'ers' and 'ums' and not feel certain about what either party would do next, and they preferred to shelve the matter.

Subsequently, the group discussed the subject of authority in the classroom, and how authority and permissiveness might peacefully co-exist. We also looked at conflict between the management function of a teacher, how he ensures that the class as a whole learns what needs to be learned and the pastoral role, how he identifies and meets individual personal problems which have repercussions for the whole class, as with Allan's student. Which has priority: the troubled individual, or the non-learning total group?

Towards the end of the session, Chloe said she was fed up with all this counselling stuff and would like the group to think more about teaching methods, particularly small group teaching. Allan supported her, complaining about immature groups always relying on the teacher and refusing to propel themselves! I intervened with a chuckle, relating that remark to the present group, suggesting that perhaps they would like to decide now what they would do next week. A discussion followed, ending with an agreement that Chloe would make some introductory remarks about group teaching next week to 'start the ball rolling'.

Process

The group was still manifestly bewildered about what we were supposed to be doing, and though hard working, most individuals were demonstrably restive. The contrast between the overt courtesy and the latent hostility was quite uncomfortable and I was relieved when the anger came out more directly toward the end via Chloe. Simon, seemingly feeling responsible for all the *angst*, was very verbal, unwittingly competing with me for leadership in order to rescue the group and take it in a direction that individuals collectively could feel comfortable with. Each time we moved into the emotional field he kept bringing us back to straightforward practical areas. I tried to check his activities without appearing too critical, but found this difficult. Several members clearly found the emotional area somewhat threatening, and the lack of conclusive summing up, as each and every aspect of Allan's 'case' was revealed, was obviously unbearable to them. The demand for neat answers, 'recipes for action' was almost overwhelming, as was the disappointment and irritation when I failed to produce a single answer, but instead insisted there were various approaches, rather than a single right/wrong dichotomy.

Much of the later discussion about difficulties which the teachers located in their own teaching groups reflected unconscious anxieties about their place in this group constellation, but to interpret that would have been an error of judgment, unfairly thrusting the teachers into a quasi group therapy situation. Although he was to alter greatly later on, Simon's fuelling of the group's resistance and my refusal to condone it made this a painful session for all of us, notwithstanding the lighter moments.

Conductor activity

My interventions were mainly directed toward Allan, helping him to be brave enough to look closer at his own feelings *vis-à-vis* this particular student. Simultaneously, I tried to encourage the other group members to participate in the discussion and offer their own opinions. They had more teaching experience than I, and I felt it was important to provide them with opportunities to exhibit their teaching skills. I encouraged humour too, for I noticed the rather 'proper' way in which these teachers presented themselves. I tried to be as informal as possible, thus acting as a counter-weight to their seriousness. Their laughter always seemed tinged with guilt, as if they felt their behaviour to be delinquent.

Impression

The group was beginning to move away from the demand for instant solutions, and introspection as a teacher-training activity was just becoming respectable. The undertow of frustration was growing stronger and occasionally burst onto the group surface in small, tightly controlled spurts.

Session 3

Content

Chloe, who was scheduled to introduce the meeting, was absent but we all sat waiting hopefully. Simon filled the breach by handing out huge cigars — to the men only. Until then I had been the only person in the group to smoke. This was a loud communication to me! Chloe did not arrive and a long rambling conversation took place about the Oxford tutoring system. This led to speculations about the law tutoring network here, and the benefits accruing if they returned to a one-to-one tutoring system. There was a good deal of talk about administration of tutoring systems and the possibility of departmental reorganization. I did not feel inclined to remind them that they were playing about in safe shallow waters so as to avoid plunging in at the deep end. I felt this might come across as a ticking off and that perhaps they needed a bit of time to settle down after the awkward beginning. The sudden predilection for one-to-one tutoring systems showed their reluctance to face the complexities of small group tutoring; instead the longing to return to the bosom of their own mother colleges predominated. I elected to let the group decide when it would call a halt to the rambling conversation.

Eventually Allan cut through the discussion by asking, 'Well, what are tutorials *for*?'. Much to everyone's embarrassment no one could adequately answer this, despite strenuous exertions. Questions then arose which highlighted, for me at any rate, the dilemma in which a teacher finds himself when trying to impart a massive amount of information whilst simultaneously taking into account the students' learning potential, individual levels of maturity, and the total group atmosphere. 'Is academic spoonfeeding a good thing?' 'Why are so many student groups clinging and helpless?' 'Why can't students address a seminar without notes?'. This was the general tenor of the meeting. This question-and-answer session represented group flight from the less well defined areas just mentioned which were too painful and confusing to talk about. Simon kept arguing about the definition of spoon feeding and supporting orthodox teaching methods as if they were under heavy attack. Susan led the 'opposition' by saying maybe we ought to start looking at how students feel in groups and why participation in them seems so hard for some of them. Stewart kept hinting that all this group process stuff was really esoteric nonsense and that he handled his groups on the basis of pure common sense. He proceeded to give a quiet but exquisite account of his skilful and positive manipulation of group dynamics!

Then came another wave of requests to me for advice on techniques. I tried to show how the uncertainty they were feeling in this group and their insistent demands for miraculous insights from me might teach them something about their own small groups. They were now students in this group — could they learn something from this subjective experience? (They were behaving very like the student groups they had been complaining about.) I mentioned the fear of speaking, the rivalries, the social anxieties and the authority struggles which happen in any student group, and how such phenomena were occurring here and now in this group. My comments did not appear to be assimilated and the group returned to a rather boring discussion about practical teaching methods. Perhaps I had pushed them too far too soon; consequently safe terrain had to be sought.

The confusion about this group's purpose came to the fore again and no one could see the point in my leadership style. There was a lot of suspicion and a remarkable atmosphere of persecution, as if they believed I was attacking them. There was tremendous intellectual retaliation against any observations made by me and endless complaints about the unspecifity of my language. While showing my appreciation of their obvious intellectual and linguistic capacities, I tried to point out that this was not a seminar in the usual sense; it was more like a play area, in which ideas could be experimented with, feelings shared, creative thoughts about education tested out against the thoughts of others. A verdict, a judge and jury were redundant here.

Susan seemed to take this to heart, for after some deep thinking she said she was worried about the 'legal mind', and how hard it was to communicate with other disciplines sometimes. She wanted to know if the lawyer stereotype was a myth or a reality. If it was real, ought we to be passing on allegedly rigid attitudes and a 'dissecting' mentality to our students? John and Stewart seemed interested to pursue this; Simon and Allan were somewhat defensive as if these remarks constituted a personal affront, but eventually they simmered down and agreed to pursue this.

Susan, somewhat nervous, realizing what she was taking on, bravely agreed to bring some thoughts to the seminar the following week to open the proceedings.

Process

There was an unconscious agreement on the part of the group to steer conversation away from any personal matters. All members welded together in opposition to me, even though much of their debate with me was on the surface good-natured and often humorous. Susan 'defected' towards the end and showed great courage in facing the polite but thinly veiled hostility that ensued.

Impression
This was the third session, usually the one which I see as the 'make or break' meeting. I was anxious about the members' lack of trust in me, and the way in which they continued to support one another in defiance of the model I offered. In inter-departmental groups of teachers there had always been less suspicion and insecurity, and a more rapid resolution of the group's resistance to new learning.

Session 4

Content
Cloe returned with apologies and the group accepted her explanation without demur, unable to examine their feelings about being let down last week. I felt the atmosphere was too fragile to bring this group avoidance into the open.

I thought that perhaps some tangible teaching input on my part might be reassuring, so I circulated a paper of mine to the group, with the option of discussing it next week. The paper described developmental phases in groups, from dependency, through rebellion, to co-operation, and finally mourning. My motive in providing written material was to assist them to relate what they read to the happenings in this group; to give them a week's privacy away from the public glare of the group; to digest their group experience and organize it cognitively. I guessed that thereby some of the anxiety and muddle could be scaled down to manageable size.

Susan started her introduction with a long apology and an admission that she lacked evidence to support the ideas she was to proffer. Her concern was that there might be some truth in the reputation that law teachers have of 'processing' bright students so as to ensure high academic attainment. She feared that law teachers might be breeding coldly analytical adults, out of touch with their feelings, and that they in turn might be passing on this culture to future generations of students. Chloe hotly denied she had no feelings, whilst the others launched into Susan, defending the need for rigorous training of law students. Allan felt he was being accused of a lack of morality, and Simon felt Susan was accusing them of a 'what is legal must be right' attitude. All the men in the group felt that good 'technicians' were vital in society, and Allan pointed out how quickly the public would become outraged if an emotionally developed but technically unskilled engineer built a bridge which subsequently fell down. Susan tried to defend and clarify her views, and when I felt she had taken enough I intervened. I said something to the effect that such defensiveness was unnecessary. Susan appeared to be asking whether something could be *added* to legal teaching, not asking that academic standards be reduced or skills removed. I ruefully suggested that maybe law teachers' reputations were not entirely unfounded, for I had seen here in this group how the members clung to their professional role and were often contemptuous or distrustful of anything to do with feeling, or any situation with students which could not be categorically defined, evaluated, and then summed up. I pointed out how effective Stewart was in his small group teaching but how he denied the importance of what he was doing, dismissing it all as 'just common sense'. I reminded them of several contributions made by other group members which had been devalued or dismissed because we had failed to come up with a 'legal' solution.

Chloe and others protested that teachers cannot be instructor, parent and friend to all their students — as well as taking them through the gruelling law syllabus. I talked a bit about the university as a total system which should cater for students' wider needs. The Law School was a highly specialized sub system — how should it relate to other subsystems in the university? How could students have their needs met without draining the teachers whose primary function was, after all, to teach? A discussion followed about how isolated/integrated the school was within the rest of the university. Simon complained politely that he never understood what I was talking about, yet he could understand his colleagues perfectly. Stewart said the group was very interesting, but useless, as it (?I) did not (?would not) tell him what to *do*, how to teach better. Chloe pointed out 'with respect' that she had no idea what she was getting from the group.

As the tension mounted and everyone contributed to the attack on me, there was a sudden and dramatic change in the group. Allan and Simon had started a private conversation — something to do with David Copperfield, literary criticism, and the trade descriptions act! Mesmerized, we all listened to and watched this dazzlingly clever argument which grew more and more intense and rarefied. After a long time, when it became clear that no one could interrupt, I broke in and told them politely but firmly to shut up for a minute because I wanted to speak. In an instructive way I revealed how this pairing activity, adopted quite unconsciously, had successfully served the hidden group purpose of arresting an emotional situation with which the group could not cope, namely an assault on myself, which I personally felt quite able to take. There was momentary stunned silence and then loud protestations, everyone denying they were angry with me. Allan and Stewart, aggrieved, said that they could not understand what I had just said — it must be something to do with 'group process' which they were still confused about anyway. Simon denied there was any such thing as a group in any case; he maintained there was only a series of individuals — 'a group is a philosophical absurdity', he said. Painstakingly I went over the events we had all just witnessed and explained again what had happened and why. Chloe suddenly cheered up and announced that at last she had learned something from this wretched group. Pairing of the kind she had just watched occurred often in her groups and now she was beginning to see how pairs can help the group avoid matters they could not or did not want to look at. John and Simon and Stewart still muttered about 'process' and 'structure' and complained about a course they had attended which was as puzzling as this. I took a deep breath and delivered a mini-speech on group dynamics to try and clarify those issues which had cropped up in this group which had confused them. This was a calculated step, necessary to counteract their growing conviction that I was purposely employing mystification and obscurantism.

The conversation returned to the 'legal mind', and I by-passed some of their comments on this as they were about to turn the subject into another semantic argument. I insisted rather dogmatically, aware that this was our fourth session, that they did have other 'minds', minds which could accommodate passion, jealousy, tenderness, and anger. However, throughout these sessions they had dismissed these other selves and had acted as if they only had the 'legal mind' to which Susan referred. What was so terrible about displaying these other selves? I felt that Stewart's non verbal reaction to my statement indicated understanding and agreement, but he then claimed it was all Greek to him. Susan was becoming very excited and seized my every point, enlarging upon it, translating it into her own words and relaying it urgently to the others. Allan was puzzled, wavering, teetering on the brink of acceptance. Simon was adamant that his and my views were irreconcilable but his contributions to the group from then on made it quite clear that my remarks had held some meaning for him. I felt something important had transpired in the group, but token arguments were still raised against my views as if it were dangerous to trust them. Allan said that the legal and therapeutic approach were too different for there to be a meeting point. I said slowly and deliberately that even if it were true, (though I did not believe it) that theoretically and philosophically we could not meet, we could still meet as people and have feelings towards one another, could we not? He asked what I thought about his 'approach'. I was not sure what he meant precisely and replied that I was awestruck by his elegantly articulated expositions of complex issues, but sad that relations with him in the group were mainly 'cortex-to-cortex' and not 'gut to gut'. He blushed violently at my compliment (everyone teased him about this), then paused to consider what I had said about the lack of emotional contact between us. Gone was his usual rapid, cleverly argued response.

The mood of the group had brightened. Everyone said in one way or another that they felt so much better after getting things off their chest, and group members seemed to look forward eagerly to next week.

Process
This was the turning point in the group's development. The open expression of anger was vital to the group's continued survival, which is why I refused to allow the behaviour of the 'pair' to continue.

Conductor activity
Attuned to the impending crisis and in touch with the collective hostility and resistance, I decided, most unusually, to resort to sledge-hammer techniques. I intervened heavily, taught didactically, reassured massively, and reached out emotionally in a very exposed way. These extreme approaches seemed to have succeeded where subtlety and patience failed.

Impression
There was relief all round; the group atmosphere had completely changed. I think my own relief and happiness was probably the greatest of all. After an agonizing labour, a group was born.

Session 5

Content
Spontaneous approval and interest was expressed in relation to the paper I had previously circulated. The climate was temperate throughout! Susan exclaimed that last week's session had been a turning point for her. From the moment I had explained about Allan and Simon's pairing, 'light had progressively dawned', and the paper seemed to have consolidated her new learning. Stewart, friendly but still distrusting, said he had enjoyed and understood the paper and was now beginning to realize the importance of personal transactions in groups, but despite this he remained convinced that he had gained nothing of any real value. Allan was still struggling to understand what had happened to himself and the group. He wanted to know, as did John and Stewart, why I could not have arranged things so that the group operated at the 'adult co-operative level' as described in my paper from the start. Why did they have to go through that awful dependent and rebellious stage which had been such a waste of time? Susan replied, explaining the inevitability of these phases, how they occur in student seminar groups, and how teachers should be aware of them and use this understanding to improve the teaching. Allan still maintained that had I provided more structure and answered all their questions at the outset, we could have circumvented the confusion and hostility. I tried to show him that if I had permitted the purely cognitive discussions he had wanted, and had given the simple advice he had demanded, I would have deprived him of the chance to see something more profound, with further reaching consequences, namely the powerful effect of emotional transactions between people and the latent but significant activity generated

137

by group life. Simon staunchly defended my approach and patiently explained to Allan the points I was making in language they could both understand, though it sounded very legalistic to me!

The group went on to discuss how students never seem to 'hear' explanations and instructions in early tutorials, but insisted on behaving in an idiosyncratic way according to some private notion of what a tutorial was supposed to be. I reminded them of the time I had explained the nature of this seminar, and how they had not 'heard' me. (We were able to laugh together about this.) Allan and Stewart immediately denied I had ever said anything of the sort and the others could only vaguely remember. I talked a bit about students' fantasies concerning their teachers, and Simon agreed that students did have strange attitudes. Inviting a limited number to a party he had pulled names out of a hat to prove fair-play, and still the rumour was that some were preferred to others. Those not invited felt personally rejected. This, I said, was not unlike the paranoid reaction of this group, whose members attributed all manner of qualities to the authority figure, myself; these qualities bearing little relation to my real personality. This led to a protracted discussion about the ways students related to staff, expecting from teachers responses and attitudes which were really characteristics of their parents. The group then pondered awhile, considering what qualities teachers might project onto their students which did not rightly belong to them, or how feelings towards a spouse or relative might be inadvertantly displaced onto a student.

Susan said that after her experience in this group she was seriously thinking about whether lawyers could inject more experiential learning into their courses, using role play or free discussion. Simon told us about a mock mental health review tribunal which he had organized with his students, and how they (like this group last week) were shocked by the sudden insight brought about by being in a live human drama. Following this event, the students were able to dissect and analyze the separate components of the learning experience. Legal education, apparently, usually consists of students having to master a series of components which they add together in an attempt to understand the total field. The disadvantage of this method is that students are often deprived of an emotional impact which can spur further more detailed learning. For the 'whole' experience of intuitive learning seems to represent more than the sum of its various components. I longed to pursue this with Simon, for that was exactly what I had meant about the group being more than a collection of individuals. The individuals form an organic whole which is qualitatively different from the mere addition of their various characters. However the group was moving on to an important and humorous recognition that we were now in our 'co-operative' phase, and could we have one more session after the Jubilee holiday to do our mourning for the group's ending?

The group members unanimously and mischievously asked if I would present a short case history, one which involved teachers, at the next, penultimate session.

Process
The conductor and group were no longer polarized and though there was still perplexity and bafflement, the hostility had virtually disappeared; everyone felt willing to co-operate with each other and myself, despite these obstacles.

Session 6

I presented a case history of a student with a chronic work block who idealized one of his teachers and loathed another in a very extreme way. I tried to give the teachers a glimpse into the therapeutic session about which they were very curious without distracting them too much from my main theme. This was the way in which this student used his teachers as repositories for conflicting parts of himself. He could not experience them as ordinary people in their own right until he had undergone a good deal of therapy.

The group discussed the handling of referrals, and looked again at matters connected with authority (this had arisen repeatedly in my case history). The work was conducted steadily and in process terms the group was uneventful.

Simon, who was attending a meeting this week had told the others he would present a case next week.

Session 7 (final session)

Simon, much mellowed, gave a moving presentation of his first ever tutorial when he had made a young student cry. He had suddenly realized that any intellectual activity between teacher and taught occurred within an emotional context, and that there was no way that this context could be conveniently sidestepped.

Simon went on to recount another episode in his career, when a pregnant Roman Catholic girl confided in him, knowing him to be Roman Catholic also, that she was unable to make a decision about abortion. Simon, rather desperate about his own inner turmoil, asked who she got on with best and when the girl replied 'my mum', it was in that direction that he steered her. Had he done the right thing, he wanted to know? Susan and John were quite clear about this matter and felt the proper thing to do was to listen in the first place and in the second support the girl while she struggled in her own mind and came to her own decision. Simon said that was all very well but his religion, in which he believed devoutly, obliged him to advise against termination. On the other hand his personal ethics dictated that in any issue people have a right to make their own choices. I pointed out how neither his dogma nor his intellect could solve this particular conflict, but perhaps the realization that he could not manage his own feelings could have helped him towards a deeper understanding of how the girl must have felt. If he could have shown her he understood her acute dilemma, perhaps this would have given her the emotional space, free from pressure, in which she could have psychologically 'roamed' and could have come to her own conclusions in her own time and her own way. The group then looked at whether it was in fact solutions or advice, or even counselling that students ask for. Perhaps it was more to do with this need for space and another person representing a safe flexible boundary around it.

There was a good deal of talk about abortion, murder, suicide, much of it involving philosophical, legal and moral speculations. It was a fascinating and highly stimulating debate in which I would have joined with much fervour under different circumstances. I intervened gently to guide the discussion in the direction of staff-student interactions, and to bring us back to looking at the teacher's function in dealing with such emotive circumstances. It was Simon, surprisingly enough, who supported me in this attempt to drag us away from the debating chamber into the more sensitive arena of personal relations. Most of the group members felt enormous respect for a student's privacy, so much so that all agreed on a policy of erring on the side of caution when dealing with all non academic matters. Whilst agreeing with this to a large extent, I said I felt that sometimes too much caution could be neglectful, especially if it really reflected the teacher's own anxiety rather than a reluctance to interfere with privacy. The desirable degree of intimacy between staff and students was examined, as well as how much or how little teachers should give advice or share their own beliefs and attitudes.

Time and again we returned to the topic of death in one form or another, and I connected this with the ending of the group which is a death of sorts. Everyone groaned, but some looked momentarily uneasy. All agreed that what I had said was absurd, yet there was some curiosity about whether other groups had discussed death towards the end. We were due to finish at 6.00 pm and just before the time came a shared silence fell upon the group. The church bell outside tolled six and no one moved, though the embarrassed eye contact as the fourth, fifth and sixth peals rang out made it quite clear to us all that we were indeed very conscious of the end. As if to deny it was really over, chattering broke out and a rapid review of the sessions occurred, the concensus being that a fair amount of rather strange learning had taken place and that time might be needed to digest it. There was some residual annoyance at the way I had conducted the early sessions. I thanked them for what had been an equally painful but very rewarding experience for me, and acknowledged the many loose ends that would now remain untied. Simon concluded the meeting by saying a little anxiously, a little jokingly 'if we really take seriously what you have taught us, how can we ever hope to tackle our jobs as teachers? Teaching would become so complex; the more you learn the more complicated it gets'. 'Yes,' I said warmly, agreeing.

Leaving the building Susan took my arm and thanked me for a good experience. Stewart and Allan each wrote a personal note of thanks a week later. Simon has become a close professional associate. I did not hear anything further from John or Chloe.

Summary

This was a particularly 'sticky' group, which is why it was so instructive. The combination of well-developed intellects with language fluency and a habitually 'cross-examining' approach enabled this group to neatly dodge emotionally charged areas of interaction with alarming ease. The fact that members shared an identical professional and academic orientation made penetration into the group culture especially difficult for myself as conductor. In addition, I was often almost seduced into joining the debates and forgetting about the group process. During the crisis period of the fourth session, I had to use unusually extreme methods; these constituted a stand-up fight with the group in which I insisted on being boss and running things my way. In interdepartmental teaching groups of this kind such an approach was never required, as many of the ideological conflicts were fought out between individual members rather than between the group-as-a-whole and the group conductor.

In retrospect, I feel these teachers may have derived more benefit in a group made up of individuals connected with a variety of disciplines. As a single threatening outsider, all the fear, suspicion and hostility, dormant in any new group, was projected onto myself, which made it impossible, in the early stages, for the membership to receive any supportive feelings from me. In an inter-departmental group, negative feelings can be spread around the group and displaced onto the representatives of other academic disciplines. Thus the group conductor may still be perceived as a nurturing figure to some extent. Another way round the problem of conducting single discipline groups might be to have two conductors, in the full knowledge that, as with the student I discussed in session six, one authority figure may be perceived as totally benign, and the other conductor as totally malignant!

One of the obvious advantages of this group was the way in which members became progressively more informal in their dealings with each other over the weeks. All of them agreed they knew each other more intimately and trustingly at the end of the sessions than they had ever managed to do in their department in the course of the academic year. This improved communication will undoubtedly enliven and personalize their tutoring system as well as model for the students a structure of social relations based on reciprocity of feeling, rather than ritualized etiquette.

The following, final, four case studies (Chapters 10-13) describe events occurring within the same overall time-span in a single department. Taken together, they attempt to show the interlinking nature of different groups within a larger group and how their interdependence might improve staff relations, curriculum development and students' learning.

A term of tutorials for students with consultant-observer

During an informal staff meeting of the Geography department at University College I asked if I might sit in on a regular tutorial as I needed to regain direct contact with a live academic situation. For months I had been listening to renditions of tutorials and seminars from the members of the staff in-service groups I had been conducting, but I was always at one remove in receipt of this information and longed to witness at first hand the teaching process to which we constantly alluded in these staff seminars. In exchange, I offered myself as a consultant who could observe the tutorial and the teacher's style, and who would then impart her impressions to the tutor in a discussion after each session leaving the teacher free to draw upon the content of these conversations if he wished, in future tutorials.

Dr Arthur Y volunteered but felt somewhat cautious about it; he was not entirely convinced that such a project could be valuable. I wondered how I would feel if he, or another academic, had asked to be present in my counselling sessions with students; my reaction to this hypothetical situation indubitably helped me empathize with Dr Y! We looked at our respective commitments, and finally chose a first year tutorial group who were due to meet first thing in the morning once a week for an hour. Later on that day, Arthur and I would confer for half an hour to go over the session that had taken place previously. (Unfortunately, half an hour was the maximum amount of time available to us both.)

Arthur explained my presence to the students who agreed that I could come along, and so at their second tutorial I made my entry into the little group. There were three females and one male; all looked very young indeed. Arthur had a comfortable but small room. We decided that since the students knew I was there to observe, it was pointless my hiding away in a corner, and so I sat with them, progressively relaxing and being able to join in with the current mood. We greeted each other every week.

Though I laughed at communal jokes and shared their inspection of teaching material (maps, census information and so forth), I did not participate verbally as I did not want to interfere with the group's natural processes. Total objectivity, therefore, was impossible; I felt that had I been emotionally cold and physically isolated from the group, that would have caused a deleterious reaction, probably of self-consciousness and resentment. As it was, I was quickly made to feel a part of it all and no one seemed troubled by my presence.

Arthur and I had crossed paths professionally before, and I liked him. He had attended some four meetings of an in-service staff seminar which was terminating, so he was neither totally ignorant of my views, nor really *au fait* with them. He was an experienced teacher in his thirties, with a natural personal tutoring aptitude, but possessed of no formal training in running small groups. His own attitude towards the study of group process in teaching appeared highly ambivalent – he professed only a guarded interest. We were not at that stage personal friends and our relations were cordial rather than close.

Before each tutorial he arranged to have the phone intercepted and the chairs were placed thus, in readiness:

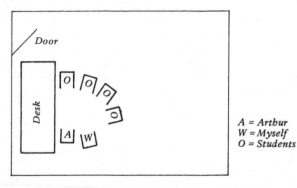

A = Arthur
W = Myself
O = Students

No external interruptions were allowed. He positioned himself more or less in equal proximity to all of us. (We agreed I should sit a little way behind him, so as not to distract him.) There was access to his desk, always heaped with papers, should he require it, but he sat adjacent to it, facing all of us. The students regularly changed places from week to week, but Arthur and I remained always in the same chairs.

Arthur usually came to each tutorial having made some academic preparation, but regarded this predetermined structure as a 'skeleton' only, leaving the group as it matured, and himself as he grew more confident, to flesh it out in their and his preferred way.

Tutorial 1

Arthur briefly introduced me, and almost in the same breath asked the students if there were any queries consequent upon the previous week's tutorial (their first). These were dealt with directly. After this, he went on to address them on the subject of books: how to acquire them, how to 'fillet' them for essential information, how they can supplement lectures, even though often out of date. He recommended a suitable 'bible' for statistics, as this was an aspect of the course which seemed to be causing concern. A question about the use of calculators was speedily answered, and having 'cleared the decks', he then asked their opinion of their first field trip. They eagerly replied, commenting on how helpless they had been and blaming this on the course organizers. On the field trip, there had only been two inches of water in the stream which had hindered the hydrological experiments; the questionnaire was faulty; they had got lost in the wood; they had not got themselves to their series of stations in the order and time required.

Then Arthur proceeded to hand back to them their first essays as university students. He gave a scrupulously fair overall group assessment, positive and negative and a constructive criticism to each individual in turn. Subsequently he gave a little talk with some humour, on how Geography related to real life, and how the students must feel free to use their sensory experience and their personal opinions when writing essays; text book reproductions were not demanded of them.

Next, Arthur prepared them for the following week's meeting. He showed them three famous journals which they were going to have to consult a lot over the next three years. He asked them to select at random one issue of each, from the past 10 years, and review it, to ask themselves: 'Who is this journal for?' 'Who and what is the organization which publishes it?' 'Who reads it?' 'Which facet of Geography does it cover?'. He advised the students about composing this piece of work, reckoning that preparation should amount to one-and-a-half hours in the library, and the actual essay ought to have one page devoted to each journal, plus a summary.

Towards the end of the tutorial he handed round huge folders of 'seminal papers', confessing that though these may be useful, they could also be seen as 'scandalous spoonfeeding'. This produced much mirth and the students appeared pleased to receive the papers.

Finally Arthur asked each person about the ancillary subjects they had elected to do (three were doing psychology and one history). At the end Laurence raised his broken spectacles in a self pitying gesture and Arthur told him there were many opticians within a stone's throw of the college where he could have them repaired.

Impressions

I found the tutorial quite breathtaking as we seemed to have hastened through a long agenda in a very short time. Although it was a conscientiously worked out agenda, touching on all the usual worries of new students, (where to find books, how to write university style essays, and what to put in them) there had been no time for the new students to identify their own worries and share them with each other. Solutions of a highly practical kind were offered before the problems relating to these solutions had even been stated, and before the students had even appreciated they were allowed to state problems. Most of the verbal input was from Arthur and the students were compliant throughout. His setting of guidelines on how to approach the homework; his emphasis on how to structure the writing itself, as well as use college resources; his stress on his own willingness to answer their doubts and queries, was excellent, as was his preparedness to recognize their dependency needs at this phase of the group's development and so 'feed' them enough advice to maintain their confidence in this new situation.

In our discussion afterwards, Arthur and I talked about the possibility of letting the pre-planned structure of the tutorials yield occasionally to the more pressing emotional needs of the membership. The urge to talk about, and hence share and then accept, all manner of anxieties concerning the course in general, and this tutorial specifically, was not really catered for. Arthur's own doubts were that if he did this the academic slant of the tutorial would disappear and no work would ever be achieved; people would just grumble incessantly.

Thinking about this tutorial afterwards, I tried to categorize some of the processes I had watched, in accordance with some of the theoretical schemes unfolded earlier in this book. The operational mode was interesting as it combined member-to-leader (dyadic) functioning with group-to-leader, in an alternating sequence. Students were spoken to in turn and they never talked to each other. Interspersed with this leadership activity, periodic mini-lectures were delivered to the whole group on matters which Arthur anticipated were bound to be troubling them. He was certainly correct in his assumptions, but unfortunately the problems were whisked away before the students had time to own them, or check whether their fellow group members suffered in the same way. (Owning and sharing of problems make for rapid group cohesion.)

The *required* relationship was one of willing and excessive co-operation (all agreed to race through the business) to avoid facing the underlying anxieties about each other, the tutorial, myself possibly, the new course and the college at large. This avoided relationship could lead to a fantasized calamity, that of being rejected or mocked by the teacher on whom they so relied at this time of great personal uncertainty. All members were equally 'busy', desperately trying to appear earnest and hardworking, to avoid being exposed as foolish or afraid before their peers.

The *basic assumption* group kept swinging between fight-flight, and dependency. The dependency was articulated through the woeful complaints about the field trip, the inability to find their way round libraries and book lists, and Laurence's plea for help with his glasses. These were not the angry complaints of challenging adults but the wails of children longing to be picked up and cuddled. On the group's surface of course, all contributions were brisk and businesslike, but this was a verbal charade, behind which lurked a good deal of emotional tension. Arthur was so actively engaged in getting through all the items he had listed in advance that he lacked the psychological distance necessary for observing his group's processes. The group's occupation soaked up all his energies. Its hyper-activity was in fact anti-occupation (ie fight-flight), in that it plainly masked the real worries which were never properly aired. Such an airing could have been identified as the group's first corporate need. Always the hardworking ethic was seized by the group to assist flight from this proper work. Process-settling preliminaries ideally precede the tackling of the official group occupation, which can then be concentrated upon in the absence of interferences, in this case anxiety about the newness of the group.

In focal conflict terms the disturbing motive was a wish for reassurance and approval from the tutor; the reactive motive the fear of disapproval and dislike if they showed any 'weaknesses'; the group solution was a collective resolve to show industrious diligence and enthusiasm and to deny all emotional and interpersonal needs in the group itself. Though not an ideal solution, for it was based on self-deception, it was nonetheless a solution which made survival a certainty, at least for the time being. There was a shared illusion that a lot of work had been concluded; the exchange of papers, handing back of essays, and waving of journals seemed to underline this. This rather frenetic atmosphere in a new tutorial is a noteworthy variation of the more predictable, totally dependent response, where there is tension, silence and agonized self-consciousness. It is probably fair to say that Arthur, like many small group teachers, played a part in imposing a characteristic culture on the group, which in this instance produced the dependency/fight-flight hybrid. He managed his own anxiety by over-zealousness, which was infectious.

The central and most important observation I made, was how Arthur always gave the impression of being a 'good guy', that is, personally authentic. He demonstrated without restraint or adornment his genuine interest in his students and in Geography, giving neither preferential treatment! Whatever technical wizardry he was to concoct, or whatever mistakes he was to make in the future, I was already sure that this authenticity would be his mainstay, so far as the students were concerned.

Tutorial 3

I missed the second tutorial owing to another commitment. I came to the third one a little early, to find all four students, and Arthur, seated, notebooks open, pens at the ready. Arthur had contacted me in the meantime, to tell me that last week had gone well. They had completed an essay for this week entitled 'How does migration theory relate to modern population problems?' (All essay topics in tutorials refer to lectures and other parts of the course — they are never totally new subjects.)

Somewhat apologetically he returned their essays, having only had time to glance at them briefly. He assured them he would give a more detailed assessment of each when he had had more time to thoroughly read them through. In the meantime, he suggested they might each summarize for the enlightenment of the rest of us, the main argument and trains of thought followed in their respective essays. I found this an impressive technique for guiding the group towards a sense of wholeness, especially as (and as we shall later see) it paved the way for a similar but more advanced exercise of actually marking one another's essays. He was obviously gradually acclimatizing them to 'public' expositions and building up their confidence in their own views bit by bit. However, he not they, chose the order in which they would speak, and as each student volunteered their summary a little shyly, he responded to them dyadically and didactically; he embellished their arguments, teasing out convoluted ideas, praising and encouraging them, while helping them understand how they could have taken their theses even further. Apart from the limitations of this student-to-tutor model, already mentioned in previous chapters, there was another disadvantage easily identifiable to an observer, but probably not so to the busy tutor. The members were hurriedly re-reading their own essays, like actors, unsure of their lines, rehearsing up to the last moment in the wings. They could not involve themselves in the two-way interaction before them, so busy were they with their preparations for their own performance. They lost an important opportunity of hearing new material from their colleagues, who had written their essays from a different angle. Had Arthur relinquished some of his dyadic activity he might have enabled them to clarify and debate each other's main essay points. They had all written about this most controversial matter from different standpoints and had quoted different references. Pooling resources rather than turn-taking could have added to their store of knowledge. In addition it might have hastened the cohesive process, by reinforcing interpersonal communication across the group, which was still leader-centerd, rather than work or group-centerd.

One fascinating development was Laurence's move from passivity and blushing in session one to out-and-out rebellion in this third meeting. (On his own, or the group's behalf, I wondered?) The only male, he flagrantly competed with Arthur for leadership, looking a little frightened as he did so, but clearly feeling some important personal issue was at stake. He opposed all Arthur's lecturettes and disagreed with all the established theories the teacher put forward, offering clever counter-arguments. Ostensibly this was an academic disagreement, but in process terms I felt it to be a challenge of authority, expressed for the whole group by the one member predisposed to risk-taking, and who, as Arthur's rival, had the most to gain from usurping the leader.

Both men seemed unable to trade their ideas, although the proprieties in terms of trading were observed at all times. Both seemed reluctant to lose face while the girls watched the jousting with coy enjoyment! The sex ratio in the group gave cause for several such competitions throughout its life. It is to Arthur's credit that Laurence was always left with self-esteem intact, yet the group was never once robbed of its designated leader. This mixture of toleration and firmness in a group leader is vital for the group members' sense of security.

Throughout the whole session, only three remarks were other than student-to-tutor. Vicky made the first of these three contributions, as the men's confrontation began to monopolize the proceedings, and her impatience rose. She stood up to Laurence on some theoretical point by criticizing him directly, but her anxious eyes were fixed on Arthur! Laurence replied rather crossly and abruptly and she withdrew, embarrassed. Arthur leapt to her defence, but may have been better advised to support her in continuing to speak for herself. After Vicky withdrew from the affray the two men were left to pair by the rest of the group who were thus absolved from ventilating their own grievances. Later they were able to express their growing feelings of rebellion against Arthur's control of the group, albeit at one remove. The library was hopeless; the computer kept breaking down; the theories taught were antiquated — in short anything in any way connected to Arthur and his role was shot down in flames. Just the same, much of the dependency remained, and there was a good deal of sisterly and brotherly competition for Arthur's favour. He asked a question and all spoke, offering simultaneous answers, each trying to express themselves louder than the rest. Then they would suddenly progress from dependency into rebellion by demolishing his ideas and revelling in their triumph. He failed at this stage to make them interact with each other, but he handled the academic material expertly, by welcoming dissent as an impetus to learning rather than a personal affront. He challenged them to look at the nature of Theory, its uses and abuses. Why bother to have theories at all, he asked? This was a new and exciting thought for them. In future lectures and seminars they will probably never again examine the very foundations of their subject like this. The first year tutorial is just the medium in which such basic but crucial work can take place.

At the end of this tutorial I felt much happier than I had in the first one, for on this occasion we had spent the whole time looking at one area only, (the conflicting opinions about migration) so that the overall effect was one of systematization rather than fragmentation.

Arthur had attended predominantly to group content, (what was actually done and said), rather than to process, (what happens to and between people, and to the group as a whole, while these things are being done and said). He seemed a little insensitive to his rivalrous behaviour with Laurence, in that he could see Laurence's competitiveness but found it hard to look at his own. All these points were discussed between us later in the day.

As the tutorial drew to a close, he asked the members to obtain a map between now and next week and to extract from it as much scientific data as possible. He asked them to select a map of a place that meant something very personal to them and to compare what they could factually discover from the information stored on the map with what they knew, assumed and felt about the place from subjective experience. 'You need a break from essays at the moment' he quipped, and his intuitive understanding of their feelings was warmly received by the students.

In our half hour chat afterwards, Arthur was feeling guilty about not having read their essays owing to a power cut, and was worried about their being deprived of his individual feedback. He was surprised that even so the tutorial had been alive and full of ideas. I tried to help him see that the power cut had forced him to give *them* the work of assessing their own essays, and that this had speeded up rather than retarded the group's progress. After we had completed our discussion I thought Arthur was beginning to feel more relaxed about shifting to a less leader-centrerd, dyadic approach. I had asked him how he saw the purpose of a tutorial and he said he had felt its chief object was to assist students with the why and how of learning itself, rather than mastering blocks of knowledge. He wanted them to learn how to question basic premises on which theories are built; to use literature and other research tools creatively; to juggle with contradictory ideas and frame their own conclusions; to seek out for themselves anomolies and conflicts in writers' works, accord their own priorities and make their own decisions about which section of geography was most important. He saw tutorials also as training workshops for reading, writing and study skills. Hoping he would not take offence, I said I noticed that he fed in a good deal of academic material; that he seemed agitated when it was not being assimilated quickly enough, and results were not immediate. His private feeling was that to properly recognize group process might lead to its 'taking over' in some mysterious way and that it could spoil the academic side of his work. He seemed to feel that group process somehow clogged the machinery of academic study, and so if he assiduously polished the machinery it would not be so susceptible to clogging! I endeavoured to stress how process, used properly, oils the machinery and helps it run smoothly. Why did he insist on running away from process to content, rapidly and collusively followed by the students? The welcoming of process would be quite in harmony with his own definition of the tutorial's purpose. He was a little shocked at this I think, for he had been worried that the group was not moving fast enough, and here was I intimating that he was driving the content along so fast that the now rebellious group were allowed no time or space to take hold of process for themselves. Where first they had implored him to take charge and make them psychologically safe, they now resented it, for they were less dependent, and willing to engage in a more adult encounter, if only he would let them. This resentment was a part process, which if ignored, would jeopardize future learning — it needed to be dealt with very soon.

Tutorial 4

The tutorial commenced with Arthur returning the aforementioned essays and spending a few minutes on each, giving to every student in turn his positive and negative criticisms. He also explained carefully what the various markings meant. (So many students complain of teachers' hieroglyphics on their essays.) In an attempt to contravene their growing tendency to revere or rebel against himself as authority he declared that when he wrote all over an essay they should not think he was speaking from 'on high'; he was in fact reacting subjectively to their work and said he would be happy for them to argue back or see him individually if his written remarks upset them in any way. Their trust in him was visibly growing as evinced by their increasingly relaxed non verbal behaviour, (which again is much easier for an observer to note).

Vicky interrupted him — the first time one of the women in the group had verbally reacted to him directly, without waiting to be asked! She had heard rumours about having to produce two 'special' essays, which would be graded and counted towards the examination result — could he explain this please? He said that grades only counted in marginal cases; that the department was much more interested in the development of students' work over a protracted period than in judging people by once and for all grades. This is not like school, he said, and different academic ethics prevail here; but he was prepared to give a more detailed assessment of her work if she did not feel she was getting enough. This exchange was very civilized, and Arthur was scrupulously fair, but there was no room for a real airing of assessment fears, which, judging from the other students' faces, was endemic to the whole group. Arthur was keen to get on with the agenda and the students sensed this and so did not press him.

He rolled up his sleeves, smoothed wayward tendrils of hair, grinned, balanced his chair precariously on its two front legs, and asked them to produce their maps, in a business-like but friendly manner. I am sure that this 'character' which he so unreservedly showed at all times endeared him to the students, as it did to me. I sat praying his chair would not collapse, chuckling at his idiosyncratic vocabulary, and joining in the atmosphere of hard work combined with merriment, which pervaded all his tutorials. This free flowing expression of his personality was worth a thousand teaching 'techniques'. He managed the impossible — taking Geography seriously, by not 'taking it seriously' too seriously!

All the students had chosen a map of their home town, and in general brought to the tutorial all manner of good and happy associations, which promoted both group cohesion and rivalrous territorial disputes. Arthur's leadership style was changing; throughout this meeting he censored many of his own contributions, and was able to wait for the students' own feelings and thoughts to emerge; he interrupted and answered queries less, so that others could carry out some of the group tasks that previously he had commandeered for himself. The object of the exercise he had set was to accentuate the difference between subjective and objective knowledge in Georgraphy, and to separate fact from personal bias when making a study of an area. Scientific method does not come easily to new students and guidance is needed. On the other hand, in Geography and related subjects, (where allocation of resources, building of community facilities and so on, seriously affects the lives of thousands of people) subjectivity and social values, and notions such as the 'quality of life' have also to be respected and discussed during the course. The students were eager to share this very personal material. This was almost certainly the first time most of them had been away from home and the nostalgia was virtually tangible. The atmosphere was expectant and the talk animated, even though people were still a little shy and unsure of themselves. Only Laurence was subdued, as if recalling last week, and wondering whether he had pushed Arthur too far. Arthur had sensed this too, and took great pains, in a delicate but casual way, to bring Laurence back into the group. In a short while Laurence seemed reassured that he had not alienated the leader he had challenged and was able to come back into the group. In handing over the choice of maps to the students, Arthur had shown his readiness to delegate some of his power; in bringing their homes to the tutorial the students had integrated deeply significant feelings from the past with their academic aspirations for the future. Homesickness was faced and managed in togetherness, without the word once having been mentioned. The working out of this communal underlying theme, at a very deep level of group resonance, bound them together as a unit. It made possible all the surface success and academic improvement which was still to come which many teachers would regard as sheer luck, or accident. As they pored over maps later in this meeting, their heads touched, and papers slid to the floor to be picked up and returned by their fellows as they smiled; there was much physical handling of each other's documents, and I felt as though I was watching an intricate, primitive, non verbal communal rite. Simultaneously the group's occupation proceeded happily, while interpersonal communications were consolidated.

Once the climate was temperate and conducive to expression, Vicky, like Laurence in the previous session differentiated herself in a provocative manner from the rest of the group. She complained that one of her colleague's maps did not constitute a village, as claimed, and was scornful of the other student's sentimental attachment to it. Jane, the quietest of the group, fought back — to my amazement. Her riposte was that Vicky's home in a small quarter of Bristol could hardly be termed a village either as it was not even rural! Everyone began criticizing others' homes, and hinting that theirs was really the best, except for Laurence, who always made a point of being different. He did not think much of his Tonbridge background, and made some amusingly disparaging observations about it. No one was convinced for a moment that he really hated it. During this competitive exchange, Arthur was almost ignored. He re-channelled a good deal of this intense feeling into the work eventually, by using it to illustrate many controversial aspects of Geography. He recognized that the group was not yet mature enough to cope with real hostility. I was sure that no other subject could have generated this much emotion in so young a group, and it successfully brought about interpersonal contact. As a by product, each student found out a good deal about the lives, habits and attitudes of the others. Formerly no introductions had been made, and so the students only had transferred fantasies about the other people in the group on which to build any sort of interpersonal relationships. Now at last the reality of each person's unique personality was on display through the manner in which they had staunchly defended their home area and all the values they associated with it. At last participants had a legitimate chance through the work itself to become acquainted with one another. Arthur also said where he was from and what Birmingham was like and this was another step towards divesting himself of his god-like mantle.

Only at the end of this tutorial, which had been conducted at a much less hectic pace, did Arthur offer a neat summary of the lessons that could be drawn from the content of their discussion. His previous habit had been to summarize repeatedly after every few statements. He then assigned them an essay on 'The Nature of Information in Geography', for which this meeting had already provided a strong foundation and again advised them how to organize it.

Our post-tutorial half hour afforded a stimulating discussion. Arthur explained to me that he had operated that day on two principles:
1 Proceed with first year students from something they know and understand (maps), to something less known such as census data. This maintains self-confidence and so secures verbal participation.
2 Give new students something practical to do as this always captures their interest.

Principle one, of proceeding from the known to the unknown is an oft quoted and sensible idea and, like the second principle, lends itself to the small group situation. These were young people, straight from the sixth form, with a competent set of academic skills appropriate to school, but not necessarily to university, and with a history of relations with teachers which might not tally at all with how teachers treat them at university. This transition from sixth form to university is most disorienting and often strips the most healthy and intelligent student of confidence. Some university teachers replicate a sixth form teaching style which eases the problem temporarily, but as the students regain their sense of security, such teaching is no longer felt as suitable, and there is a tendency to rebel or abscond from infantilizing groups. Over a period of several weeks, Arthur successfully weaned these students from one learning model to another.

I was very pleased by Arthur's lack of emotional stress when he realized there was insufficient time that day to take them through census data. 'It will keep', he said. The group's occupation, and its processes too, had this time been given equal emphasis, and some very useful spadework had been done towards the essay. The next item on the agenda could wait for a week; at least the members had now undoubtedly become a group, even though Arthur was still holding on to conventional leadership for much of the time.

The second principle was much more potent than it first appeared. Setting a practical task which only they can carry out is tantamount to transferring authorship of learning to the students themselves. They then undergo the 'Look, I did it myself' euphoria, which strengthens motivation towards new attainments. If they receive predigested learning which they perceive as teacher or institution owned, their motivation towards new attainments will be limited. 'Who owned the learning?' is a question all group teachers need to ask frequently as they mull over their group work at the end of the day.

Tutorial 5

The students were already assembled, when Arthur dashed in waving the *Guardian* front page, showing a picture of two of the department's staff carrying placards at an AUT demonstration. The students eagerly took the paper from him for a closer inspection and chattered excitedly about the previous night's televised interview with one of the other geography academics who also taught them. This gossipy start set the tone for the rest of the tutorial, in which the hierarchical divide between Arthur and his students shrank perceptibly.

He returned essays, and commented on them, this time giving more prominence to common faults and virtues. For the first time, he solicited their own opinion of their work and asked how they saw the main trends in their essay writing — were they improving their writing skills or getting stuck, for example? Amanda looked awkward and uncomfortable but took courage and, blushing, requested some lessons in writing essays, as she had failed to get the hang of it. Amanda usually complained piteously about the inadequacies of the department, when in fact it was she herself who was finding it hard to cope. She had led the group in its displacement activities (blaming the college for all difficulties); but now, as a result of the more co-operative and relaxed atmosphere, she was able to dispense with this defence mechanism and express one of her worries directly. In many groups, students permanently rely on such mechanisms as displacement for personal survival, and the teacher never discovers their underlying anxieties; they do not surface, owing to the lack of cohesiveness in the group. To my delight, Arthur turned to the other students and asked for their help. Vicky had had such lessons in the sixth form and summarized the main headings under which she had been trained. Jane, normally reticent, offered sensible and practical suggestions about structuring, and Laurence laconically (but with secret pride) added his comments too. This participation was vital to the continued cohesion of the group. Had Arthur delivered one of his off-the-cuff mini-lectures in essay writing, the others may well have bcome bored with the tutorial and irritated with Amanda who could, from then on, have the more easily become the scapegoat. Competent group conducting means preventing unwanted process from developing, as well as managing it deftly when it does threaten to override the work. Amanda experienced support and interest from her colleagues and was reassured about her own imagined stupidity and the others benefited from the recognition of their corporate usefulness to one of their members. All the skill and knowledge did not, after all, reside in the tutor alone. Arthur took much more time to allow a thorough discussion of this subject, and waited until all had had their say before summing up and adding one or two pieces of advice of his own. He then described how he and some of his colleagues prepared papers for publication and what a nightmare the re-drafting and amending process was. This was excellent for showing the students that they were not atypical if they filled their waste bins with discarded papers or if they suffered inexplicable creative blocks. After a further exchange of anecdotes related to essays, Arthur teasingly warned them that he was beginning to feel they were ready to read and comment on each other's essays. Everyone grimaced and laughed accepting his tribute to their growing academic maturity, and accepting the peer tutoring suggestion too, though not without anxiety.

Arthur had demonstrated in this matter how a tutor can reduce assessment fears by combining personalized teaching with an honest acknowledgement that work has to be measured in some way. He formed an *alliance* with the students. They did not feel duty bound to appease him with high marks, as if he were a judge. Each of these students were now seeking their own academic level, not Arthur's, and were plainly unafraid of him as a person and authority figure. He told them that whatever their other faults, all the recent essays were packed with individual feelings and opinions, so unlike the thorough but deadened A-level work with which he was often confronted. He admitted his surprise and pleasure that in essay writing they were, on the whole, progressing faster than most other students under the same circumstances. They beamed at this compliment. I was privately amused by his puzzlement. He could not see that their accelerated progress was the result of his improved teaching. In our discussion afterwards he still maintained that fate had been kind in apportioning him a group of especially gratifying students this year!

Two important features of teaching might be noted here; firstly, the reluctance of British teachers to reward students' endeavours with glowing approval, and secondly their taboo on complimenting themselves after an insightful piece of teaching. A positive approach to these two features will bring about attachment feelings in a group which are central to the building and reinforcing of group cohesion, and they should never be dismissed as trivial sentiment. Arthur found no difficulty in praising his students, but later was acutely embarrassed when I tried to persuade him of his improved approach to the group.

Arthur wound down the first half of the tutorial by reminding them that they should not regard their essays as finished and deserving of disposal as soon as they were marked. He drew their attention once again to the fact that disagreements between them could be talked about in the tutorial or individually, and that just because he was their tutor, this did not mean he was automatically right about everything. This repetition by the teacher in a tutorial is a vital if tedious part of the job, for students often fail to 'hear' such reassuring speeches, because their 'hearing' is interfered with by other anxious preoccupations. A tutor must repeat himself to ensure he is heard and properly understood. This is especially true of a dependent group where there is a built in member resistance to taking any autonomous action. Deafness becomes rife as the tutor tries to inveigle the students into independent action.

Arthur circulated census data which he had collected for each of the home areas the students had examined last week. They were keen to investigate facts about their own background further, and the tables were hastily skimmed for pertinent information. Arthur's aims had been to generate an interest in and help them find their way around such complex tabulations, but little effort on his part was needed. The students quickly absorbed the data before them, firing rapid questions at Arthur when they failed to understand a code, or abbreviation, or how the material was organized. They drew upon Arthur as a resource, so as to use his minimal replies as an aid to finding their own route through the census. A stimulating argument developed about the moral, social, economic and political implications of assessing and describing citizens by class. Opinion was divided on this matter. Some felt that a statistical collection of this kind was essential for planning and administrative purposes, and so long as it was not abused citizens could be helped by the census. Others retaliated by insisting that grouping people together in social classes led to prejudice and worse. Arthur spoke occasionally, as leader *in*, not *of*, the group; voicing opinions on his own behalf, rather than acting as a mouthpiece for others, — for though this had been required earlier in the term each student was now well equipped to speak for his or herself. Arthur could safely propound views of his own, without their feeling he was speaking *ex cathedra*.

Showing consideration, Arthur asked what other academic demands were being asked of them at the same time by other staff, and in the light of their answers refrained from setting another essay. Instead he asked them to 'brush up' on their knowledge of general systems theory and to make certain they were clear about the differences between it and systems analysis. He referred them to one or two papers which discussed this distinction. He reminded them too, that it was time physical rather than human geography was studied in the tutorial, and they all groaned, looking disappointed, except for Amanda who cheered up at the prospect of a familiar topic. This good-humoured group groan was evidence of the trusting and affectionate relationship they had with Arthur. He had carefully balanced the themes 'understanding the census' and 'writing good essays' with looking after each separate student's need for contact with himself; while at the same time casting his 'third eye' over all the group as a single whole. He had monitored the ebbs and flows of process, stemmed tides, and tugged at waves to increase their magnitude, as and when the occasion demanded. His verbal input was severely reduced, and his tight control relaxed, so that the group functioned more independently. Conquering the urge to talk so much seemed to be the most trying obstacle for Arthur. The post-group discussion revealed Arthur's refusal to believe that he had beneficially exploited the group process, and also that the work itself, far from being damaged, had been taken further than he had anticipated! It is a common fallacy that intervening in group process (or deliberately desisting from doing so), in order to promote cohesion and engineer preconceived styles of communication might harm the academic work, or at least restrict output. Once this collection of four people had become a group, they managed in a single hour, and with no pressure from Arthur, to teach one member how to write an essay; to offer her compassionate understanding and moral support; to deal with the census; to look at more socially relevant issues thrown up by an investigation of the data; to prepare for the work next week; all this at a leisured pace interspersed with humour.

Arthur had not envisaged there would be time for debate, nor had he bargained for Amananda's problem. However the group completed his agenda and also these two items, on their own. A cohesed, resonating group works very fast indeed and does not need to be driven along by a parental authority figure.

Tutorial 6

Exhibiting great sensitivity to their needs, Arthur asked how they were getting on with the rest of the course. He had been reviewing the departmental timetable and it had seemed to him that they had extremely busy periods, interspersed with slack periods and that this must diverge greatly from their school experience.

I noticed Arthur's singular skill in settling them down each week during the first few minutes; there was always a little friendly preamble before the official work was started. These minutes were used as boundary reinforcers, helping the students into the group from outside, and gradually adapting them to the new secure setting. They always visibly appreciated his concern for their other academic pursuits and it was pleasant to watch a tutor who did not teach as if the boundaries of his own little group were the boundaries of the world. The students enjoyed bringing vignettes of others' lectures, or humorous incidents from other classes, offering both their criticism and praise of the rest of the course. It was as though Arthur was a special teacher among other teachers. They entered the tutorial room much as children come home from school bubbling with news about the day's events that they want to share with an interested parent. In this and the next meeting they brought along pictures, maps, documents and such like from the preceding lecture, and bustled into the room in mid-conversation about them, drawing Arthur into the discussion quite naturally and relaying to him all the gossip they assumed he would be interested to hear.

After these preliminaries Arthur said we must try and work towards some kind of conceptual clarity with regard to general systems theory and systems analysis. He could see they all looked a bit uncertain about it, and so started not by demanding definitions, but by asking each to tell the rest of us how much or little of general systems philosophy had been taught at their school. He confessed he found it a troublesome subject, because seldom did his students speak a 'common language', owing to their different A level subjects, and the type of teaching undergone before they had come to university. They felt better once this shared problem was spoken of and each realized just how patchy their fellow students' knowledge was. By clarifying and refining their hypotheses, asking each other questions and requesting amplification of various points, some limited common understanding was arrived at.

Arthur did not lecture at them or offer ready-made definitions, nor did he fill the gaps in each person's understanding. He enabled them to find satisfaction in helping each other and in putting together the pieces of the puzzle as a team. This leadership behaviour was in great contrast to his style at the beginning of these tutorial sessions. When he did interpose, it was to ask open questions such as: 'Where do you think that leads us?' or 'What might the repercussions be?'. Or, he would say 'So?' or 'Well?', or merely extend a hand or react non verbally to a statement so that the persons speaking felt it incumbent on them to explain themselves better. Slang expressions were used by all and the sprawling or slumping sitting positions showed how much more relaxed the students felt in Arthur's and each others' company. Laurence said 'pass', as if taking part in a TV quiz game, when asked to explain a point, and

everyone laughed. This kind of informality would not have been possible a few weeks ago.

A rather obtuse debate sprang up as to whether general systems
theory was really the key to the universe, but I felt this sudden immer-
sion in intellectualism hid a real uneasiness with the subject, which became manifest when Arthur suggested an essay about it. Just as they
were beginning to enjoy themselves in a rather self-congratulatory way,
the illusion of safety and atmosphere of fun was removed, and they
were faced with unpleasant reality. For the first time in this group, no
one spoke and the atmosphere was thick with tension. Eight seconds into this silence Arthur must have panicked. He said breezily 'never mind,
never mind, — let's go back to human systems as Vicky has been egging
us on to do'. With relief the entire group colluded with Arthur's 'flight'
basic assumption response and co-operated with him in a high-flown
conversation about human systems, — the basic conceptual framework
of general systems theory having not been thoroughly understood by
them all, and the essay problem remaining. I sympathized with Arthur
as this sudden silence had been totally unexpected, but he rescued them
too quickly and did not help them take responsibility for the learning
problem they all shared, which with his support they could have solved.
Immediately following his 'flight' from leadership he paired with Vicky
in animated discourse. This pairing between a teacher and the most
extraverted member of the group is very common in most groups, and
is often an indication that some major group problem connected with
leadership is being avoided. Although the material the two were discussing was very appropriate to the tutorial, none of the others derived any
academic sustenance from it, as they were regaining their composure
after having been so abruptly thrown off balance. They looked unhappy and self-conscious. Resistance reigned and no one was learning
anything; cohesion appeared to have vanished.

Arthur gradually got a grip on the group once more and started to
talk and gesticulate less. He wanted to change this over-anxious over-
active leadership behaviour and discourage monopoly by Vicky; yet to
simply flop back in his chair and ignore her and the rest of the group
did not seem the best way to win their trust or induce feelings of safety.
We had been talking in an anthropological vein, and Arthur, now calm,
swiftly adopted a position that was neither authoritarian, nor passive
and distant. He enthralled us with a brief story about a researcher he
knew who lived with aborigines and studied how they made use of their
primitive local environment, and how they also craftily manipulated the
socio-economic system to safeguard their interests. It was a fascinating
little yarn, ostensibly a first-rate living illustration of systems theory,
but in practice a 'pied-piper' like spell woven to bind his children together into warm kinship. When we talked later, I think he found this
impression of mine rather fanciful, so I asked why he thought he had
done it. 'It just felt right' he replied. Unconsciously he had rapidly

assessed the situation and had come up with a solution which bore his personal stamp. Story-telling is not necessarily recommended to every tutor as a panacea for group emergencies! Each tutor will accumulate his own store of emergency strategies. To use someone else's strategies would not be an expression of genuine concern for the students. What is important here is an accurate diagnosis of the group's process problem. Intuitively, Arthur saw and understood the loss of group cohesion and the reasons for it. He appreciated that when cohesion becomes diluted (though this is not the language he would have used) and when the leader loses control, the group momentarily becomes an unsafe place for its members and strong rather than gentle leadership is temporarily required. He had us sitting in rapt attention, like kids listening to daddy's bed-time story, and soon bonhomie crept back, as we all united through our leader! Arthur conducted the rest of the meeting with renewed confidence and dropped this group-to-tutor model of operation. This episode had lasted about seven minutes, after which we returned to our original struggle to understand general systems theory.

Amanda really could not grasp the essentials of the theory, and was quite upset about it. Again the others helped her out good naturedly, despite growing impatience with her stubborn resistance to the concept of a system. I am sure that a teacher in an individual tutorial would have despaired, but between Arthur and the group, the general idea finally percolated through to Amanda and everyone looked pleased with themselves. Bashfully Amanda smiled her gratitude. This 'let's-help-Amanda' campaign would never have got off the ground in the earlier climate of that session which was one of tension followed by fight-flight, then pairing. Arthur's speedy first-aid had made this new learning of Amanda's possible. Had the earlier climate continued she could have been a serious casualty.

Arthur filled the last 10 minutes working out with them how to structure the last three tutorials before Christmas. He unashamedly put in his own bid and stated clearly what he felt the students ought to cover by Christmas; they then announced the areas they felt needed further scrutiny. By negotiation a compromise was reached as there was insufficient time to meet everyone's demands.

This was an instructive session, a good example of preventive group tutoring. It might be worthwhile to contemplate what might have happened had this tutorial been taken by an ineffective tutor. I have given an edited account only of what occurred, so the reader is asked to trust my judgment. Laurence might well have become petulant, lazy and sullen, which was his stock response to stress; or, had Arthur opted for passive leadership during the 'crisis', Laurence might have seized the authority in the group, only to have felt miserable and guilty later when and if Arthur had regained control. Amanda might have been rejected, and her fears of academic inadequacy confirmed, possibly leading to depression and absenteeism. Jane might well have withdrawn into her shell, never to have emerged. Vicky, always wanting to hurry the pace, might have become fractious and rebellious. In those circumstances the situation would have become chaotic within a few weeks. As it was, Arthur prevented anything like this nightmare happening!

Tutorial 7

This was straightforward, with little resistance observable. A good deal of solid academic work (central place theory and rank size rule) was accomplished, and Arthur responded to a request for information and advice about what to study in the holidays, and how to prepare for next term's work. Everyone was in good spirits. Written essays on systems theory were exchanged among the students, ready for group discussion the following week. Arthur had read them all, but preferred to keep his counsel till he had heard their views on one another's efforts. Arthur was conscious throughout that the end of term drew nigh. He took pains to assist each one integrate their first term's experiences, through contact with him and each other. He also firmly persisted in asking them to check whether they had understood the rationale behind the many projects, essays, and field-work they had been assigned by other tutors. They gave him a good deal of feedback about other course constituents, and their impressions of the comparative value of each. In the tutorial environment it was easy for them to share their criticisms and assessments of the whole course, as Arthur was more intimately known to them than any other teacher.

This constant evaluation of the entire course, through reports from all students, in all the groups, is another vital function of the tutorial. Arthur and his colleagues (providing they saw their tutorial groups from a similar perspective) would be able to feed back to one another their own speculations as to how the course structure and content was being received by students, as well as to relay the students own views about the multiple teaching methods currently practised. Such staff feedback could cause offence and wounded pride unless it was granted to each other in an atmosphere of mutual respect and personal trust. In chapter 13 readers will see how delicate and time-consuming the building of such a supportive interpersonal staff web can be. It is not a simple matter of arranging a staff meeting; many of these meetings are ineffective because little of real import is shared, as people are afraid to give or receive honest opinions on sensitive teaching matters. A good many teaching difficulties turn out to be personal issues for the tutor. These can only be exchanged in a staff meeting if there *is* genuine trust between teachers.

The tutorial is only one small social system, interlocking with several other teaching and learning systems; the 'mother' system of the department is nourished by frequent exchanges between the leaders of these academic sub systems. In managing tutorials the tutor should never forget that this little group is related to, affects and is affected by, positively or adversely, the main departmental system to which it belongs. The tutors need tutorials about tutorials with each other, if they are to improve their own skills and enrich the course content.

Tutorial 8

This was the penultimate meeting of the term, (although no 'work' was to take place in the final tutorial as Arthur was planning to surprise the students with Christmas punch!) Sadly, it was my last visit to the group, as I had another professional engagement the following week.

Arthur suggested that the students introduce one another's essays by making a short 'public' critique, in clockwise rotation. He seemed a little on edge, as if afraid things might get out of hand, and offered a good deal of guidance about how to gauge the content, style, presentation of the written work they were evaluating. Eventually, he allowed them to start and they each gave a discerning and stringent analysis of the others' work. The criticism was franker and more penetrating than I had ever heard from Arthur, who though honest, always displayed great tact and delicacy when recommending improvements. The students took no such pains with each other, but though extremely strict their criticisms were neither brutal nor malicious. I was, and I suspected Arthur too, astonished at their ruthless exposure of their colleagues' weaknesses, yet gratified that such honesty was possible. Although eager to proffer their opinions, they nonetheless reverted to addressing the leader in this rather tense climate, and referring to their colleagues as 'he' or 'she' being unable at first to tackle the object of their criticisms directly. Arthur did not point out this evasion, but nonetheless each person quickly began defending their own essays, explaining why they had written them in the way they had. The critic would then protest the validity of his or her assessment, while the one criticized, including quiet Jane, persevered in hot rejection of some of the negative remarks. It was interesting to note that they were never able, either in or outside of the tutorial, to fight back with Arthur partly because it was impossible to get angry with such a nice, fair discerning person. At least sometimes they must have longed to argue with him, as they were now doing with their fellow students. Arthur appeared a little alarmed and kept making nervous reassuring jokes; refereeing a lot, as if he wanted to guarantee fair play for all. They mostly ignored his helpful overtures, so impassioned were they. Some of the criticisms were greeted as fair and acceptable, others were smartly repudiated. No one was vulnerable during this exchange and I was pleased to see Jane and Amanda holding their own in this tussle, without waiting for Arthur to rescue them from their distress. However, Arthur was not enjoying himself nearly so much as I was, and found it unacceptable to delegate peace-keeping functions to the group. He continued to see his relationship to the group in a paternal manner, as if the students still languished helplessly in the early dependent phase. I felt they were now in a position to tolerate this cross fire in the group, but Arthur did not altogether agree, when we talked it through later.

Contemporaneously with these tutorials Arthur was attending my teaching effectiveness seminar (see chapter 13), in which competitiveness between the participants and power sharing was currently proving painful for all involved. I wondered whether some of Arthur's over-protectiveness of these students was linked with his own personal intolerance of, or distaste for, competitive or power seeking impulses in himself. Many teachers accurately predict future instances of student discomfort with their leadership role. These instances, whether associated with group hostility, depression, eroticism, power struggles or other features, are clues about unresolved personal areas in the tutor's life which might profit from private inspection. In certain cases such 'blind spots' can deeply affect teaching. No one can declare with absolute certainty that I was over-optimistic about this group, or that Arthur was wrong to play down the group conflict so as to assuage students' alleged fear of attack. However, the desirability of tutors' insight into their own personal make-up remains a fundamental principle of good teaching especially in groups.

The students moved on to argue among themselves about the best essay technique. No longer was Arthur expected to bestow handy hints upon receptive compliant freshers; now they instructed each other, or queried one another's methods. When Arthur gave his view they found something to disagree with in that too! This was a very adult-to-adult challenging session, rather like heated political quarrels that happen frequently between great friends of different persuasions.

Towards the end calmness descended and the group fell to musing about groups in general. Various members found themselves comparing their own behaviour and academic input in the several seminars and classes they were obliged to attend and assessing the various sorts of teaching they had witnessed. Jane said she was glad that at last she could state openly how, even in this informal group, she felt intimidated. No one rebuked her for this as they understood her feelings only too well. But how many students in other groups would dare to say this kind of thing? How many cloak their feelings of inferiority in silence, or even absence? In this group, however, each of these students explained how their contributions to different teaching groups varied; they might be silent in one, talkative in another; sometimes they felt tense and anxious, while in other groups they became excited — and in others they were totally bored.

This was a useful juncture for including me in the conversation, and Arthur suggested they might like to spend one tutorial with me next term to ask me about my observations and impressions. They all agreed that they were curious about me, and would like to know exactly what

165

I had been up to throughout the term. (We did in fact meet the following term and reminisced enjoyably.)

Conclusions

This tutorial was the central pivot of the first year course, and provided a much needed opportunity for making the psychological and academic transition from school to university, in manageable degrees. Firstly, the tutorial was analogous to a small supportive family, in that it created in the students a sense of belonging, while they adjusted to the large new department, many staff, and the unfamiliar institutional attitude to study. (A good many students withdraw from university at the end of this first term as a result of inadequate negotiation of this transitional process, and this is more likely where there are no small group tutorials. An individual tutoring system is better than no provision at all, but almost all freshers are too afraid to visit an unknown tutor privately, to shamefully confess that they cannot adjust to university life.) Secondly, in these tutorials, students were confronted with the task of examining and questioning the fundamentals of the subject; its philosophy, theory, political and social remifications, its language, and its basic premises. This foundation would equip them with the confidence to decline allegiance to antiquated, or reified knowledge, and assist them root out prejudice and faulty constructs, replacing them with a more personally truthful version of the facts. The learning they underwent was in the end self-directed. In Geography as with most other disciplines, new knowledge quickly lapses into obselescence, and teachers will not always be on hand to divulge the latest research findings. This tutorial paved the way for self-propelled study. Thirdly, Arthur taught them how to become productive group members, so they would be able to take advantage of new group teaching situations. Perhaps they would even model themselves on him a little, when they themselves were allocated a position of leadership!

I hope that my report proves the efficacy of study skills training when it is practised by a tutor who cultivates a conducive atmosphere, and has a good relationship with all his students. For example, Arthur's intimate acquaintance with the academic subject, and long experience in assessing students' work qualifies him more than any centralized counsellor or psychologist, to free his students from the hamstrings of school learning and study habits which are now outmoded. A pre-packaged skill kit on how to pass exams, handed out by a central authority figure to whom the students have little or no attachment, is no substitute for good departmental tutoring which includes help with study skills.

Despite the bleak weather, characterized by the usual November flu epidemic, there was not one absentee and no lateness. This was not fortuitous; rather, it expressed the magnetism that the group exerted for its members, thanks to a competent tutor.

Finally, I felt much closer to Arthur at the end of the sessions, even though we had not once discussed our private lives, or socialized outside the group owing to pressures of time. Our transactions had been purely professional, as are tutors' with their students, and yet should I ever need a friend to confide in, I would have no hesitation in contacting Arthur. I am certain that the four students felt exactly the same, and would always be sure that there was someone trustworthy to whom they could turn in time of need over the following three years. Arthur had not counselled or interviewed any of them, and had used no institutional procedures or devices to exhort them to confide in him. He had had no training in therapy, psychology or counselling and had never once stepped out of his role as tutor. He ably demonstrated that proper tutoring eliminates the need for amateur psychiatrists and armchair counsellors. However, the tutoring function is a complex one and it requires insight and experience brought about by regular consultation with colleagues. (See Chapter 13.)

Chapter 11

A term of seminars for students with consultant-observer

Jack invited me to join part of a rural geography seminar programme, which was to run for five sessions between Christmas and Easter. During that term he also continued to attend the teaching effectiveness group reported in chapter 13. Lest readers feel that imitation of these combined events in their own institutions is prohibited by time constraints, let me assure them that all my in-service training projects at University College were conducted under great pressure and with rather frantic preparation. Jack for instance had an extraordinarily heavy teaching load, and was engaged in research of his own. I was running a counselling service for students single-handed, during one of the busiest periods of the year. Both of us accorded the highest priority to our joint venture and so sacrificed other activities to make time available, though conditions were far from ideal. Most of our practical arrangements, as well as advance discussions concerning the purpose of the venture, were planned and effected through the internal mail, and via telephone messages; post group reviews were held in corridors or over hasty cups of coffee, for we were intent on finding at least one opportunity to share our impressions after each session. I would not wish to mislead the reader into any assumptions that these case studies arose from a carefully pre-organized overall research project, or that any special allowances were made for the tutors involved. With sufficient motivation, and a consultant or college counsellor experienced in group work, one department can gain tremendous benefit from taking a little time each week to study their several groups, including their own staff group. Readers need not feel too disheartened by the ubiquitous scarcity of people and shortage of time. With effort and good will, as my colleagues have shown, some learning about group tutoring can be acquired despite a full timetable. Just the same, all colleges should benefit from an evaluation of their teaching standards and an estimation of resources required for their remedy and/or improvement.

I asked Jack to let me have some background information to the seminars, and to try and explain what he was aiming to achieve; this would enable me to make some sense of his subsequent conductorship when I observed the five meetings. We were unable to get together face-to-face, but a note duly arrived, showing clearly Jack's well thought out aims and objectives for the seminars.

'For each session two students will present very brief reports on their personal research topic and two other people will introduce the discussion which (usually) broadens out. The idea of the seminars is as follows:

(1) to overcome the fact that 48-50 people do the course and would otherwise only have lectures;
(2) to let them talk to me and to each other in a semi-formal, but less 'pressured' atmosphere;
(3) to ensure that they *do* some personal work (it counts for 50 per cent of the grade);
(4) to enable me to advise on particular issues, and for each participant to share information and common sense.

It has to be rather structured, since there is a fairly precise programme of work to get through'.

Each day a different sub group of the course members met with Jack for a series of five seminars, so that in all he led five seminar groupings each week for the duration of the autumn term. I was to sit in on only one of these groupings for five consecutive weeks. Jack gave me identical documentation to that which the students had received. There was a detailed 'map' of the meetings to come; who would present material or lead discussion on which day and on which topic; and a detailed handout describing exactly how term papers should be presented — length, binding, title, layout, number of copies, arrangement of footnotes and references etc. At the end of the term they were to write a paper to conform with these regulations. The main academic function of the seminar was to assist them to bring this paper to fruition. Each person was asked to present an early draft of their ideas, and themes they hoped to work on in more detail for the final submission. In fact, almost all the students offered an over-long, almost finished essay during the seminars. After putting in so much work prior to their 'public' performance, the realization that drastic revisions or changes in the direction of their argument might be needed must have been demoralizing for them.

In the main, the membership consisted of four men and three women, all second or third year, Jack and myself. They knew one another vaguely through having shared lectures and other groupings, but this was the first time they had met in this particular constellation. They knew Jack as someone who had lectured to them, and as a personality in the department, but none of them were on intimate terms with him. This proved significant later on, as the problems he was to meet in future weeks were not reproduced in other seminars of the same course unit where students knew him better, and did not exhibit evidence of extreme fantasies about his personality. Jack's serious and conscientious approach was easily discernible, and these students were to read much more into the personality traits he displayed than was warranted. Whether their suppositions concerning his character were correct, no one but Jack perhaps, could say. The point I am making however, is that students do react in very subjective ways to the self-presentation of a group leader with whom they are not already closely acquainted. Such group perceptions, whether correct or erroneous affect the group process; this in turn sometimes obstructs work which in other circumstances the students would be competent to deal with.

Session 1

The first session started with Jack ensuring that he had attached all the right names to the right people and saying he hoped that they would not regard him as the fount of wisdom, but would feel free to discuss all issues openly. I was surprised at how relaxed everyone appeared, contrary to the tense climate I usually expect to observe in a new group. We had been asked to abandon our room right at the start, as it was double-booked. We then migrated to the professor's room, settled ourselves round his table in rather cramped circumstances, only to have him return unexpectedly with a guest. We then had to remove ourselves once more. The students accepted all this philosophically, and trailed about after Jack until new premises were found. I realized that the relaxed atmosphere had much connection with Jack's over-protective, highly structured organization. Throughout the early meetings, everything seemed so pre-ordained that the little community was at all times passive, calm and accepting. There was so much safety in the group that it often became soporific. Jack always came up with answers, a reference, a bit of background knowledge, despite his insistence that he was no expert. One of my general impressions was that the students felt they had no role to play except reading their papers, or dutifully asking a question if it were their turn that week 'to lead discussion'.

The first member who presented a paper read an erudite, witty piece on landscape gardening, which Jack told me later was not appropriate to this course, though it had been packed with lots of good quality information. No one laughed at the jokes and quotations; the material was over-prepared and too long (22 minutes!); his colleagues appeared to listen politely to his quite animated performance. No one took notes, save Jack, and occasionally people's attention wandered. *There was no eye contact between anyone throughout*, although the presenter sought to elicit it, and spoke faster and with more urgency each time he failed. Is this one reason why so many students presenting seminar papers become so fearful of 'performance'? Verbal participation is denied the audience for a long time and they tend to respond with social hibernation; the 'performer' consequently feels ignored, apologetic and embarrassed. For the duration of the speech, I felt as if the group as a corporate identity had disappeared. It reappeared later, when the leader reinstated himself and interaction became permissible; it was as if the ritual had been observed, and it was now safe to return to life! The boredom lay not so much with the subject – they all discussed that pertinently enough; it seemed rather that boredom resulted from being isolated on seven different 'islands' without communication for the 22 minutes, which was a third of the seminar time! There was not even any mischievous behaviour (doodling, note passing, surreptitious eating, for example). I suspect this was due to the enormous respect for Jack's earnestness, and his high academic reputation. Were the teacher less in control or less respected, I am sure there would have been giggles and other such behaviours occuring as a way of breaking the monotony.

Perhaps the student could have made four main points, and discussed each in turn, with his peers, so as to involve them at regular intervals? 40 out of the total 60 minutes were used in presentation, for the second presenter repeated the monologic pattern of the first! This left Jack with 10 minutes to conduct two post-presentation discussions; a considerable waste of his talents, as I knew him to be adept at handling group discussion. I found several questions arising unbidden in my mind, as I sat with those students during that first meeting. In other seminars, were they perhaps asked for completed pieces of work and had they assumed that this was the same kind of group? This was hard to believe, as Jack's detailed preparation for the students included instructions on this matter. Did they want to put on a 'good show' before comrades, feeling that a declaration of weakness or asking for academic help was shameful, or was it that Jack must be impressed at all costs? Ought the seminar time to be increased to one-and-a-half hours so as to create more time for discussion? Perhaps length of presentation could be cut, or abandoned all together and papers pre-circulated instead? Is it fair to expect students to identify with and enthuse over a special topic which has been thoroughly researched only by the presenter? No wonder he was left to his own devices when offering his material; the data was in no way viewed as shared property – how then could discussion of it be deemed a shared responsibility? As these thoughts preoccupied me, Jack warmly thanked the students who had read out their essays. This reinforcing of students' self-esteem and recognition of their efforts is a straightforward but vital aspect of group tutorship, especially when there is little positive feedback from fellow group members who are bogged down in prevailing resistance.

Jack managed well what little discussion arose after the first presentation. He explained to the student in a direct manner the inappropriateness of his work, whilst enthusing over its fascinating content. He criticized the work, without making it appear a judgement on the person, or the person's values. He made an alliance with the student and together they focused on the piece of work to try and improve it. It was obvious that Jack wanted a high grading for the student as much as did the student himself. Afterwards in the general discussion, Jack spoke little, except where an essential piece of information needed to be given, and after it became clear no one else was going to provide it. He used not his own but their own previously expressed ideas, however muddled, to draw their attention to this new data, with such remarks as 'Coming back to Jane's point . . .', 'Following what John said . . .', 'The converse of Anne's proposal suggests . . .' He provoked them into thinking through issues from their own base of knowledge, not his. This was excellent training for future situations, when they would have to think for themselves, without a handy tutor always around to bail them out with his wisdom. He began to address the group-as-a-whole (strengthening the *we* corner of the TCI triangle) when dyadic communications looked as if they might take over. 'How would you (the group) have improved upon this presentation?' he asked, after ensuring he had first bolstered the young man's esteem enough for him to withstand colleagues' criticisms. Back came the hesitant replies: 'I would strengthen that introduction a bit, I think', and 'I would sort of tighten it up, throw out some of the literary allusions, get it back to rural geography, rather than historical geography, which is a separate course, nothing to do with us'. Jack enabled them to experiment with helping one another, by distancing himself enough to view the group as a single social unit capable of 'team' functioning. In some respects this session seemed too good to be true; it seemed to be running like clockwork, and as yet I could not understand my discomfort. Thinking about it afterwards I realized that some of my unease had been connected with the 'cultural conditioning' these students appeared to have undergone. As has already been stated there were to be two presentations. Both were over-long. They represented individuals' special interests, with which other group members had been plainly out of touch; no one had challenged the format, even indirectly. These were quite senior students, no one having experienced less than one-and-a-half years in the department, and some considerably more time than that. It did not seem to occur to them that there might be alternative ways of carrying out their business together.

After exactly 10 minutes discussion of the first paper (Jack had put his watch on the table) he asked the second student to make her presentation. Before she began, he asked the first student to come and see him for some extra individual tuition, so as to tie up some of the loose ends which time did not allow in the seminar. He accepted that a single seminar session could not cope with everything but was sufficiently generous to offer complementary support where needed. This could also have the effect of making students feel their work was expected to be perfect and all-encompassing, that impossible standards were being set. He did not follow up the first student's worries, for if he had, he would have denied Anne her full 20 minute quota. It was this structural rigidity which, though based on a sound rationale, was making me feel uneasy. No negotiation of boundaries seemed possible and predictability seemed to be the keynote. I decided to wait and see if future meetings produced the same ultra safe but unexciting climate. Anne gave a lively account of tourism on farms, which was greeted with dutiful responses in the 10-minute period allocated for discussion. I was astonished at the manner in which the discussion imitated Jack's own 'editorial' style! Careful weighing of one stance versus another, factual, analytic, objective, evaluative. (In chapter 12, I show how another seminar group takes on the characteristics of their tutor in a similar way.) In the middle of this brief discussion, after one of Jack's overtures to the group-as-a-whole, Joe voiced a mild disagreement in connection with Anne's paper, claiming that she had said such-and-such, but would it not have been better if she had looked at it in such-and-such a light? Jack noticed that Anne's posture suggested she was defensively withdrawing, but instead of answering for her and referring to her in the third person as Joe had done, he gestured towards her with an expression of interest and concern on his face. Granted this permission and support from the leader she replied to her critic. Thereafter all questions about the topic were addressed to her, rather than Jack, and her confidence grew as she dealt with each. Jack looked on, remaining passive but far from uninvolved. This small gesture to Anne from Jack meant a great deal and changed the group from group-to-leader functioning to member-to-member operation. When the questioning of Anne stopped, a discussion between individuals ensued and Jack faded from the group picture for a few minutes. Sadly, and this was to be the pattern of all the meetings, just as cohesion and group authority at last gained prominence time was up and we had to end.

After this meeting I talked with Jack, who, like so many other tutors I know, failed to congratulate himself on those subtle and crucial qualities of leadership which had assisted him in managing the group process. (For example, the gesture towards Anne, which was an excellent example of decrescendo leadership.) His main criteria for assessing the success of the seminar was the degree to which he had succeeded in helping them upgrade their papers. My impression was that these students were over-conscientious, to the point of feeling obliged to identify with Jack's academic earnestness (exemplified by their careful, very detailed papers). Jack was far too strict with himself about the 'results' he felt he ought to be getting from his students. If a little more of the charm and humour that he expressed in other settings were injected into the seminar, the atmosphere might be freed sufficiently for heated debate, and intellectual play might evolve, rather than the polite no-conflict discussion I had just witnessed. I fully agreed with Jack's conviction that extra security measures, firm boundaries and clear procedures are vital for a short life group, if members are to get down to work quickly without too much time-wasting preamble. I wondered though if perhaps this important principle had been adopted too rigidly, and whether its relaxation might improve the climate and enliven the discussion, thus increasing learning potential.

Session 2

(Is not reported as the group processes were much the same as in session 1.)

Session 3

Five students were present plus Jack and myself, totalling four men and three women. I should like to digress here, to remark upon the relevance of this composition for group discussion. The group had an ideal size and a balanced sex ratio for social interaction: seven or eight people usually constitute a group intimate enough for sharing and risk taking, but large enough for people to hide in from time to time. It is populated enough for participants to select allies; members can retain a sense of personal identity, yet feel they belong to a unit which does not swamp them. This composition is conducive to the rapid establishing of a communication and feedback network, other process factors being equal. Group size is a significant variable in determining group development; there is no 'magic number' which guarantees success but the size must be considered by the leader in relation to the goals he espouses for his group; the goals or size may need adjustment before the group ever meets.

Jack was pleased to announce that he had been able to find us a regularly available room. Chairs with detachable swivel table-tops were dragged from their rows, at his request, and arranged in a semi-circle. He sat in the center of the gap, facing the arc. I was pleased at the giggles and jokes which accompanied the furniture moving and the Chaplinesque clowning with the table-tops. The re-arranging of the furniture permitted laughter in the group. Students took the opportunity to weigh up one another's personalities via shared amusement. They were beginning to test out their previously distanced images of one another against reality. (The introduction of humour into a group at an appropriate point in its development is an essential tutoring skill.) This release lasted two-and-a-half minutes.

Solemnity, reduction of eye contact and withdrawn body posture started, while private signalling ceased the moment the first presenter opened her folder to read. Once more there was no possibility for interaction during the ritualized performance; the student looked at no one, did not pause once, and never attempted to speak extempore. We passively waited until, cheeks flaming, she completed her self-conscious task. She gave us a detailed and well-prepared lecture on tied cottages, but she had investigated the topic so fully that there seemed little for us to add. Jack was forced to ask her to amplify and invited her to consider other detailed aspects; tedious silences were thus avoided. This was a long 10 minutes indeed! Leader and presenter were left to pair, and the other students appeared very comfortable with this state of affairs as no one seemed to have any competing ideas to offer. I had the distinct impression that they felt all knowledge of the topic resided in the heads of Jack and the presenting student, so that there was no point in joining in the discussion. When Jack rather desperately tried to stimulate their interest by asking questions, they offered dutiful and minimal replies before again retreating into their audience role. The student reading received none of the special advantages normally available in a group; she found herself in the same situation as that of an individual tutorial. She had been set a task by her tutor, had thoroughly prepared it, had presented it and then had discussed it with him. No doubt some benefit as well as embarrassment accrued to her from this exchange with Jack, but in essence this was not a group experience for her at all. Group potential had been wasted. I was by now convinced that the main difficulty was this prescribed period of presentation which choked any possibility of interpersonal contact, particularly as the topic for the day represented the real interest of only one member.

The second presenter for that occasion was unable to attend. The brief discussion of the previous paper dwindled away, but there was still half-an-hour seminar time left. Later Jack explained to me (showing his sensitivity to student needs) that to close the seminar there and then would have been perfectly legitimate, but he had not wanted the students to feel personally rejected, as if he only valued their presence when they were slaving away at academic work. He attempted to create a more informal ambiance by asking them to comment on their other assignments and to say what they felt about the lectures they had been given, what their opinion was of the course structure as well as its detailed content. Interestingly, this deviation from the usual seminar routine threw the members into some confusion and ambivalence. They were reluctant to answer his queries yet were noticeably interested in what he was saying and looked at each other to see who would dare voice an authentic opinion. One or two ventured critical remarks and quickly checked them; others looked properly alert for the first time, as if they wished very much to speak, but opted for silence nevertheless. This was not a bored or angry silence, but a silence which I saw as a solution to a focal conflict. Participants wanted to discuss and criticize the course. They knew Jack whom they revered to have a huge personal investment in the course and feared if they gave license to their wish to criticize, their leader would be too vulnerable to withstand the attacks. Jack said repeatedly, 'I welcome criticism', 'I won't be offended', 'I can't be hurt', which exerted the exact opposite effect to the one intended; unfortunately these remarks seemed to convince them that any real challenge would wound him terribly. He was as good as his word, in that all the hesitant and very slight criticisms made, he welcomed and considered, humbly and patiently justifying the reasons why the course was so arranged. For instance, he told us that the written material and lectures he used were altered regularly as he gained more experience and knowledge, and because he did not want to regurgitate the same old stuff year after year. Some of the group members looked a little embarrassed or guilty at his rather apologetic and self-justifying tone.

To lighten the proceedings I imagine, one student asked his opinion of a book, which Jack, who is very well versed in his subject's literature, dismissed as profitable only for novices. There was once again embarrassment all round when it became apparent that the book had been recommended by Jack's senior colleague. Instead of sticking to his viewpoint, (thus challenging a senior colleague's opinion) Jack tried to undo what he saw as 'damage' by qualifying his earlier quite definite statement. We all laughed nervously at his attempts to rationalize away his *faux pas*, but he had confirmed the image he sometimes projected, of a rational sensitive man unwilling to attack anyone, or involve himself in heated conflict. This prevented his group from exercising any strong feeling, or confronting authority either. They saw him, probably, as an introspective vulnerable young academic dedicated to his work, and I sensed a shared wish in the group to 'look after' him. Pranks and rebellious behaviour was eradicated and only behaviour guaranteed not to upset Jack's careful organization was allowed. But suddenly here was Jack inviting them to confront him! The conflicting wish to speak out versus the wish to be silent for fear of hurting him was almost palpable. In our discussion afterwards Jack said he had felt it too. As a tutor it is essential not to be too 'good' and to let oneself be seen as fallible; it is vital to have one's own biases, blind-spots, off-days, bad tempers, a sense of humour and to be ready to break all the rules occasionally. Jack was a little too saintly and therefore difficult for students to fight with or model themselves on. Superficially they adopted his group style, but this was owing to a focal conflict solution not a genuine identification with the leader – it was resistance masquerading as resonance. The student who had shown most courage in airing negative views approached Jack, on leaving the session, and apologized for his criticisms, (which had been exceedingly mild) assuring Jack (in Jack's own verbal style) that despite his nasty remarks about the course he knew he had no better alternative to offer so he really had no right to complain. I felt this young man spoke not only for himself but also on behalf of the entire group. He seemed truly afraid that he had damaged Jack, who reassured him all the way along the corridor that, on the contrary, the negative comments had been valued and welcomed. Perhaps if Jack had been less reasonable, and had fought the objections and challenges (such as they were) instead of baring his breast to the students' critical arrows, they would not have felt the need to protect him.

There is another valuable lesson to be learned from this instructive session. Looking again at the first half of the meeting it is evident that all the positive, reassuring, information-giving functions were fulfilled by Jack, to and for the presenter, and a little later to the group-as-a-whole. This left any negative expressions to the members, and rather than be the 'bad' counterpart to his 'good' leadership, they usually preferred to keep silent. They must have felt somewhat superfluous, as all the emotional and academic nourishment was *actually supplied by Jack*, although he appeared to be asking them to supply this. If Jack could have allowed himself to be less perfect, more negative in his attitude, then the students could have seized some of the positive, supportive group functions. The security of knowing they could be helpful to each other would make it safe to then complain to the leader and demand changes. This polarization and allocation of 'good' and 'bad' functions to different factions is dangerous for the group's continued survival as an integrated system. The more common picture of polarization is found in a group where the teacher is allocated all the initial disciplinary functions, and the students monopolize and mobilize supportive and rebellious ones, using them to herd members together against 'the tyrant' leader or the 'establishment' for which he is an emblem. But in the case of the seminar described above, Jack was the 'good guy'. He was too perfectionist to allow himself to be seen as 'bad' — academically ignorant, angry, in disagreement with anyone, or standing up to authority — as in the case of his senior colleague's recommended book. All his and all their negative feelings were suppressed beneath a facade of collaboration.

Session 4

This meeting proceeded along much the same course as before: I say this to indicate to the reader that none of my conclusions were made as hastily as the earlier part of the chapter might suggest. Jack had given much thought to our post group conversations and was trying to show a more definite side of his personality; his contributions were increasingly colourful and opinionated. The presentation ritual, however, was retained. During a long speech I found myself drifting into a reverie. A poor student had invested hours of work in writing the paper he now read aloud, but none of us seemed able to concentrate; we all stared out of the window stultified by the group process. There was desultory discussion after the presentation, but no contentious statements were made and time passed slowly. The *required* relationship was one of 'keeping the peace', to *avoid* any conflict, debate or high feeling. This would circumvent one or two, or both, the following *calamities*. First, that Jack would crumple psychologically in response to any defiance; or second, that any conflict or argument with him or each other would result in their personal defeat and humiliation. (For Jack seemed to know it all and have an answer or 'ah but' for any comment, so what was the point?)

Later on in this session, an important piece of displacement took place, when Jack made suggestions for the two papers' improvements. He indicated that his criticisms were designed to help the students meet the demands of the external examiner. He thus displaced unwanted critical aspects of his own personality on to the 'bad' examiner. In this way he remained 'pure' and silenced any incipient opposition, for who can fight with a faceless, distant external examiner? Jack unsuccessfully tried to stir up controversial issues by listing some of them but as *he* took no stand on any of them, the students did not either. If he were to revive this group (which was rather dull, but had promise, and after all the standard of work was undoubtedly high), I felt that the introduction of conflict, *sanctioned and modelled by the leader* was urgently required. If, in similar circumstances, such first aid measures should daunt the tutor-reader, he might profitably reflect upon his private feelings about conflict and authority. If he himself cannot confront authority or endure conflict, then his group teaching will certainly have been affected.

Session 5

This was a most rewarding session for me, as consultant. Jack was drawing upon all the precepts we had discussed as a result of sharing our feelings and observations about the meetings. He was implementing all the principles of good group tutorship. Both presenters kept within 12 minutes, which created much more discussion time and this made an enormous difference. Jack redeemed the group as much as he could: he spoke less, tolerated silences better, took a stand on academic issues, and related all the specialized topics that each had presented over the weeks to each other — forming a common *academic* matrix, in which it became possible for the students to experience a *social* zone rather than each individual inhabiting separate space within the group. He made them see they were neither academically nor personally isolated from each other; their topics had common qualities. This brought them a little closer together and the atmosphere improved slightly. Not a great deal could be changed at this stage as it is harder to stimulate and change a fixed culture than to build a fresh one in a new group. Jack could not be expected to reverse an entrenched position in one session. Nevertheless, there was a distinct improvement.

Treated this way for another five sessions, the group would have really come to life. In this session, more questions were being asked of the presenters and talk between students occurred, (though always in twosomes with the others watching, as if this new student-student dyad were imitating the earlier student-tutor dyad). During the seminar, (which still ran along pre-ordained lines which the students passively accepted) three minor incidents convinced me there was real potential for a cohesive group. Firstly, their chatter continued when Jack came in, because he joined in the leg pulling of one student who arrived each week in a suit and waistcoat, having attended job interviews. Snow had fallen heavily that morning and we all commented on this too. The sense of belonging was uppermost, and it included Jack. However, we lost this group cohesiveness as soon as the presentation started. Secondly, a student from a neighbouring room crept in to borrow a chair halfway through the first presentation. His furtive posture was comical; immediately there was interest, eye contact and much discreet signalling between group members. Thirdly, one of the seminar participants arrived late as trains were snowbound and this provided a welcome distraction while we found him a seat, helped him off with wet clothes, and found somewhere to deposit his squash gear. Jack welcomed him and gave us time to settle him, a service which we rendered as a group amid conspiratorial smiles at the secret enjoyment of the disruption. The group seemed far from despair; it only needed a small stimulus for it to become alive. The group's inflexible structure was the main impediment to cohesion, rather than individual personalities; given the right environment they seemed to get on very well together. Jack was a caring and relatively informal figure, willing and eager for contact in the group, but he too seemed inhibited by the format he had designed.

During the last 15 minutes Jack displayed splendid teaching ability and capacity for change of style. He invited the students to suggest how the seminar might be improved. (This was the only seminar they were currently involved in.) On this occasion he was not apologetic nor was he eager to defend himself. For the first time in five weeks they discussed an issue with each other and the tutor in a non dyadic fashion! Between them they made the following points, which I have summarized. These confirmed Jack's and my appraisal of what had been going on over the weeks.

1 Could we have advance photocopies of one another's presentations, which should be shorter? To listen, absorb and at the same time comment on new material is asking rather a lot of us.
2 A major problem (strong agreement here) is that the presenter knows his material and has researched the subject assiduously. We, the listeners, have not so who are we then to criticize? If we do, the presenter rightly feels that the criticism is founded on ignorance, and if we knew and had read what he had, then we would see things his way too. In other words we doubt that value of dealing with the group's academic work in this manner.
3 (Here, apparently, was a contrasting view to the second point.) Some of us appreciate the *general* feedback when we present work, but not the questioning by colleagues who have not studied the material. By general feedback, we mean the raising of wider social, economic and

philosophical issues concerning the topic. (I guessed that what they were really saying was that specific peer criticism is polite and well-meaning, but useless in terms of improving grades; it was Jack with his knowledge of the exam marking system who could give useful hints as he was the only person to have made the general remarks which were so appreciated. This clarified for me how the dyadic interactions between Jack and the presenters had been constantly reinforced, and why it had been so hard for him to break this pattern. He had been subjected to immense pressure from the presenters to operate like this, for academic as well as psychological reasons! The group's occupation had combined with its process to force him into unwanted leadership behaviour. The students had no belief in their ability to derive help from one another. That each had conducted his researches alone suggests, sadly, that this was a correct perception.)

4 We would like to know how previous years' students felt about your seminar. (I felt the real question behind this statement was, 'How honest can we be with you — can you take criticism after all?') Jack in reply to this question said, 'I don't know — their academic work was always good, so I never asked them what they felt about the group as such. I felt that our group this year has been very polite, and we all have been over-protective towards each other. How can we get more interaction going in a group like this?' (This was, for Jack, a very emotional statement, to which they reacted with surprise, uncertainty and pleasure. Everyone looked animated, even the silent ones.)

5 We think the seminar should definitely be continued. It is valuable. We want more personal contact on the course, between ourselves and our teachers and this is one of the few places where we feel it could be obtained.

Jack made some moving parting remarks about his appreciation of their company. He explained that he was a fairly prolific writer and that sometimes he saw himself as a 'lone researcher'. Seminar work brought him into the social side of things. He added that their papers had shaken some of his long-held concepts and he was grateful. Clearly he was going to miss the students despite the relief of coming to the end of a long and arduous term. The students were visibly touched, pleased and embarrassed by his expression of feeling for them. At literally the last moment group cohesion triumphed; we came together finally in the sadness of parting.

Jack managed the good-byes sensitively, acknowledging the worthwhile as well as the painful aspects of his association with them. Departure is a delicate matter, and its management can shape the students' attitudes towards future groups. It is often in saying good-bye that unresolved struggles are suddenly dealt with; the tutor, too afraid to refer to the awkward fact of the group's death, may miss a golden opportunity to do his most inspired work in it. Jack's final session illustrates the necessity for breaking the prohibition on openly facing feelings about loss, regret and separation; feelings which, however uncomfortable, release so much urgent energy: there are last minute tasks to be completed, quarrels to be healed and foundations to be laid for more effective participation in future groups. The manner of a group's death shapes to some extent the birth of every new group which its members will join.

Chapter 12

A single seminar session for students, with consultant-observer

This short chapter features an unusual teaching situation Here, the group tutor was already proficient in handling group process, having worked hard in two in-service training seminars which I organized at the college. Despite his knowledge and understanding, the session to be reported still posed serious teaching questions concerning the function and structuring of the traditional seminar.

14 third year students taking a Latin American studies option of a Geography degree convened, as usual, in a large classroom. (The seminar format itself and the group's leader were familiar to them.) Steve, the tutor, had prepared the room in advance by rearranging the furniture into a square consisting of four long tables, with a large square space in the centre. In the corner of the room a coffee urn bubbled and spluttered cheeringly, and the proceedings started exactly on time. Someone informed Steve that Angela, who was scheduled to do the first seminar presentation that day, was at the dentist, but would try to come along later. I could not help wondering whether the well-timed dental appointment signified some kind of anxiety about the performance expected of her.

Steve reminded the students briefly of the seminar's occupational task. They all knew the routine backwards, but the object of these introductory remarks, as Steve confirmed in a later discussion with me, was to enable them to separate from whatever activity had gone before, and to escort them across the external boundary into the group space where the membership work awaited them. While he spoke papers were shuffled, bags emptied, pencils sharpened and jackets removed – all boundary-crossing rituals, after which the participants settled down and applied themselves to the job in hand.

As members began to communicate, I started to explore my environment, which everyone else in the room took for granted. I believe very strongly that environmental factors do affect a group's ability to work, even though tutor and students may be unaware of them. The white strip lighting was glaring and intrusive, so that to 'hide in the shadows', which we all need to do from time to time, would have been impossible. I felt very exposed, and wondered how much the lighting in this and other teaching groups contributed towards students' feelings about having to 'perform' publicly. The acoustics were abysmal. The noise of the coffee urn plus traffic, and the chasm (12 feet wide) which separated one side of the square from the other, made speaking and listening difficult. Voices seemed to come from far away, and the tables constituted an added barrier to communication, particularly if one wished to talk to someone opposite, for two tables, one's own and one's interlocuter's, had to be surmounted. Several obstacles to open communication, inherent in the group's structure from the beginning, ensured that throughout the seminar the verbal exchanges took place in two small sub groups of three people each. Each sub group was located at a diagonally opposite corner of the square, where conversation between neighbours was easier and less hampered by distance and other intrusions. Periodically the opposing sub groups took pot shots at one another across the room before retreating once more to their own corner. It is probably fair to surmise that the talkers selected where and with whom they would sit. This is one of the main problems which arise when the seating offered is anything other than a circle; physical arrangements where students are not equidistant from each other and the tutor, always increase their tendency for sub grouping, and furniture can easily be used defensively as a barrier behind which to hide. This unwitting abuse of the setting by the students tells the tutor about their psychological fears of interaction. Steve wanted to have as free a discussion as possible, and his subsequent management of the group, when they attempted to force him into the role of didactic teacher, revealed his skill in dealing with the latent process. That limited manifest discussion and debate was possible, owing to inhibiting structural factors, must have been disappointing for him. A circle offers opportunity for unrestricted development of group process, which this tutor would have been quite capable of dealing with.

The first presenter, Mary, had obviously carried out an enormous amount of reading and research, and offered us a carefully worded talk about credentialism in urban Latin America. (All three presentations were to demonstrate different aspects of unemployment and underemployment in Latin American cities.) After the seminar all members were to write an essay covering the whole topic, not just the aspect they were presenting; everyone would have access to the three presentations which were to be copied and filed for this purpose. In addition, Steve had circulated several pages of notes summarizing the subject, and had lectured on it also. It seemed to me, therefore, that thorough notetaking in this seminar was not necessary, and that clarification and discussion about this very controversial and complex issue ought to be the main focus of the meeting. Mary's presentation was, as asked, only 10 minutes. It was a self-effacing offering, delivered in a shy monotone, so that many people on my edge of the square, opposite to her, became fidgety towards the end and a little bored, principally I suspect, because it required such an effort to hear. Steve listened attentively and took notes. Those sitting opposite him (the non talkers) made copious notes simultaneously. After her speech Mary (whom I identified as one of the 'talkers') argued her case fluently and with great passion, when some of her colleagues queried her statements. This Mary was very different to the demure creature who had talked at us so formally a few minutes ago. This does raise some technical questions about the seminar format. Is formal presentation really worthwhile? If so, ought the tutor and other students train one another to give confident and accomplished presentations? Why do students argue vehemently in discussion, but sink under the floorboards when called upon to show their mettle before their colleagues? The external pressure to perform and the internal urge to discuss frequently bring out contrasting responses in students.

When Mary's presentation was over and questions from the others had been answered by her, there was silence. Steve invited further comments. They did not reply to this and the room became very quiet for a good half minute or so. Steve looked relaxed, and yet managed to convey that though he was exerting no pressure on them, he himself felt no need to break the silence; nor was there any need to enter into a battle of wills and force them into speech by using the weapon of hostile muteness. Eventually the students' discomfort increased. The reluctance, shyness, fear or whatever it might be about speaking became gradually less daunting than the prospect of a continuing silence, and so someone finally spoke. Steve acknowledged the communication non verbally and looked round the room with raised eyebrows. A lively discussion between a sub group of four (all seated next to each other) followed, with occasional input from Mary on the other side of the room. Steve refrained from any comments, yet the students were acutely aware, as I was, of his presence, his interest, and his concentrated attention. Without speech, he still communicated so much. Here indeed was competent process management. I noted throughout the seminar that all the discourse and many of the mannerisms, linguistic habits and ideas expressed were very like Steve's own. Even when his known views were opposed, the counter-arguments offered were couched in the terms he would have used! This was more than a mere shared use of sociological jargon — the unconsciously imitative behaviour was quite marked, though Steve said afterwards he had never noticed this. This behaviour again underlined for me how powerful a model the tutor is.

During the next 30 minutes Steve intervened on four occasions and never spoke more than two sentences. These were in terms of clarifying, questioning or elaborating — never instructing or arguing. He ensured that they took over that particular responsibility to and for each other. (Readers may feel that four interventions in 30 minutes seems average, but were they to ask a colleague to sit in on one of their seminars and time the number and extent of their interventions, I am sure most tutors who subscribe to the ideal of true group discussion would be horrified by the amount of verbal control they exert over their students.)

In the ensuing 20 minutes when once more the same five discussed, another four listened carefully and wrote prolifically, while the remaining five oscillated between day dreaming, writing, and making the occasional remark. Steve interjected twice, this time to give a couple of 'mini-lectures' summarizing all that had gone before, emphasizing the main points, and drawing in topics which had not been given sufficient thought. He complimented those individuals who had made salient remarks, and helped others who had not fully understood certain points. His summaries were taken down almost verbatim by the silent scribes; he encouraged them to talk once, and then gave up, when the usual five took over the discussion. The latter, (three of them forming the real core) were all bright attractive vivacious people with interesting ideas and an enjoyable sense of humour who were gratifying to listen to and talk with. Steve responded warmly to them. (I felt that those who neither scribbled nor talked may have seen themselves as 'poor relations' to this sparkling sub group, which Steve so clearly enjoyed.) Steve managed to pull back the talkers to the subject in hand when they threatened to wander off into a fascinating, but (for the purposes of the group's occupation) irrelevant political debate. He did this by means of a joke, in which he subtly suggested he too would like to join in an argument about political implications, but that such a discussion would be more fitting for another seminar on the course. This ability to keep students within the group's boundaries without resort to punitive remarks is a delicate skill which takes time to acquire. Most tutors of my acquaintance prefer to forget the boundaries, and hence dilute the learning rather than use disciplinary measures against students. Steve did not do either, for he had cultivated the art of boundary maintenance, and the students respected his wishes in this matter without any evidence of regret or resentment. His presence exuded both his professional and personal attributes so that he came across as warm yet authoritative (as opposed to authoritarian). He used anecdotal material from his own field work in Latin America whenever the discussers became bogged down in sociological constructs and abstract theorizing — again without direct criticism, bringing them back to the seminar topic. The five 'dreamers' became more animated whenever Steve's real experience in Latin America was referred to. The sharing of research material in this way played an important part in the seminar, and brought the subject itself alive, and the group members into greater communion. The personal bonds between learners and teacher were also strengthened by this sharing of his personal experience.

The second presentation, so Steve confirmed for me afterwards, was packed with remarkably rich material, all the pros and cons beautifully sorted and cogently argued. Alan was telling us about the advantages and disadvantages of using intermediate technology as a solution to underemployment problems. Once more this splendid piece of work was delivered apologetically, almost in a mumble. Just as he was getting into his stride, two members of the talkers sub group decided spontaneously, without cues from elsewhere, to make and distribute the coffee, along with clattering spoons, sliding sugar bowls and urgent whispers. I suspected that their motive might be envy of the excellent content of Alan's talk. The two concerned, a man and a woman, were obviously much enamoured of their tutor; both Steve and I later felt they had been working extra hard to 'help him out', as an observer was present — but they wanted to see themselves, and be seen as, his favourites. The coffee ritual was a welcome distraction for most of us, but must have been greatly upsetting for Alan. His current communicational tie with Steve was more or less broken by probably jealous comrades, although Steve valiantly endeavoured to concentrate on his presentation despite the intrusions. I am certain the two students who initiated this minor revolt were totally unaware of their motives for so doing. Rivalry such as this in a group is very normal, but in terms of tutoring skill the design of the seminar should preclude, attenuate, rechannel or contain the destructive enactment of such impulses. Later on Steve and I chatted about the session, and agreed that while the provision of coffee was an important symbolic gesture on the part of the tutor perhaps a separate time could be scheduled for its consumption, so as to avoid abuses.

Meanwhile, Angela had returned from the dentist. By now we were over an hour into the seminar. Steve had explained to me previously that the seminar lasted officially one hour, but unofficially two. Students were obliged to attend for an hour, but thereafter were free to leave, stay, smoke and drink coffee as they wished. Usually four or five left and the others remained. Today was no exception. Angela was asked by Steve to give us her account of problems of data compilation. She was extremely nervous, and seemed not to have prepared the work very coherently. Blushing and stammering she struggled through her notes, as Steve looked increasingly worried. One or two people left, as they were now entitled to do, and those remaining showed increasing signs of restlessness. We were tired; her reasoning was hard to follow; her embarrassment was embarrassing. As Steve came forward to rescue and support her, gently and sensitively guiding her through the material in dyadic protectiveness, so we gradually withdrew our emotional investment from the group, leaving Steve and Angela to cope on their own. Even the note-takers ceased to scribble, and many of us began doodling or making secret signals to one another, or looked at our watches. Angela was aware of all this peripheral activity and was growing more breathless and anxious with every sentence. In retrospect I feel there was nothing else that Steve could have done. He was forced to sacrifice group needs to the needs of an individual student in temporary crisis. In a smaller group, with fewer communicational barriers and less sub grouping, the participants themselves might have found resources to support and guide a colleague in distress. But this group was too big and impersonal to mobilize collective support. The helping facilities were trapped within the boundaries of sub groups, and Angela did not belong to any!

I was very perturbed indeed by the loose termination arrangements. Each time someone left, the seminar felt distinctly depleted; communications became fragmented; sub groups and pairing increased and the conversation no longer strictly surrounded the work. There was a half-hearted attempt to continue with the academic material, but I had the feeling that, of those who were left, several would have liked to leave but dared not, or had nowhere better to go, and so thought they might as well stay. I felt that Angela, who had enough problems of her own, was also caught up in a boundary 'incident'; members drifting off, and those staying losing interest. Coupled with this was a general fatigue. She could easily have related all these responses to her own inadequate presentation. A definite end-point to the seminar would have been more desirable, possibly with an option for another, more informal meeting after a short coffee break. (Two separate one hour seminars for two populations was worth considering.) If the seminar were divided into distinct segments, people could take their leave after an hour without affecting the atmosphere they left behind. Another advantage in apportioning the time like this would be that the functions of note-taking as against discussion could be separated. After the seminar proper in the first hour, there could be a coffee break, followed by an opportunity for those who wanted notes or verbal clarification to meet these needs, while those who wanted to leave could do so. It is unfair to commence new topics during times of sanctioned absence. The question of numbers could be usefully reviewed, as 14 people, under these conditions, achieved only a limited amount of work. Are there other ways of structuring time and routines so as to channel process into more productive directions, or is 14 too many students for a discussive type of group?

Numbers of participants, physical setting, group boundaries, conflicting usages of group time (note-collecting versus discussion) were the main issues which presented themselves to me as an observer in this group. There are no simple answers to these problems, but a good teacher at least realizes that such questions need to be asked. This chapter has, I hope, underlined the necessity for providing and maintaining a group structure in which the process can be cradled and nurtured. Structure and process, as stated at the beginning of the book, are totally interdependent and interactive. Neglect of one results almost always in damage or malfunction of the other.

Steve relayed the substance of his and my post group conversation to the students during the following week's seminar period. Following this consultation with the students, the room itself was changed, chairs were arrayed in a circle, the lighting was improved and even the coffee making ritual was reorganized. Assessment anxieties were allayed and the writers helped to talk a little more. The time was broken up into two separate hours. According to Steve the group members felt much happier with the new arrangements and the work, which had always been adequate, improved further.

Chapter 13

A regular departmental staff group for the examination of teaching effectiveness, with consultant-conductor

Three members of my inter-departmental seminiar for teachers conferred with two of their senior colleagues a year later to see if there might be professional gain in some kind of departmental follow-up. They were all keen to recruit new colleagues, for whose personal well-being and teaching standards they felt responsible. They were anxious lest the suggestion that they attend a training group appear as criticism, and yet were concerned not to abandon their new or isolated fellow teachers in a 'let them sink or swim' attitude. I met the five to discuss the format of the proposed gatherings. Though there was unanimous agreement that we should meet on the teachers' own territory, to reduce any suspicions that meeting in my own room might generate, two contrasting points of view evolved. The first suggestion was that I should be identified as a visitor, who nonetheless could somehow 'infiltrate' the meetings' proceedings, and have a hopefully positive effect upon the staff, while one of their number would 'chair' the meetings. The other was that it should be seen as my 'course', and that I alone should take charge of it, even though it would be conducted within the environs of the geography department. Towards the conclusion of this preliminary discussion my thoughts were clearer. I expressed my agreement that the venture should be a shared one, but said I was sure that boundaries ought to be defined openly, one way or the other. I was prepared to be present at what amounted to regular staff meetings, as a guest and commentator, but we would need to bear in mind that such a role would severely restrict my interjections and behaviour, as my activities would be subject to protocol. Alternatively, I said, I was willing and eager to conduct the group under my own leadership, but would like the intended participants to decide upon the projected group's title. A meeting of this caucus plus future participants was duly convened, in my absence, and both these proposals, namely my involvement as guest, or involvement as leader, were considered by all. The impossibility of my functioning both as respectful guest and unhampered leader was explained. I was content to submit to the authority of a departmental chairperson and to the norms of a departmental staff meeting, but could not operate within such boundaries as well as running the group in the same fashion as the previous inter-departmental one in chapter 8. Finally, it was decided that I should conduct the group in my own way, with no chairperson, and that we should have as our title 'teaching effectiveness'.

The group consisted of seven men, one woman and myself; they represented 'junior' and 'middle' status in the academic hierarchy, and varied widely in ages and length of service, though three of them were very young and new to the profession. Arthur (who was our subject in chapter 10) and Ginny had at different times been allocated official responsibility for the overall welfare of students in their department, and were therefore regarded (rightly) as possessing a wide experience with students and colleagues, and with the institution's workings generally. Arthur loaned us his room and was well disposed to my requests about the layout of the furniture and other rituals to be observed, in order to secure privacy and peace. Throughout the first term, there were many jokes about the ceremonious atmosphere; any deviations from the normal arrangements were noted instantly, and there were lengthy discussions of a humorous kind about the exact positioning of the central coffee table! We contracted to meet weekly for one term, and then to collectively review the situation. Owing to time-table problems, we had exactly one hour available to us, which I knew could adversely affect our deliberations. However, harsh realities must always be faced; an hour was better than nothing, and perhaps we could explore new times later on. My anticipatory feelings were optimistic for the following reasons:

(a) the teachers already knew each other fairly well (I thought);
(b) a sub group of 'culture carriers' was already established who could help and support those members unfamiliar with my approach;
(c) everyone had been given an opportunity to express their wishes about the group before its inception in a very democratic manner;
(d) conducting the group on home ground should have promoted feelings of security;
(e) the invitation to take part in this exercise had come from them, not me, which pleased me greatly.

My optimism led me to suppose (and experience was to correct me) that this group might work at a faster pace and at a more personal level than other staff groups, and that cohesion would be almost instantaneous, with less resistance to new learning than is usual for this sort of group. I failed to gauge the degrees of shyness, or fears of ridicule and disapproval which resided in many individual members underneath their often talkative, sociable exteriors. That friendly links already existed between them was obvious; the fragility of those links, and anxiety about their breakdown under stress of truthful revelation only showed itself later, when nervous jocularity and circumlocution increased in a desperate and collusive effort to preserve individual anonymity.

Session 1

I introduced myself to those participants I had not previously met, and talked a little about my style of leadership. I stressed the importance of us all trying to keep to the times stated, as we only had an hour for each meeting. I reiterated the group's theme, saying that members were free to respond to that theme at any time in any way they wished; that the organizational aspects of the seminar within the few boundaries I had provided were entirely up to them.

The atmosphere was warm and people seemed eager to work. Much curiosity was shown about what other members actually did when managing a small group of students in a teaching situation. Participants realized quickly with some surprise, that they had never watched the others teach, and had no idea how one person's teaching might compare with another's. Attention soon became focused on Jack, (see chapter 11) famed for his 'group circus', as Arthur (see chapter 10) put it. (This remark produced much mirth.) No one could understand the alacrity with which he broke up large numbers of students into small groups, thus greatly increasing his contact hours and running the risk of exhaustion. The remarks addressed to him were tinged with admiration, and some shame that emulation of his technique was not a terribly attractive proposition in view of the work involved. Arthur told us that he enjoyed running small tutorials, but felt wary about seminar groups of 8-12 like Jack's. He thought this number was too unwieldy for teaching purposes. Ginny said that in my inter-departmental seminar last year she had picked up some useful hints on tackling middle and large sized groups, and perhaps that would be one subject we could study in this group. She seemed to feel the need to organize an agenda speedily before she could feel safe in the group. Meanwhile the men were comparing their small group teaching approaches in a way which suggested each might be privately ranking himself against the others. At the time, I reckoned this jockeying for position to be competitive and group specific; in retrospect I understood that the rivalry was covering up chronic individual fears about making the grade professionally, fears which some members had been carrying for years. To my own and others' amazement, Jack confessed that his 'group circus' was not so much the result of dedication to a group teaching model as a fear of inadequacy when confronted by a vast number of students to whom a formal lecture must be addressed! This made it easier for the other members to tentatively consider their own fears. James complained that, try as he might, no students would give him honest feedback about his lectures and seminars.

The difficulties and exasperations created by the small group were retained as this meeting's dominant preoccupation. I commented on my observation that curiosity, envy, fear of looking silly, hopes of finding the 'right answer', rivalry, were all being expressed in this new, uncertain ambience. I asked them to consider their own teaching groups, and how students might experience these same phenomena in a new group, and might also cover up these feelings to avoid being vulnerable. Even though academic work is attempted, these feelings may well affect how and to what extent work is successfully achieved. This remark resulted in a discussion of the relationship of 'latent' (hidden) group activity, to its 'manifest' (directly observable) interactions, and how the academic work and the group's interpersonal processes interact with each other.

'Bidding' then began. Each person tried to crystalize in his or her own mind and then communicate to the others, what they wanted to use this group for. Ginny wanted to look in a practical way at teaching, whereas Jack felt the 'whole person' of the teacher was deserving of attention, and was hurt by Ginny's assumption that teaching *per se* was the most important area for study. Steve, (see chapter 12) a most politically conscious man, wanted an ideological exploration of who we were educating, for what and why. As the argument intensified in a mutual 'leg-pulling' way, I again related this group to a typical student group, where interests clashed, and members felt claims had to be staked. One member was often left out, perplexed, unsure about what was going on and reluctant to fight. As I said this, I smiled at Gerald who had not spoken. He joined in the discussion, saying he would like the group to talk about lecturing, as he feared his lectures were over-prepared and dull, no matter how accurate and comprehensive the content. Throughout these sessions, I wanted to intensify each member's awareness of his/her own group functioning style, so he/she might change it into a more effective one where needed. This subjective experience of improving competence could assist them to train students in membership effectiveness. That was one reason why I brought Gerald in at that point; the other reason was purely humane — he looked so unhappy.

A rather serious and complicated conversation then took place, about whether it was justifiable to always teach in a certain way, just because the course members seemed personally stimulated by it. Was popularity really that important? Ought they to mind if their students did not like them, or their lecturing style, or the work itself, providing they obtained good grades? I said, jokingly, that they seemed very guilty about enjoying themselves. What was so sinful about job satisfaction or wanting to like and be liked? This was by way of drawing attention to the sometimes quite absurd premises on which we build our work habits. A puritanical conscience and denial of pleasure can be counter-productive to rich teacher-learner relationships.

The first meeting ended with Ted assuring us confidently that he got on well with students, and there was no feedback problem. Horace engaged in a long discussion with myself and others about practical preparations for lectures, and the right balance of flexibility and rigidity in delivering them: when should a lecturer dispense with notes, wander off the point on purpose to widen the topic, abandon careful strategies designed to ensure adequate coverage of the material? I found Horace very warm and lovable but rather hard to follow, and hoped the group would not use his lengthy and rather rambling speeches to avoid facing painful matters. (They did subsequently use this manoeuvre several times, but when Horace's lengthy comments lessened over the weeks and became succinct and to the point, the group was thrown into confusion and was forced to seek new avoidance devices elsewhere.)

This first meeting did not display the usually overriding feature of dependency on the leader. They knew in advance that the group would not be led in the traditional style. Though I sensed the dependency, my observations told me that they were looking more to fellow group members for indications of solidarity or rejection. It was as if my reputation had reached the group before me, and the members had given up any hope at the outset of my possibly being a source of comfort or security. They co-operated in a quasi-adult way, striving to push away perfectly legitimate fears and anxieties in a superhuman effort to be seen as a 'good group'. I had not bargained for this artificial robustness!

Much later, it became apparent that several members were 'putting on a good front' in the department too. A teaching culture reigned in which individuals felt obliged to convince self and others that all was well; no private or professional doubts were expressed, and a cheery facade between staff and staff and students was maintained at all times. It took some months for real fears or conflicts to be expressed in this group.

Session 2

Ted was absent. All the others rushed in a minute or two late, apologetic and breathless, urging their various excuses upon me. These I accepted, impressed by their appreciation of my boundaries. We then looked at timing *vis a vis* seminars and tutorials. We discussed the many possible meanings of a student's habitual lateness and the underlying 'message' that is often being emitted by a teacher who is persistently late, or keeps changing the time or venue of a teaching group. Each group member then began to compare in some depth, his/her preparation for tutorials. Arthur recounted his technique which was helping students mull over a topic with him in a tutorial, and out of this discussion a pertinent essay title would emerge. This would be written, then marked and returned to the writer and discussed in a further tutorial very shortly afterwards. Horace said airily that he had no particular structure and did not expect regular attendance or predetermined contributions; it was all played by ear. Steve talked about pacing the material; how to assess a group's mood and its readiness to gobble up new information; how to feed students according to appetite; how vital advance academic planning was, in order to induce a sense of expectant excitement as new data was anticipated; how pride was registered as course goals were systematically achieved by the students. There ensued an interesting and mutually helpful exchange of ideas and guidance about programming a course, and using teaching aids.

Gerald, hitherto silent, volunteered the problem of the quiet student member of a teaching group, as well as the silent whole-group. Why are they silent? What should he do about it? I tried to show the futility of taking one particular group problem out of context and trying to solve it in the abstract. There is no single technique applicable to all situations. The key lies in understanding causation. Why is the group or one of its members so silent? What is promoting learning resistance? What part of the group's total process requires intervention? 'But they all *want* to work or they wouldn't be in the group', someone said, taking silence to infer a refusal to co-operate. Declining involvement, I agreed, did not, on the face of it, square with a desire to learn — but let us look at *this* group, and see if there is anything we could deduce from the disparity between our members' wishes to work hard and their subsequent mode of self presentation. I suggested they thought for a moment about their hopes, fears and fantasies about our group and about me, before they had come the first time and that they looked at their previous behaviours and experiences in other learning groups. All those memories and fantasies must have coloured the way they were now interacting. Their actual behaviour at this early stage in the group's life almost certainly failed to tally with the behaviour they had hoped to show. Fearful experiences in the past lead to expectation of fearful experiences now. A silent student or tutor may be waiting for some awful event he is sure will occur, and tries to ward it off by being mute. His silence may have little to do with the academic work, to which he can boast a very hale and healthy attitude. Students' group behaviour is by no means always related to the work. Horace, James and Arthur seemed embarrassed and shocked at having to look inside themselves, and dismissed my contribution with much smirking and self-consciousness. Horace found the prospect of having had prior fantasies about this group particularly preposterous, even though he had turned up 40 minutes late for the first session, and this despite having no competing engagement. Silence and absence often have much in common!

Jack complained of my 'extreme' and 'exaggerated' ideas, and was to continue doing so throughout the term. He seemed to want insight into the group's process, providing I could defuse it first! Mastering information is less frightening to many academics than facing muddled feelings. James backed him up in this, and denied having fantasies, as if private imaginings, (to which we are all subject) were inadmissable, even distasteful and that only the world of fact has validity. It proved a very

hard task indeed over the months to enable these academics to welcome their fantasy life as a valuable prerequisite to good teaching, and a
good tool in making human relationships work. Jack grumbled that so
far as he was concerned, fantasy did not enter in any way into his lecturing. All he wanted was to please and stimulate the bright students,
lead the rather dumb ones, entertain the bored ones, and so forth, all of
which he maintained was very down to earth. I begged to differ over
this, and invited him to look at whether his fantasy of himself as a perfect teacher, which he constantly tried to live up to, was one of the
reasons why he quaked at the thought of giving a lecture, and preferred
instead to be ringmaster of his more controllable 'group circus'. If he
could cease driving himself towards fulfilling an unrealistic, omniscient
and omnipotent fantasy of himself as a teacher, he might find lecturing
easier, perhaps even fun. Jack looked rather shaken, but pondered over
this idea, while the rest of the group went on to argue about whether
atmospheres in groups were accidental or brought about by the teacher's stance; whether a tutor should concentrate on the tutorial group as
a single entity or on discrete individuals within it. Horace claimed that
this discussion was wasteful, as a tutorial was not really a group anyway — it was too small. 'When is a group not a group?' I said smiling,
and then left.

After this and future sessions those members who did not have to
rush away continued the meeting informally, and I often wondered
how helpful or destructive this was. An hour's session did not seem long
enough, but I was not comfortable about the group continuing after my
departure, unless all members were present to avoid boundary confusion. However, perhaps group members were moving closer to each
other away from the public glare of the group which might later
improve its functioning. I decided to wait and see.

Session 3

Ted was absent once more, this time sending apologies. (Otherwise all
the members were present.)

A strange conversation opened the session, with participants speaking in vague and confused terms about what a group might really be, if
indeed it exists, and how the individual relates or not to it. The lack of
concrete information available, or exact formulae and management tactics for group work, irritated everyone, and I suspected this generalized
hostility would soon seek a target. Horace, as I had predicted, was
selected as the object for displacement. He was encouraged to describe
his tutorials in detail and then was criticized in a teasing way, which
tottered unsteadily from affectionate ragging to rather nasty jibes and
back again. He responded to the 'fun' by feeding the other members the
exact information which they could seize upon and make jokes about.
It was impossible to detect from moment to moment when they were

laughing with him or at him. Any cruelty was unintentional, but the thinly veiled attack was really aimed at me and my 'lack of structure' and 'inadequate leadership', not his. Arthur too was looking uneasy and began to try to reason with Horace, forcing him to clarify, simplify, say precisely what he meant. In so doing, Arthur became rather garrulous and the two were left to pair while the others, with great glee, watched them argue. I then intervened and said simply and without value judgment what I thought was going on and pointed out that I was the real target of their anger. Everyone except Ginny and Steve hotly denied displacing anger onto Horace. Steve sympathized with Horace, saying that he, Steve, had felt 'set up' in the same manner last week. He felt he had been nominated by the group as the over-structured, over-active, too interventionist teacher, and had been contrasted with Horace (who used hardly any structure). On that occasion, both of them had been pilloried as examples of 'extreme' teaching. The others protested that no such thing had happened, but when Steve insisted that that was why he was so quiet today and told them of his wounded feelings during the week, they gradually began to look at their own conduct as a group. I tried to reduce the remorse a little by suggesting they use this experience to help them understand scapegoating and pairing in their own student groups. At least they could not now remain blind to such group resistances as they themselves had been actors in this group drama.

The displacement behaviour stopped and questions about dependency came to the fore. The subject was how to deal with silent or passive students who were forcing the leader to be more active and traditional in his approach. Does one give in to their determination to be dependent; does one talk to them directly about how to share authority in the group, or does one 'sit it out', matching silence with silence, until they are forced to speak? Someone remarked that if the teacher does refuse to teach in the manner to which students are accustomed they get very cross, and the teacher is seen as a 'bad' unlikeable person. At an unconscious level this discussion related to their anger with me and their fear of expressing it. However, I did not say this, as it could have resulted in more heated denials and a retreat from a painful but important issue. So once more I connected up the discussion with the teaching process by saying that the giving and taking of genuine anger was a vital part of any relationship that was really alive. Trust was necessary before anger could be safely expressed, and if neither student nor staff could trust or be angry with each other in a group, there was little hope for anything other than contrived superficial respect and cordiality between them.

This tacit permission to exhibit hostility enabled James to break out of his rather conventional mould a little and grumble at me to my face about this group. We were not getting anywhere, he complained; could we not take turns in presenting material each week as in proper seminars? Or perhaps an agenda or series of topics planned in advance would help us get round all this time-consuming muddle? The tension and conflict in the group which he found so painful and longed to by-pass was, for me, the most central part of the group's occupation, and was not, as he thought, just an interference with the 'real' work. Sadly I was not able to communicate this to him and the others seemed to understand this notion only in a rather hazy way too. I was beginning to admit to myself that I was perhaps pushing the group a little further and a little faster than I ought. As he received little support, James began to withdraw emotionally as well as verbally. By tactfully but firmly silencing the others and physically leaning towards him, reaching out an arm, I created time and space for him to at least give vent to the feelings he had been bottling up within a very polite and amenable exterior for some time. He became quite eloquent and indignant, verbally courteous but colouring up facially and clenching his fists, betraying his deep feeling about the group's and my shortcomings. I was sure that my ability to withstand his annoyance without any apparent harm was a crucially reassuring experience for him. Thereafter he had no trouble in giving his opinion, loud and clear. I felt, and I am certain the others did, judging from their reactions to him that he suddenly became a much more attractive, imaginative person, and a more valued member of the group when he finally showed his anger. 'The way you carry on Wyn', he said indignantly, 'anyone would think we were all secretly working out which of us is the best and worst teacher in the department, and that is just plain crazy!' 'Is it?', I asked the group in general. Everyone laughed, recognizing the irony of James' outburst, and the atmosphere became calm and companionable, as if we each of us had had a secret thought, only to find everyone else thought it too and were now able to share it with each other. Only James failed to clearly understand the event, preoccupied as he was with an internal upheaval of his own.

Later I was able to show that ritualization in group teaching, (turn-taking, agendas, prescribed sequences of behaviour) is often used to mask a dominant shared preoccupation, such as the fear of personal exposure to ridicule, or the wish to be angry. In a tight group structure, feelings are banished or suppressed. Without feelings there can be no interpersonal matrix in a group, no trust, and therefore no relationships over and above the aridly formalized. Conversely, a complete absence of boundaries and structures leads to insecurity and lack of cohesion between members, which is equally disastrous for learning and relating. In this staff group we could decide to have a structured seminar format, devoid of emotion, if that was what was wanted. However, in my view, effective teaching (which was after all our main theme) rested on a foundation of seeing, understanding and managing our feelings to others, and confronting the images of ourselves, which we project. Transmission of the knowledge in our heads was only a small part of

197

effective teaching.

Horace meditated on this little speech, and then in a serious, cautious tone said that he was worried; he thought some of his students found him unintelligible. Jack, once Horace's student, hastened to reassure him — 'only occasionally Horace, not all the time'. Horace wished he could teach like Ginny. 'I hear such marvellous reports of your lucid lectures', he said to her. 'Yes', replied Ginny. 'But I can't get conceptual stuff over. Everything I do is logical and itemized, but I'm not creative and philosophical in my teaching. How can I learn to be that?' Many participants had heard of Ginny's high reputation among students and were surprised to hear her self-criticism. James added to the conversation by sharing his fear that though he loved his special subject, his lectures were just downright boring to the students. Gerald felt that he lectured at students too much — in the lay sense of the word 'lecture' — allowing no room for discussion between students.

The group made a decision, with varying individual levels of commitment, to bring to next week's session the image each held of their own style, ('boring' 'simplistic' 'unintelligible' etc.) This discussion, they felt, would meet the demand for a bit more structure in the group without outlawing the free exchange of feelings. As so many of the members had revealed personal doubts about their teaching it was generally felt that trust was beginning to grow. At the same time, confusion about the group process still reigned, and much of the irritation was not expressed verbally.

Session 4

Ted returned for this, the fourth session; Jack had another academic appointment; Steve was very late for the same reason. Our changed composition as a group affected people's composure and idle chat was used to delay a serious start to the meeting. The group seemed reluctant to work; perhaps it was still adjusting to last week's rather jolting session. Arthur jested about how he had forgotten everything which had occurred, although his memory was normally excellent! Ginny said she believed she could remember — but her account was very different to what had in fact happened. She said that we had ended the session by agreeing to evaluate our teaching this week. She then proceeded to assess her own, by looking at what students said and did, examination results, seminar performance and so on, regardless of her own feelings about herself. Academic objectives, suitable class and seminar numbers and practical teaching methods were then discussed affably, everyone in the group joining in the great pretence that this was our agreed topic for the day. I interrupted, to everyone's annoyance, after this talk had persisted at great length. I said what a pity that last week we had come so near to trusting and confiding in one another. Real colleague support, sharing of direct feelings, and asking for personal help from one another, had seemed possible. Now we had relapsed into safe formalized discussion which precluded intimacy. I may have put this clumsily for Horace and James reacted with some alarm. They argued vehemently about how wrong they felt it was to project an artificial dramatic personality and put on some kind of excessively personal 'performance' for students. 'We're not exhibitionists!', said Horace offendedly. James, returning momentarily to his earlier tendency to neutralize or evade conflict, (so as not to have to vent anger) said, 'Look, talking frankly to each other here about what we think of one another is just too delicate and may cause offence. Perhaps we could discuss other absent lecturers, like Dr X for instance. Everyone praises his lectures. Why are they so good? — Couldn't we analyze his technique?'

To my relief, most of the others refused to support this blatant attempt at leading the group in basic assumption flight activity. Instead, they discussed whether or not an academic should be expected to effect personality change in the service of good teaching; it seemed to be asking a great deal of the lecturer concerned and in any case no one seemed to know how to do it. I reminded them that change or development was not so unattainable. You had first to recognize the way you are, the impression you give, the response your teaching elicits from students. Acquiring new teaching attitudes and skills, developing or toning down certain personality traits could only be accomplished if colleagues, in a setting like this, could give you accurate feedback about yourself, and if everyone trusted each other enough to share the good and bad things about one another's teaching. Efforts could then be made to modify or change personality quirks here first before extending the 'new' self into the classroom. Gerald, our most silent member, appeared hopeful and afraid simultaneously, and repeatedly asked if personality change were possible. He made an emotive plea: 'I *know* the academic stuff inside out, but *all* my teaching problems are to do with my personality, and its all so hopeless, unless one can change'. I believed in the possibility of change, I said, though it does take a long time and can only come about in a trusting, safe, interpersonal environment, not by flicking some kind of switch, or resorting to gadgetry.

James, formerly so defensive, now came forward and told us of his depression some time back, a depression which he had felt there was no way of relieving. There had been so little support from the students for his course unit that he deduced he must be a rotten teacher. Dedicated though he was to his specific subject he seemed to be unable to communicate his enthusiasm. He had become more and more miserable, and had unburdened himself to no one but Gerald, as he had not wished to show 'moral weakness'. Finally, he had thought about leaving the college. The group was shocked at this revelation, and especially at James' solitary suffering for all those months. They seemed rather guilty about not having picked up the depression at the time, for they prided themselves on being a caring department. I said that it was not a case of uncaring cold colleagues failing to help one of their number — rather, it was to do with the lack of intimacy and trust which is typical of any large group where relationships are defined in terms of professional roles and hierarchical divisions, and where teaching performance is equated with personal status. Reputations in academic circles can be made and broken very easily. How hard it must be to confess to doubt in any university teaching environment. Slowly and painfully the group groped towards this issue of inter-colleague support and all resistance melted. It returned later when doubts were expressed about my claim that 'trust-and-soulbaring' (as Arthur called my technique) could be of help in improving teaching standards. 'We must take your word for it', James said. Arthur echoed this, as if wanting to believe me and hoping that I was wrong at the same time.

Ginny and Steve felt that giving feedback to each other was all very well in principle, but in practice no one really watched their colleagues teach in the classrooms as this was tabooed. Ginny felt strongly that they should correct this right away by arranging to sit in on one anothers' lectures before the next session, and then to discuss impressions next week. There was a mixed reception for this idea — relief that a practical suggestion had been made, and fear of exposure before one's colleagues. Ted, who had spoken rarely, but always with some bravado and apparent confidence, butted in and said, 'Just a minute, if we do watch and discuss one another, someone might get destroyed'. Some dismissed this rather dramatic utterance while others looked rather glad he had said it. Ginny eventually summarized the discussion by saying they were obviously not yet ready to carry out this exercise as people were seemingly afraid of being judged. Steve and James denied this and challenged anyone from the group to visit their lectures. The intensive debate about the pros and cons of observing each other's work continued as I left.

Session 5

Arthur delivered a message from Gerald with great relish: 'he regrets he has a cold, which he insists is not psychosomatic!' We all giggled at the joke, and then the group fell silent, everyone looking at me for guidance. Now that we were approaching really personal matters the dependent need for a strong leader rose to the surface. However, I felt it was vital to their growth as a group that they should use the group resources and inter-member support network which they had produced last week, so I demonstrated my faith in them by remaining acutely attentive but silent.

For half-an-hour they argued about the desirability or otherwise of sitting in on each other's lectures and individuals became even more exasperated at the group's inability to decide. All complained of 'our pussy-footing attitude', but no one was really prepared to do anything about it. Certain members would almost give assent to the proposal, only to retreat at the last moment into the whys and wherefores of how it could be time-tabled, what observers should look for and how they should 'score' colleague's performances. It was even suggested that perhaps issuing questionnaires to students might be more profitable than watching each other teach! Attempts at voting were sabotaged by a whole array of 'ah but's'. Those who had reservations about being watched found ingenious ways of disrupting the decision-making process as the advocates became more aggressive. Arthur, as was often the case articulated both sides of the conflict. One moment he urged other members to ask the students, as well as colleagues, to monitor their teaching progress; he suggested all sorts of practical ways of collecting information about their teaching. The next moment he was wrinkling his nose and scratching his head, advising us all to 'examine ourselves'. He said he felt rather frightened about all this 'introspection lark', but was sure that in some way he could not yet fathom that it must be important. This prompted an affectionate laughing response, as this tendency to see both sides of the question in a valiant try at 'fair play for all' was very characteristic of Arthur, as was the rather convoluted language used.

Steve thought we were deceiving ourselves if we pretended we needed to watch each other at work before being able to comment on teaching ability. He felt that the other members' personalities generally, and their behaviour in this group specifically, made a definite impression on him of how they must each of them teach. His interpretation of our recent behaviour was that we were running away from studying our interactions here in this room, by conspiring to set up some pseudo-scientific experiment elsewhere. He felt we should look more at what was happening between us in the group and strengthen the bonds of interdependency which were slowly growing. Arthur, a bit puzzled but rather pleased by his insight, shared with the rest his realization that they themselves were duplicating the small group situation with which students faced them every day, and as they were now the students they may as well exploit the possibilities of this situation rather than take flight into external activity. He agreed with Steve that they must each have a vision of how colleagues in the group teach. James was astounded. He invited the whole group to sit in on his lectures, to prove he was not being defensive. He insisted with great passion that he had no idea at all as to how any of them taught. I felt that here again was evidence of James' need to kill off any fantasy life, so as to avoid realizing rivalrous or other negative feelings which fantasies about colleagues might produce. He was obviously sincere about his lack of imaginative pictures of his fellows at work, and I was sure this repression of feeling was at the root of his teaching difficulty, though it would have been premature and possibly hurtful to say so just yet. He begged the others to tell him what they thought of his singularly different reaction to this question as he desperately wanted to better his teaching. No one had the courage to respond, presumably for fear of upsetting him, as he had already told us of his propensity for depressive feelings about his teaching.

The atmosphere was becoming more tense. Ted dealt with this awkwardness by using his characteristic 'let's call a spade a spade' method. He announced that he had lived in hall for ages, was of a similar age to students, dressed like them, and moved about socially in the student culture, and knew jolly well how all the teachers in the department were regarded by students. Questionnaires were superfluous. It was mad to suppose that no one knew anything about anyone else; of course there was such a thing as common knowledge. Why were we pretending not to know what was obvious to everyone else? There was momentary shock and then all the group members clamoured to be told about their reputation. At first Ted resisted but then became excited by the role he had been given and the power vested in it as he had everyone's rapt attention for the first time in the group. At this point I became aware of my own stress. I was remembering that it was Ted who had previously talked of group members being destroyed. The group now seemed to be setting him up as a 'prophet' with privileged information consisting of messages for them from the student body. The fate met by many prophets prompted me to seriously think about breaking up this group process. I looked at Ted carefully and decided he, too, was aware of the danger, and would accordingly proceed carefully. The demand for and fear of reliable feedback had been mounting for weeks and here it was offered on a plate. Should I wreck this opportunity, knowing it might never return, or should I risk emotional casualties in the interest of the group's overall progress? I opted for the latter and felt very tense indeed about it. I said nothing; then gently, sensitively, carefully, but with total frankness Ted went round the group and described the teaching style of, and student reaction to, every teacher in the room. Had a pin dropped during that monologue I would have heard it! Horace, he said was dogmatic and brooked no interruptions or differences of opinions. Students could take or leave what he had to offer and the way he offered it. Arthur was over-effusive and not specific enough in his academic presentations. James's lectures were full of solid material, but rather dry and too much like A-level material. Jack was over-prepared and over-factual, a bit intimidated by the students, and over-anxious to please. Ginny was very popular indeed as a lecturer for those who wanted to do well in exams and toe the departmental line, but the student who wanted a philosophical debate was unable to have any satisfying discussion. Steve was also very well liked, for his stimulating and controversial seminars particularly. He had been rather nervous and self-conscious at first (this was his first job), but had gained great confidence over his first year. Gerald was solid and over-prepared and rather earnest. Everyone looked at each other, blinking and smiling, as if a bright warm light had suddenly shone upon them. 'But that's just what we thought of ourselves all along!' would sum up the collective responses. The relief was tremendous and I was greatly touched by the ensuing lively discussion about the best way to bring an academic subject alive for the students. It was not what was actually said that moved me; it was the mode of the discussion, the real appreciation of one another's teaching problems and the genuine support given. Here indeed was a resonating group.

James was metamorphosed, eagerly gesticulating, eyes shining, posture fluid, facial muscles relaxed. Horace looked content, and sat quietly. He no longer gave long speeches in order to earn his place in the group. The common nervous hilarity which was so typical of this group gave way to authentic humour. Arthur's talk consisted of single exact sentences without the anxious habit of over elaboration. Steve did not feel the need to rouse everyone's consciousness and push them forward to self-revelation but could relax for a change, and Jack seemed more authoritative than before. In a state of resonance this group, like others, operated at an adult co-operative level, with individual participants shedding compensatory façades which had now become redundant.

Throughout this session I had not spoken a single word, but was left exhausted, having followed every utterance, and having empathized closely with each person, in order to assess the need for intervention. I felt very much that I had been an active member, and was proud to be associated with them.

Session 6

The group's preliminary regression at the beginning of every session convinced me even more that the pace was a little too fast. Each time we took an important step forward, a step backward would invitably follow, although the overall trend was progressive. I had quickened the pace partially on account of my somewhat faulty prediction of instant trust, (though there had been some cohesion). It was partly owing too, to my constant awareness of how little time we had, both in the individual sessions of one hour, and in the number of weeks till the Christmas break, namely eight. I do not recommend accelerating group process in this way, but like all teachers, I had to make judgments about ensuring the group achieved certain goals by the end of term. Moving at the ideal pace could have brought the group to Christmas with no real understanding of process and therefore no motivation to continue the meetings so as to explore this field further. The other aspect to my dilemma was that the necessary if undesirable forcing of the pace might raise the anxiety level so high, people could elect to terminate the group at the convenient Christmas break. Pacing is a crucial and much neglected facet of group conducting — too fast or too slow a pace can lead to group disruption, apathy, or termination!

Ginny looked pale and fatigued and was conspicuously quiet. There was the usual edgy laughter and bluster at the beginning, which finally developed into a group grumble about what we were all here for. People kept referring to the 'real issues', but asked too what these could conceivably be. Arthur referred to 'Wyn's dark hints', and said that 'real issues' are probably not the listing of techniques, or laying down of practical guidelines — after all we had all been told about and had been practising those for years; so it must be something else that Wyn thinks this group has to offer. As people tried to puzzle this out, Steve and James announced proudly that they had taken matters in their own hands and had actually observed one another's lectures since last week. No one was inclined to pursue this, and the two looked rather crestfallen. Even so, Steve was determined to stir up some movement in the group, and so asked the others to decide if we were to continue after Christmas or not. If we were going to finish in two weeks' time, he said, he did not want to miss out on the 'mourning' phase which he had read about in my book. All laughed, and then dismissed his point by saying there was heaps of time left and there was no need to decide just yet. (This was a classic 'group flight' basic assumption in efficient operation.) Pairing conversations, containing very little of substance, took place in sequence — first one pair, then the other. Onlookers seemed bored but unwilling to interfere. The rather woolly discussions were fulfilling the group's wish to escape ambivalent feelings concerning continuation of the group into next term. I felt too, that the level of obscurity attained by individuals perfectly capable of clear thinking, reflected their need to slow the pace a little; I tried to respect this.

Gradually dissatisfaction grew, as the rather disinterested discussion about what constituted 'real work' in the group meandered on. I wondered out loud about the abstract nature of our talk and why we could not meet individuals' needs this week. We had been embarrassed about James' private unhappiness, and had expressed the hope that such a thing would not happen again. Yet here was Ginny in our midst looking awful. No one had said anything about it. Steve said he had been very conscious of it but was reticent about asking her the reason. By now her wretched appearance had turned to grimness, and I felt sure that whatever else bothered her, the group certainly had some part in her unusual silence. She at first assured us that she was just tired and overworked and there was nothing to worry about. I encouraged her to talk more freely, for I felt definitely that we the group were in some manner responsible. She then aired her disappointment about the collapse of her idea about observing each other's lectures. She just could not see any direction or movement in the group and felt all at sea. I said I wondered if under that nice friendly exterior for which she was so well liked another side of herself lay bound and gagged. Was she angry at being the only woman member in the group; always being used to drag straying conversations back to the point; always turned to for practical suggestions, and then repaid by having her proposed structure for the group rejected? Perhaps she was tired of being helpful and understanding all the time? (She had a reputation in the group for pouring oil on our troubled waters.) A grin reminiscent of the old Ginny spread across her face as she agreed she had gone on strike today, and was cheesed off with enacting the maternal role allocated to her by the rest of the group.

Ginny wanted to know if the others felt stereotyped too. James leaned over to Gerald and asked if he felt lumbered with the silent member role. Would it help if we allowed him a word in edgeways? Gerald thought a bit, and then said that change would have to be his own decision; other people always expected him to remain silent, and so never asked him anything and never urged him to alter himself. In lectures and classes though he thought he spoke too much and too dictatorially. This contrast in his own personality disturbed him. I gently intervened, offering Gerald the hope that over time if the group carried on, he might learn to bring these two facets of himself together in the group among caring colleagues. Perhaps this kind of change was one of the 'real issues' everyone seemed so anxious to label. This idea of helping one's personality blossom struck the group as very novel and rather ambitious — although I had been alluding to it for weeks. Constant repetition of central concepts is very necessary in teaching. Often a group is blocked from 'hearing' the conductor introducing them to new ways of understanding because of group or individual resistances to learning, and he must persevere with these ideas until they finally register. This group at some level understood the notion of personal change very well, but some inhibition about daring to be really ambitious and adventurous prevented them from 'hearing' me until the seventh or eighth time it was mentioned. It is for this reason that many ideas in this book are stated and restated in different chapters.

An argument erupted once again about whether such change, however desired, *could* occur in a group like this. Ginny dismissed this question as nonsense. 'Why, James has already changed. He is letting go of his feelings now, which makes him more real to me'. She said that prior to this group she had categorized him as an isolationist. What she now wanted was to work on her relationship with Gerald, whose shyness made her shy, so there was no progress. Arthur interrupted politely to say that while he valued what he called my 'method', he thought this group could not progress much further because of the already cemented formal and informal relationships which went on between them daily in the department. Steve was astonished and amused. 'Come off it', he said, 'you've changed more than any of us, and it shows in the way you think and talk about yourself and the students. You just want to rest on your laurels now. But don't we deserve a chance to catch up with you?' Arthur looked pleased at the implied tribute. James said he was now at last enjoying the sessions but could not see how they were actually helping him. Gerald could not quite work out what was going on, but believed he should persist, to see what might come out of it. The group seemed dispirited, for it was setting itself too high a standard. I assured them that in my opinion we were doing quite well and shared with them my own feelings that I was rushing them a little. We had only met a few times, and it was impossible to achieve everything all at once.

Session 7

Everyone except Horace was late, for this the penultimate session. It was not without significance that we had agreed today to make a decision about the group's ending or continuing. Ted said he had to leave early owing to pressing business, (but in fact did not leave early). Arthur was very late indeed and seemed flustered and preoccupied, 'after what has been a hectic day', and was unable to switch off and relax for the one hour group period. This was group flight on a large scale from a difficult decision. The multiple lateness generated a long and fruitful discussion about how the length of time given to this and other academic seminars affected what learning could be accomplished within set temporal boundaries. I was conscious also that this very serious conversation was being used to avoid making the life or death decision about this group. Group members went on to look at the use of alcohol in various departmental groupings, social and academic, and how helpful this provision often proved. I interpreted with a smile this unconscious dependent wish that I would pop them a pill or a stiff scotch; then perhaps they could throw off inhibitions painlessly, and become close to each other without having to even think about it, or face any of the obstacles to communication with which we had been struggling for weeks.

Ted and James were very rebellious on this occasion and demanded more structure, criticizing my 'sloppy' leadership. I felt that what they really feared was leadership which encouraged rather than protected them from intimacy. They declared that as I refused to take my leadership responsibilities seriously, (although they were sure I meant well!) the group must find a way of organizing itself without me. James was most annoyed with me, complaining that there was no way they could all share power equally without conflict, or all have their own needs amicably met over what subjects we talked about. I agreed that competition, conflict, power-seeking, and having to fight for one's rights were facts of life, but that I was not prepared to protect them from exposure to the facts by becoming the wished for authoritarian figure. Yielding to their demand for a parental chairperson who would eradicate the need to make these awful decisions, (who would in fact decide for them) would only perpetuate an authority dependency relationship with them, thus creating the very group situation here from which they begged to be released with their own students! I also defended Ted's imputation that I abdicated leadership. I did not mind the criticism, but in case the idea that no leader was present spread, which might intensify insecure feelings, I explained that I was very much in touch with my duties as group leader. However, I chose to use my conductorship in a way which might assist them to examine *in situ* their membership of a group, as well as looking from a distance at their teaching. This meant my declining the mantle of authority, even if hostility resulted.

There were further requests for an agenda and proper seminar format. Ted headed the revolt he had now been chosen to lead, with James as able second-in-command. I waited until everyone had expressed their feelings at some length and then reiterated my own view, — not to win a case, but to help them see the implications parental leadership, or its absence, could have for their student groups. This issue is the very cornerstone of group teaching, and raises fundamental questions about the purpose of Education. I suggested they had been allowed great freedom within the group to organize it how they wished, but that lack of parental discipline had forced them into collisions with each other, from which they preferred to be protected. After all, how could they both lean on and yet compete (for time and attention) with each other? Better to have an arbiter. If they could not begin to adjust to this difficult but more democratic model of group functioning, I asked, how can they ever hope to wean the students from dependency on themselves? They blamed the students for leaning heavily on the staff, yet here they were, doing it themselves. Could they now envisage dependency as a *group phenomenon*, not as a nasty attribute of individual students? Presented with freedom, staff are as emotionally bewildered as are students. The withdrawal of authority is a delicate operation. James insisted, despite this little speech, that they should have more guidance from me. Horace, who had taken my point, quipped to his comrades that before we knew where we were, James would be asking Wyn to set them essays on group teaching and mark them; it must, he said, surely be time for them to grow up.

The teacher stereotype was then talked about, and I commented that teachers often felt obliged to act as the repositories of wisdom and strength; they could not allow the vulnerable 'student' within themselves any breathing space, just as students were often not allowed to be their own teachers. Steve postulated that in this group everyone spoke as if they were conscious of their professional status, no matter how relaxed or light-hearted the talk: to admit to 'not understanding', or to feeling insecure was not congruent with their perceived role. Hence the appeal for strong leadership, which was supposed to rescue them from uncomfortable feelings, which in fact they needed to experience, if they were to really learn about teaching effectiveness. Jack ignored this, objecting to my comments instead, which he found 'gross and over-simplified'. Nevertheless, within a minute or two he found himself in touch with the 'troubled student' within himself, and dropped his teacher facade. He had indeed 'heard' his colleague's salient remarks! He spoke to us quietly and with great sadness about his own academic/ psychological problems in his research area; how he, like James, had suffered severely from depression associated with the job, and had told no one. He had established a high research and teaching reputation in the college which had to be preserved. Thus, even at the expense of his own happiness, he had confided in no one. This had been the only setting in which it had been permissable to speak. That, he said, was why Ginny had hurt him very badly, when right at the beginning, she had asked that we confine our attention to the teaching job *per se*, rather than other circumstances which could influence it. Warmth, affection, support and advice were immediately forthcoming, and participants seemed to be seeing Jack properly for the first time. The little remaining time was spent investigating Jack's feelings and the background to his problem. (It is here worth noting that I have never seen teachers' expectations of rejection fulfilled, after admitting to problems, in any group I have ever conducted.)

Session 8

Jack's demeanour was more peaceful, the tense facial expressions and taut posture gone. Horace continued to take a relaxed observer position, speaking little and only when appropriate; he was no longer prepared to offer himself as a scapegoat, and he had acquired an air of dignity and composure. Gerald spoke a good deal (for him) and was more animated than usual. All were present and waiting as I arrived and immediately got down to business. After much toing and froing it was decided to continue the group next term, for a longer period of one-and-a-half hours — but this was to be confirmed later! I inwardly chuckled at this ploy to keep options open even now, but said nothing. I was greatly pleased by the decision.

Ted resurrected his fight for more structure and said he would leave if it were not granted. He was quite prepared to have a group rule which coerced everyone into taking turns at confessing problems and placing their doubts before the general assembly of the group, whether they liked it or not. We were all too lily-livered to volunteer, so we must be forced, he said. No one followed him this week; indeed no one could believe their ears, and he was asked to repeat himself — which he duly did. The more he attacked the 'cowardly' group, the more the others, save James, defended it. They drew to his attention how many times he had been absent and how he had managed to stay away during most of the group's emotional periods, just as he kept out of departmental activities on similar occasions. He therefore forfeited the right to complain. The upshot of this confrontation was that Ted told us angrily and with much pain, why he affected a tough and independent manner. It concerned the denial of certain longed-for conditions to do with teaching and research, which had been verbally promised him earlier. The decision to deprive him of these opportunities had been taken in secret and without consultation with him. He had been smarting over it ever since. The history of this event was overhauled, in terms of his disappointment, anger, and understandable rebellion, rather than in the historical facts. The others showed him how his solitariness and brash behaviour encouraged others to ignore him. Just the same, they very much wanted him back in the social as well as professional scene in the department. All this time they had left him in peace, (which he had interpreted as rejection) because they had thought he chose to be distant and diffident. Ginny was most upset, because she had fought terribly hard for him on a certain committee and he seemed not to notice that, but instead had rejected her along with the rest, as well as now turning down any help the group might offer. Ted's anger had by now evaporated in the face of all this understanding and firm confrontation about how he appeared to others. He became serious and thoughtful, and in saying goodbye for the Christmas vacation, I expressed my hope that he would rejoin us next term.

Postscript

Ginny left the group, giving domestic commitments as her reason. Ted continued, as did all the rest, until the end of the academic year. The group played, fought and worked hard; relations in and out of the group deepened, as I tried to avoid the increasing polarity between the structure versus non structure factions during the early months. Resolution was achieved at around the ninth month. Despite chronic conflicts, the mutual respect, real sharing and completely new type of learning which occurred between members was extensive and undoubtedly worthwhile. Most agreed that their teaching had been greatly influenced by the group, though not at all in the way they had anticipated! Each member was concerned in varying degrees with reassessing undergraduate teaching in the department, and acting as a catalyst of discussion and change with their colleagues who had not participated in these meetings. Definitive steps are being taken in this direction, at the time of writing this chapter. In this respect the group will live on long after its formal termination.

Conclusions

Those readers who have studied the whole text will readily appreciate the main features which distinguish the competent group tutor. He has mastered theoretical group-concepts; he has acquired long and wide experience in a variety of teaching and colleague groups; he is himself consistently involved in peer group learning via in-service support schemes and informal contact with colleagues. From time to time he participates in a training or therapeutic group, designed to provide subjective experience of group process. Finally and most important, with regard to group work he has attained internal changes in his attitudes, philosophy and perceptual boundaries, alterations and realignments of feeling and thinking which are unique to him. In the absence of such personal change, all that is written in the book has but rhetorical value to the tutor.

Understanding a group as a result of this change is quite superior to, and distinguishable from, the naming of concepts, labelling of processes, and the identification of boundaries and conflicts around and within them. Understanding marks the difference between a person who turns a knob on a television set knowing that a picture will be produced, and a person who is familiar with the interrelationships of the many components inside the set, who realizes how and why the picture comes about. He can repair the set or improve the picture, whereas the knob-turner randomly twiddles knobs, bends the aerial, and looks up the instruction manual, before declaring the set is rotten, the weather is affecting the picture, or sending urgently for the maintenance man. Thus he turns away from understanding, failing to make any connection between himself and the faulty television set. He regards himself as blame-free, for he has not built the set, any more than the tutor has fashioned the personalities of group members. Yet in both instances what brings about improvement is an appreciation of *how the system works*, rather than the application of technological aids alienated from the user's understanding. The tutor who supplies academic data as automatically and unfeelingly as pressing a button, and who always expects a perfect picture of group learning in response, is as ill-equipped to maintain his group's optimal functioning as is the frustrated television viewer.

What is the nature of this 'personal change', of this inner journey; where does it lead? Each tutor must travel alone and reach his own series of destinations, but perhaps these concluding remarks may serve as signposts. This book is intended as a map and must on no account be mistaken for the journey itself; cognitive knowledge and a new group language in the absence of altered feeling and outlook is worthless, mere jargon, as far as the handling of human groups is concerned.

Four cardinal ideas, extracted from the book and stressed again here at its conclusion, may point the reader in the direction of change. When *first* applied, these preparatory precepts may produce a temporary reduction of data absorption and more general learning in the groups. The new group tutor must deliberately allow himself to be sidetracked, and must force himself to observe process, boundaries and personal reactions — possibly to the detriment of the work agenda. This transition of emphasis from manifest work to latent group phenomena is anxiety-inducing, for the tutor naturally feels more secure on academic ground than on unknown process territory. If he can fight the resistance to learning group tutoring that this fear promotes; if he can tolerate rather than eject these initial doubts and uncertainties and the sometimes adverse effects on the work itself, he will gradually come to see and feel for groups in quite a new way. His consequent actions may lead to a vast improvement in students' work. At first the clumsy, contrived, and almost exclusive monitoring of all the systems-activity in the group is exhausting, but eventually this observational habit is absorbed into the tutor's repertoire of other more unselfconscious teaching skills, and the fatigue and stress recedes. The balance between the old-established aptitudes, and the new proclivity to process management is redressed: all the tutor's educational arts begin a mutually enhancing co-existence. It is at this stage in the tutor's professional development that academic results are striking. Education for the tutor with insight has become symbolized by the *I we it* triangle discussed in chapter 3. His teaching is no longer *it* determined neither are his transactions with colleagues. Insight is not *bestowed*, but is *discovered* by the searcher, through his own experience. The tutor is invited to carry with him the following essential precepts.

Working with the group's inherent potential

Cultivate the art of drawing out innate social and learning potential from the group, rather than assaulting it with directives, imposing method, techniques or anxiety-inducing procedures on the members. Help the members cope with and develop the existing interpersonal environment, until they are cohesed and academically motivated enough to withstand the burden of additional procedures should these prove educationally necessary. But offer sufficient boundaries and procedures to reduce isolation/disorientation and so provide the means by which members can tentatively reach out for contact with each other and yourself. Prepare yourself for members' silence in the early stages; for their embarrassment, dependency and competitiveness. Welcome these manifestations as normal and healthy in a new group, even if uncomfortable. Minimizing or negating this discomfort by resorting to academic rituals and excessive verbalization ensures that unease is driven underground and prevents it from ever being resolved. Chronic observance of increasingly hollow rituals usually results, ensuring that the primary interpersonal tensions cannot surface.

Developing receptivity/passivity

Endeavour to locate in yourself, whatever your personality type, qualities of psychological stillness, receptivity and calm. This will help you 'see' and 'hear' with your third eye and ear, what the group, its sub groups and pairs are latently revealing. Wait and watch for the group pattern or picture to appear of its own accord. The interpretation of how the group is operating will inevitably be influenced by your own private transferring and displacing tendencies, and the valency for certain leadership styles. This underlines the necessity for you to understand your own personality foibles, as well as the theoretical underpinnings of group work. Each group is unique, but bears the stamp of its leader, just as children, however independent, show traces of their parents. Straining towards scientific objectivity in assessing group functioning would be like trying to bring up a child by computer. You can afford to make mistakes, just as parents can, without disaster ensuing. There is no need to maintain hectic activity: passivity, (allowing the group to act upon and use you) is a much more sensitive instrument in group teaching; it is greatly underrated, and often misconstrued as lack of enthusiasm. The degree of overt leader activity is often in inverse proportion to the extent of student learning! A receptive passive attitude creates more time and space for observation, reflection and diagnosis of group behaviour. In a crisis however, you must be able to convert the knowledge gained through passivity into speedy and potent action.

Increasing systems-observation

Discipline your perceptual apparatus to view the group (large or small, staff or student) as a social system, a single unit capable of corporate action, sharing common preoccupations, able to elect members to speak or act on its behalf. Should one individual develop or regress in his functioning, this will affect the overall interactive pattern; a change in one component of the system affects the system as a whole. Similarly the total group culture will affect how individual participants express themselves and relate to each other and to you. Survey the whole field of group forces rather than itemizing separate pieces of behaviour and attributing these only to the person exhibiting them. You should constantly ask yourself the following questions. 'How does this single contribution to the group fit in with its operative processes?' 'How does the process inhibit or exaggerate this person's utterances; does he speak and act for himself or herself, for me, for the group, for a sub group or for a combination of these?' 'What boundaries round the system have I built?' 'Are they too rigid, or not rigid enough?' 'How permeable is the major internal boundary between leader and members?'

Welcoming emotionalism in teaching

Most important of all, you should combat any prejudices you may have against the emotional explorations demanded of you if you are to excel in this work. You have been trained in a scientific culture, which has exalted the observer-observed relationship, and demoted the shared emotional-social experience. Resuscitation of this world of feeling (Passion) in the hearts and minds of individual academics is very greatly needed, as well as its reinstatement in the canons of our major teaching institutions. Publicly restored to its place alongside Research and accumulated Knowledge, we can then begin to combine the three. (That is, Research, Knowledge and Passion.) Thus we may regenerate teaching, so that it imbues men and women with socially responsible impulses, political integrity and moral vision — as well as with facts, skills and a hopefully marketable qualification. Research and Knowledge alone will not educate humanity about how to live more fulfilling lives. For that we must add Passion. Those who have crossed the frontiers of Knowledge have often been scorned or censored in the past, because their awesome discoveries threatened to disturb their society's equilibrium. Is Passion so dangerous, that it must meet with the same fate in our own scientistic times? You yourselves as teachers are the people who will answer this.

Selected readings

Chapter 1

Benne, K D and Sheats, P (1948) 'Functional Roles of Group Members'; *J Social Issues*, vol 6, no 1, pp. 41-49, USA

Bramley, Wyn (1977) *Personal Tutoring in Higher Education*; SRHE, London

Chapter 2

De Board, Robert (1978) *The Psychoanalysis of Organizations*; Social Science Paperbacks, Tavistock Publications, London

Durkin, Helen E (1972) 'General Systems Theory and Group Therapy: an Introduction'; *International J Group Psychotherapy*, vol. 22, pp. 159-166, New York, USA

Miller, E S and Rice A K (1967) *Systems of Organization*; Tavistock, London (currently out of print, but available in most libraries)

Miller, James G (1965) 'Living Systems: Basic Concepts'; *Behavioural Science*, vol 10, pp. 193-237

Rice, A K (1969) 'Individual, Group and Inter-Group Processes'; *Human Relations* vol 22, no 6, pp. 565-584

Von Bertalanffy (1973) *General Systems Theory*; Penguin, London

Chapter 3

Cohn, R (1969) 'The Theme Centred Interactional Method'; *Group Process* (Formerly *J of Group Psychoanalysis and Process*), vol 2, no 2 pp. 19-35

Schaffer, John B P and Galinsky, M David (1974) *Models of Group Therapy and Sensitivity Training*; Prentice Hall Inc, New Jersey, (chapter 12) pp. 242-263

Chapter 5

Bion, W R (1961) *Experiences in Groups*; Tavistock, London

Ezriel, H (1967) 'The First Session in Psychoanalytic Group Treatment'; *Nederlands Tijdschrift voor Geneeskunde*, Amsterdam, vol 3 no 15, pp. 711-716

Heath, E S and Bacal H A (1968) 'A Method of Group Psychotherapy at the Tavistock Clinic'; *International J Group Psychotherapy*, vol 18 no 1, pp. 21-30, New York

Higgin, G and Bridger, H (1964) 'The Psychodynamics of an Inter-Group Experience'; *Human Relations*, vol 17, no 4, pp. 391-446

Whitaker, D S and Lieberman M A (1964) *Psychotherapy through the Group Process*; Atherton Press, New York

Whitaker, D S (1962) 'Interpersonal Concerns during Early Sessions of Therapy Groups'; *International J Group Psychotherapy*, vol 12, no 1, pp 14-26 International University Press, New York

Chapter 6

Bales, R F and Strodbeck F L (1951) 'Phases in Group Problem Solving'; *J of Abnormal Social Psychology* vol 46, pp. 485-495, New York

Bales, R F (1970) *Personality and Interpersonal Behaviour* Holt, Rhinehart and Winston, New York

Bognadoff, M and Elbaum P (1978) 'Role Lock: Dealing with Monopolizers, Mistrusters, Isolates, Helpful Hannahs, and other Assorted Characters in Group Psychotherapy'; *International J Group Psychotherapy* vol 28, no 2, pp. 247-262

Durkin, H E (1964) *The Group in Depth*; International University Press, New York

Foulkes, S H (1964) *Therapeutic Group Analysis*; Allen & Unwin, London

Foulkes, S H and Anthony E J (1957, revised 1965 and 1973) *Group Psychotherapy: the Psychoanalytic Approach*; Penguin, London

Foulkes, S H (1975) *Group Analytic Psychotherapy, Method and Principles*; Interface Books, Gordon & Breach, London

Geller, Joseph J (1962) 'Parataxic Distortions in the Initial Stages of Group Relationships'; *International J of Group Psychotherapy*, vol 26, no 1, pp. 27-34.

Haskell, Robert E (1978) 'An Analogic Model of Small Group Behaviour'; *International J Group Psychotherapy*, vol 28 no 1, pp. 27-54, New York

Kraüptl, Taylor F (1953) 'The Scapegoat Motif in Society and its Manifestations in a Therapeutic Group'; *International J Psychoanalysis* vol 34 part 2, pp. 253-365

Chapter 7

Abercrombie, M L J and Terry P M (1978) 'Reactions to Change in the Authority-Dependency Relationship'; *British J Guidance and Counselling* vol 6, no 1, pp. 82-94

Kernberg, Otto F (1978) 'Leadership and Organizational Functioning: Organizational Regression'; *International J Group Psychotherapy*, vol 28, no 1, pp. 3-25

Redl, F (1942) 'Group Emotion and Leadership'; *Psychiatry* vol 4, Nov pp. 573-596, USA

Chapter 8

Menzies, I (1977 reprint) *A Case Study in the Functioning of Social Systems as a Defence against Anxiety*; Tavistock pamphlet no 3

Redl, F (1942) 'Group Emotion and Leadership'; *Psychiatry* vol 4, Nov pp. 573-596, USA

General Interest

Abercrombie, M L J (1960) *Aims and Techniques of Group Teaching, third edition*; SRHE, London

Abercrombie, M L J and Terry P M (1978) *Talking to Learn*; SRHE, London

Berne, Eric (1966) *The Structure and Dynamics of Organizations and Groups*; Grove Press, Evergreen paperback, New York

Blackham, H J (Editor) (1978) *Education for Personal Autonomy*; Bedford Square Press, London

Bramley, Wyn and Donnachaidh, I (1977) 'Students and Group-Analytic Psychotherapy'; *British J Guidance and Counselling* vol 5, no 2, pp. 198-206

Cooper, Cary L (Editor) (1972) *Group Training for Individual and Organizational Development*

Hamblin, D H (1974) 'The Counsellor and Alienated Youth'; *British J Guidance and Counselling*, vol 2, no 1, pp 87-95

Main, T F (1957) 'The Ailment'; *British J Medical Psychology* vol 30, part 3, pp. 129-178

Redl, F (1966) *When we Deal with Children*, The Free Press, Macmillan, New York

Ruddock, Jean (1978) *Learning Through Small Group Discussion*, SRHE, London

Skynner, A C R (1974) 'An Experiment in Group Consultation with the Staff of a Comprehensive School'; *Group Process* vol 6, no 1, pp. 99-114

Thomson, Sheila and Kahn, J H (1970, reprinted 1976) *The Group Process as a Helping Technique*, Pergamon International Library of Science, Technology, Engineering and Social Studies

Index

219

DATE DUE

DEMCO 38-297